INDIAN NATIONAL ARMY
A Documentary Study

INDIAN NATIONAL ARMY

A Documentary Study

(In 5 Volumes)

Volume-IV

(1944-1945)

T. R. SAREEN

GYAN

GYAN PUBLISHING HOUSE

NEW DELHI - 110002

INDIAN NATIONAL ARMY—A DOCUMENTARY STUDY

Rs. 4,500/-

ISBN : 81-212-0833-5 (Set)
ISBN : 81-212-0847-5 (Vol-4)

Published in 2004 in India by
Gyan Publishing House
5, Ansari Road, Daryaganj
New Delhi-110 002
Phone-23282060, 23261060, Fax-23285914
Email : gyanbook@vsnl.com
Visit our Website at : http//www.gyanbooks.com

Lasertype Setting by: Tact Computer Graphics, Delhi
Printed at: Chawla Offset Press, Delhi

To
My Parents

List of Documents

Introduction

The period November 1944 to the end of war in August 1944, which this volume covers was very decisive for the future of the I.N.A. Bose had realised by the end of October 1944 that the drive of the I.N.A. towards India was virtually over due to the advance of the Allied forces. Reports were coming from I.N.A. commanders about the failure of the Japanese liaison agency the Kikari-Kikan to supply even the minimum war materials and rations. In view of the difficulties Bose realised the need for re-organising the I.N.A. and make it somewhat independent from depending too much on the Japanese for help. To further solve the problems involved in it, Bose also decided to go to Tokyo and have further discussion with the new Japanese Cabinet.

Bose left for Tokyo towards the beginning of November and spent about a month in the official negotiations with the Japanese Cabinet under Prime Minister General Koiso. Bose placed the demands before the Prime Minister saying that I.N.A. should be strengthened and the Provisional Government of Azad Hind should have direct access to the Cabinet through an Ambassdor. He re-assured about I.N.A. determination to launch a fresh operation against the British (Doc.1, 2).

What transpired in Tokyo has been graphically recorded by General Kawabe in his memoirs (Appendix II). For the Indian side of the story, it will he worth while to consult the interrogation report of A.M. Sahey and his memories given in the next volume. Sahey accompanied Bose during the visit and even served as his interpreter during the negotiations.

During the visit, Bose also had the opportunity to sense the helplessness of the Japanese military authorities and their vulnerability against air bombing of Tokyo by the Allied powers. Even under these adverse conditions still, Bose was hopeful of the victory of Japan. In his speech and press interviews, Bose gave out that as far as I.N.A. was concerned, it would fight shoulder to shoulder with the Japanese army (Dec.3). While in Tokyo Bose had the time to express his views about the fundamental problems of India and how these could be solved after freedom was attained. He expressed his view in a series of talks which he gave to the students at the university of Tokyo. These talks summarized his political ideology and were in fact stood for the philosophy of the I.N.A. He made it clear that India could never achieve independence without the help of some foreign power. Once this was achieved, the economic and social reconstruction of India would start under a government that will function as the servant of the people and will have full powers to put new reforms concerning industry, education, defense etc., in free India. Caste and communalism in his view would have no place in such a state (Doc. 4).

Throughout the war on the Imphal front, it was propogated by the British that the Japanese and the I.N.A. forces did not recived any help from the local people. Conceding that the assistance from the Nagas was not substantial, but the reports of the Political Agent, Manipur show that there were number of local people who directly or indirectly were supporting the Japanese and I.N.A. and how they were punished by the British. (Doc 6-8, 11).

Bose after coming back tried to mobilise the resources for the fresh offensive against the British forces. From February to April 1945, I.N.A. attempted to put up a strong resistance against the formidable thrust of the allied forces. The reports of Dhillion and Sahgal even hinted at the heroic deeds of the I.N.A. But it was not possible to resist the British who had superior weapons. (Doc. 22-23). Against heavy odds, the I.N.A. soldiers began to surrender in May, 1945 (Doc 35-36).

Bose tried to stop it by issuing special orders, but it was of no use. Desertion and surrender became a daily occurance. After capturing I.N.A. soldiers, the British began to interrogate them in order to find out the motive of Bose and I.N.A. (Doc. 25, 28).

After the situation became critical in Burma, Japanese authorities persuaded Bose to leave and go to Bangkok and then to Malaya. Bose left Burma reluctantly and in a series of special orders, positively predicted that there was no power on earth that can keep India enslaved (Doc 34). He expressed the same sentiments even in subsequent special orders he issued before his death in a plane crash (Doc. 44-45).

The military career of the I.N.A. was over by the end of May 1945. Bose concentrated his efforts to frustrate British efforts to negotiate with the political parties. In a series of broadcasts, Bose appealed to the leaders of the Congress to reject the proposals offered by the Viceroy. Lord Wavell to end the constitutions dead-lock. Bose was releived when the talks at the Simla Conference ultimately failed (Doc. 49).

Even during the war, the British government had been following a policy towards the I.N.A. soldiers, who were captured on the Imphal or Kohima front alongwith the Japanese. While the Japanese were treated as prisoners of war under the Geveva Convention, the I.N.A. soldiers were considered as traitors. They were classified into three categories of "White", "Grey" and "Black" depending upon the involvement with the I.N.A. For instance those who joined the I.N.A. with the intention of desertion or sabotaging it from within were classified as "White". Those who yielded to pressure and joined the I.N.A. were treated as "Grey" and third category of "Black" were those who joined the I.N.A. willingly out of patriotic motives. Appendix I gives a comprehensive account of policy pursued during the war and how these soldiers were utilised or treated. The need for a definite policy towards I.N.A. arose after the war came to an end, when it was discovered that majority of the soldiers joined the I.N.A. out of their love for Bose and their country.

The British were now confronted with a problem of dealing with more than twenty thousand I.N.A. soldiers. In a series of high level meetings the political implication of prosecuting so many soldiers were discussed (Doc 37, 47-49). On account of pressure from the British officers of the army, it was decided to takes action against all of them and a communique was issued, which stated that the government was considering very carefully the treatment to be given to the Indian soldiers who joined the enemy. This was followed by another communique towards the end of August, which was slightly mild in tone. The policy of the government of India had to be modified in the face of mounting political agitation. Almost all the soldiers of the I.N.A. who were repatriated from south-east Asia were interrogated at one stage or the other by the officer of C.S.D.I.C. Their reports are available with the National Archive of India. Here the report of one of the senior officer is given, who joined the I.N.A. with a view to sabotage it from within. The report show as to how the office brought about the rift between General Mohan Singh and the Japanese military forces and how it led to Mohan Singh's arrest and dismissal (Doc 47). Like him there were other officers, who remained loyal to the British and provided necessary information to their former masters.

As mentioned earlier, this volume also contain two appendices. Appendix I gives a detailed account of the steps taken by the British government to check the impact of the I.N.A. an the Indian Armed forces.

This report also gives the indication of how seriously the British were concerned with the threat to the security of India, which the collaboration of the I.N.A. with the Japanese forces had created for them.

Appendix II is an English translation of the relevent portions from the memoirs of General S. Kawabe. These memoirs are based on the account compiled by General Kawabe for the Japanese foreign ministry entitled "Subhas Chandra Bose and Japan". This was prepared on the basis of Japanese official records. Kawabe was commander of the Burma Area Army and was closely associated with I.N.A. and Subhas Chandra Bose. As such, his description of many aspects of I.N.A. is more revealing than the accounts compiled by other Japanese commanders.

By for the greater portion of the hitherto unpublished documents included in this volume, as in its predecessors, were selected from difference archival repositories in India and abroad. The documents are supplemented by private memoirs. Copies of the private memoirs were collected from the individuals as were as from various organsation. I am particularly obliged to Anand Mohan Sahey, S.A. Ayer, General Mohan Singh President, Netaji Subhas Chandra Bose Academy, Tokyo, and I.N.A. Relief and Enquiry Committee for their help and cooperation for providing me documents and copies of memoirs included in this volume.

T.R. Sareen

1

Bose's Activities in Tokyo[1]

3 November, 1944

Subhas Chandra Bose Head of the Provisional Government of Azad Hind, proceeded to the Imperial Palace at 9 a.m. Thursday and entered his name in the Register. Following this, Netaji Bose visited the Yasukuni Shrine.

At 10 a.m. the Indian Leader called on Prime Minister General kuniaki Koiso at the latter's official residence to exchange greetings on the occasion of his present visit to Japan. Then at 10.30 a.m. he called on General Yoshijiro Umezu, Chief of the Army General Staff, and later conferred with Field Marshal Gen Sugiyama, Minister of War.

Netaji attended a luncheon given in his honor by the War Minister and the Chief of the Army General Staff at the War Minister's official residence at 11.30 a.m.

Furthermore, at 1.20 p.m. Mr. Bose conferred with Admiral Mitsumass Yonai, Navy Minister and Admiral Koshiro Okwa Chief of the Naval General Staff.

The members of the Netaji's suite who arrived in Tokyo on Wednesday are Colonel M. Z. Kiani. Colonel A. C. Chatterji and Lieutenant Colonel Habib-Ur-Rahman.

Greeting the Japanese nation over the radio soon after his arrival in Tokyo Wednesday evening. Netaji Subhas Chandra Bose Head of the Provisional Government of Azad Hind, reaffirmed the solemn resolve of all freedom loving Indians to continue to fight shoulder to shoulder with Japan until the common enemies are brought to their knees and final victory is achieved.

The text of the Netaji Bose's radio message follows.

Exactly one year after my last visit, I am now setting foot on the soil of Nippon. It gives me indescribable satisfaction and joy to greet once again the nation at whose hands the Indian delegation and myself received

1. *Nippon Times* 4 Nov, 1944

such a worm and friendly welcome last year. For the people of Nippon, I am also bringing with me the most cordial greetings of all freedom-loving Indians who have solemnly resolved to fight shoulder to shoulder with Nippon,under all circumstances until our common victory is achieved.

Last year, while addressing the General Assembly of Greater East Asiatic Nations in Tokyo, I said that in order to create a New Order, we would have to shed our blood on the same battlefield, in fighting our common enemies. I am now happy and proud to be able to say that since then our Army—the Indian National Army—has gone into action. Side by side with our valiant comrades of the Imperial Nipponese army and the Burma Defence Army we have been fighting the Anglo-American and their allies since February last for the achievement of our common goal. Having had the opportunity of taking the measure of our enemies our confidence in our final victory has increased a hundred fold.

I have often said in the past—and I say it once again on my arrival in this great city—that no matter how long and hard the struggle may be we shall go on fighting till the last, until victory is achieved. As for Nippon so also for India there is but one path ahead of us—the path of uncompromising struggle. For the Indian people to compromise with British Imperialism will mean a compromise with slavery. We have therefore no other alternative but to fight on under all circumstances regardless of the suffering and sacrifice that we may have to face.

During our short stay in Nippon, I and my colleagues will have the honour of making personal contact with His Excellency the Prime Minister and the other Honorable Members of the New Cabinet. We know that their one aim and resolve is to bring about a total mobilization of all the resources of this country in order to win a speedy and complete victory. Our visit to Nippon will therfore afford added encouragement and inspiration to us in our future campaign in the meantime, the Provisional Government of Azad Hind has also set up a War Council, with a view to intensifying and coordinating the activities of freedom-loving Indians for the early achievement of India's for the early achievement of India's Independence. Some of the members of this War Council are accompanying me in this tour.

Though we have no illusions about the magnitude of the task that awaits us and though we are aware that in a war of this kind ups and downs are inevitable, we nevertheless face the future with a feeling of unshakable optimism. This optimism has been further heightened by the recent battles in the Pacific. In the waters off Taiwan and the Phillippines. These victories of the Imperial Japanese Navy in the Pacific have heralded the third and final phase of this war—during which the initiative will pass into the hands of our allies. Our enemies know as much as we do, that time is now working against them. That is why they are becoming more and more desperate in their vain attempt to end this war before their morale breaks down.

When we first took the solemn pledge to fight shoulder to shoulder with Nippon. we did not do so as political weather–cocks, or as fair weather friends. Our motto then was—We shall sink or swim together." in reality we shall not have to sink together. Justice is bound to triumph and, through the grace of Providence, together we shall swim, together we shall fight and together we shall win.

2

Address by Bose Expresses his Conviction in the Ultimate Victory for East Asia Under the Leadership of Japan (Extract)[1]

4 November, 1944

Brothers and Sisters!

Exactly one year after my last visit to your great city. I stand before you today in the same Hibiya Hall, to offer you the heartiest greetings of all freedom loving Indians who are engaged in a grim battle, along side of your people and of your brave fighters on land, sea and air. This day the third of November is the birthday anniversary of the great Emperor. But the 3rd November of this year is also an auspicious day for the people of Asia. who are now fighting your enemies—our common enemies— the Anglo-Americans. I call this an auspicious day for all freedom loving Asiatics, because I am firmly convinced that we now stand on the threshold of the third and final phase of the present war. The recent victories of the Imperial Japanese Navy in the waters of Taiwan and off the Phillippines are an unmistakable indication that new chapter of the present war is about to begin.

Friends! We have already passed through two phases of this war During the first phase Nippon and her Allies had a sweeping victory on every front and everywhere our enemies had to suffer shattering defeats. In the second phase of this war, our enemies started their counter of view. This second phase is nowcoming to an end and during the third and final phase of this war the initiative will, once again, pass into the hands of Nippon and her Allies. I am happy to be come to Tokyo again—just when the truning point of this war is at hand.

---

1. 1.*Nippon Times*, 5 November, 1944. The above address was given by Bose under the auspices of the Imperial Rule Assistance Political Association at the Hibaya Hall, Tokyo.

The only thing that grieves me on my arrival in Tokyo is that the reverted and venerable Toyama[2] san is no longer in our midst. Through his death, India has lost one of her greatest friends in this world. Throughout his long and eventful life he was not only a friend and well wisher of India, but he was foremost among those who dreamt of—and worked for—the emancipation and unity of all Asiatic nations. However, we have this consolation that the ideal for which he lived and fought is now firmly planted in the hearts of millions and millions of people—only in this country but throughtout Asia as well.

Friends! You will remember that when I was here last year, I oftern declared in private and in public that a New Order can be created only, if we fight together and shed our blood on the same battlefield in combatting our common enemies. I am happy and proud to be able to say that since February last Indian soldiers have been fighting shoulder to shoulder with the valiant soldiers of the Imperial Japanese Army and the Burma Defence Army, on the same front. This is a proof that for the achievement of the great idea that we all have in front of us—we are prepared to pay the price with our blood. When we are fighting for justice and morality and when we are prepared to pay the full price with our blood—no power on earth can stand between us and our final victory.

The Anglo-American know, in their heart of hearts that they are not fighting for a noble cause—as we are, Consequently they lack the spiritual strength that we possess. Their only hope is to win the war with the sheer weight of their steel and armour. But this war of the past—will show once again that in the last resort steel and armour cannot prevail against the human spirit. Because our enemies are relying solely on their steel and armourl and they are making a vain attempt to end this war before their morale breaks down. The tactics that they are now employing are those of a desperate gambler. But as against the desperate gamble of our enemies—we are calm and collected and are pursuing our fight with grim determination and with the fullest confidence in our final victory. What strengthnes us all the more is the consciousness that time is no longer working for the Anglo-Americans. Time is now working for us, and against our enemies. Consequently, however long and hard the struggle may be, nothing can ever depress or demoralize us.

So far as the Indian people are concerned, they are already prepared for a long and hard struggle. We know what India means to the British

2. Toyama Mitsure was a great political leader and President of Block Dragan Society, who were interested in the freedom of the Asian people.

Empire. We know that the emancipation of India will mean the end of the British Empire. We know, therefore that the British will fight hard in India in order to save their Empire. Consequently, the Indian campaign will not be like the campaign in Malai or Burma. There is another reason why we expect a long and difficult struggle in India. It took the British full one hundred years—from 1757 to 1857— to finally sunjugate India. Now when we want to expel the British from India, we cannot do so within one month. It will naturally take us some time. Further, the freedom of India will mean the liberty of one-fifth of mankind. For such a gigantic task for liberation of such a vast country, the full price will have to be paid and no Indian can, therefore, grudge a long and hard struggle. I can assure you that as long as you may have to fight, we shall be with you—in fair weather or foul. We are neither opportunists nor fair weather friends. When we have once pledged ourselves to fight anlongside of you, we shall do so under all circumstances—no matter what the suffering or sacrifice involved may prove to be.

Friends! I have remarked before that I am confident of our final victory. I have also said that the third and final phase of the war will soon begin. But that does not mean that in future, we shall have smooth sailing until the day of our victory. On the contrary I expect that there will be some ups and downs even in the last phase of the war. In some setbacks from time to time. Nevertheless, the initiative will remain in the hand of Nippon and her allies and this will continue until our enemies are finally overthrown in a war of the present magnitude, only a fool will expect smooth sailing along the road to victory when the present war comes to an end, we shall see a completely new order in this world. This New Order cannot be created without suffering and sacrifice, without trouble and tribulation, without many ups and downs. The greater the price that we pay, the more valuable will be the victory that we shall ultimately achieve.

Here in Nippon, in order to prepare for the final struggle you have a new cabinet, whose one aim and object is to bring about a total mobilization of the entire nation and of all its resources. The results of this supreme effort on the part of your nation are already visible in the brilliant victories recently won by your indomitable navy. The unflinching determination of your nation to sacrifice all for the sake of victory has been manifested in the glorious achievements of your "Divine Wind Unit" and it is impossible for our enemies to show anything that can stand a moments comparison with such glorious achievements. The supreme efforts and sacrifice that you are now making has served as a great inspiration to all other nation that are engaged in the present struggle. Speaking for my countrymen, I may inform you that we have recently formed a War Council of the Provisional Government of Azad Hind.......

3

Statement of Bose regarding the Present Situation in India[1]

6 November, 1944

Subhas Chandra Bose released a statement to the press, Monday afternoon at the Greater East Asia Guest Hall to which he clarified the objectives of his latest visit to Japan. The main point of his statement follows.

The purpose of my visit to Japan this time are briefly as follows: Firstly, to make personal contact with His Excellency the Prime Minister and the members of the new Cabinet. Secondly to meet once again the many friends, I have in this country. And thirdly, to discuss with the representatives of the Government and of the armed forces of this country the question relating to our mutual cooperation in the political and the military sphere in the future and thereby help the successful prosecution of our common war against the Anglo-Americans.

The Provisional Government of Azad Hind declared war on Britain and America on October 23, 1943.

During the last 16 months Indians in East Asia have been trying to executive the program that I placed before your—the program of "total mobilization". Much has already been achieved—but much more remains to be done. My Government has, therefore, set up a War Council the sole aim and object of which is to vigorously push on this work of "total mobilization". In every sphere so that we shall not lag behind any other nation in the matter of war-effort or sacrifice.

The military operations on the Indo-Burma frontier and inside India have afforded us a valuable experience as to the comparative strength and weakness of our enemies and of ourselves. I expect that in the Indain campaign the stiffest fight will take place at and near the eastern frontier of India—for it is there that our enemies have built their Maginot Line. But though the fight for India's emancipation will be long and hard, we have not the slightest doubt about the final issue of that struggle.

1. *Nippon Times*, 7 Nov, 1944

"The breakdwon of the Gandhi-Jinnah talks has clarified the political atmosphere of India and it is welcomed by the overwhelming majority of the Indian people. The Indian people firmly stand behind the 'Quit India' resolution which was adopted by the Indian National Congress in August 1942. But it is now clear to everybody in India that mere civil Disobedience, or any form of non-violent activity, will never force the British to quit India. Therefore, all hopes are now centered in the military operations that have been going on the east and north-east of India, since February last. Even the blind and orthodox supporters of Mahatama Gandhi's policy of non-violence are fast realizing that for the achievement of Independence, the Indian people will now have to take up arms and fight.

4

Bose's Address to the Students of Imperial University, Tokyo on India's Fundamental problems; gives a frank and vivid account of realities which India was Facing and how these could the Solved[1]

7 November, 1944

I do not propose to speak to such a distinguished gathering on the commonplace things that you hear or read about India. I think it would be far better if I speak to you on the more fundamental problems of India. Having been a student of philosophy myself, I am naturally more interested in fundamental problems. I hope you will also agree with me that I should rather speak to you today on some of the fundamental problems that face my country, both in the present as well as in the future.

In my travels abroad, I have often found that people generally have a wrong and sometimes a rather funy idea about my country. For instance among the people in Europe, the general idea about India is that it is a land in which three things can be found: snakes, fakirs and maharajas. Among those who have been influenced by British propaganda, the fighting among themselves, and where the strong hand of Britian is required in order to maintain peace and order among the people.

If you approach the Orientalists in Europe, that is, the experts in Indology, you will find that they look upon India as a land of mystics and philosophers, a land which at one time produced a very rich philosophy, but which is today as dead as the ancient civilisations of Egypt and Babylon are dead today.

Now the question is, what is India in reality? No doubt we have a very ancient civilisation, but unlike other ancient civilisations, such as Egypt or Babylon, Phoenicia or even Greece, the ancient cultural and civilisation of India is not dead. It still lives in the present. And we Indians

1. *Nippon Times*, published this address of Bose to the students of the Tokyo University in four instalments on 8, 9, 10, 11. December, 1944. Bose spoke in English and it was translated into Japanese by Mr. Kakitsuba

of today think the same thoughts fundamentally, and have the same feelings, the same ideals of life, as our forefathers who lived 2,000 or 3,000 years ago. In other words there is a continuity, historical and cultural continuity extending from the ancient times till the present day—which is in some ways a very remarkable thing in history. Now, in order to understand India, this fundamental fact should first be understood, namely that the India of the past is not dead. India of thefacing past lives in the present, and will live on in the future.

Against this background, this ancient background we see changes in our national life from age to age. During the last 3,000 years, people have come into India from out side with new ideas, sometimes with new cultures. All these new influences, ideas and cultures have been gradually absorbed into the national life of India, so that in spite of the fact that fundamentally we have the same culture and civilisation as we had several thousand years ago. we have nevertheless changed and moved with the times. Today, in spite of our ancient background, we are able to live in a modern world and adapt ourselves to that world.

Those who have been influenced, whether consciously or unconsciously by British propaganda, have the impression that India was very easily conquered by the British and also that after the British conquest of India our country was for the first time politically unified. Both these notions are entirely wrong and without foundation.

In the first place, it is not true that India was easily conquered by the British. It took the British 100 years, from 1757 to 1857, to finally subjugate India. Secondly, it is also an entirely wrong notion to think that India was politically united by the British. The fact is that India was for the first time politically unified nearly 2,500 years ago under the Buddhist Emperor, Ashoka. In reality the India of the time of Asoka the Great was even larger than the India of today. Asoka's India included not only modern India, but also Afghanistan and a part of Persia.

After the time of Asoka, India has gone through many ups and downs in her national life. There have been periods of decay, followed by periods of progress and national upheaval but throughout these ups and downs in our national life, we have been able in the long run to keep up our progress. About one thousand years after Asoka, India again reached the zenith of progress under the Gupta Emperors. This was followed by another glorious epoch in Indian history about nine hundred years later under the Mogul Emperors. Therefore, it is worth remembering that the British notion that we have been unified politically under British rule is entirely wrong. All that the British have tried to do during their regime in India is to divide the Indian people and to weaken, disarm and emasculate them.

I shall now present before you a problem which will interest scientists, and in particular, students of sociology. The question is whether the Indian people have any right to live as a free nation. In other words, have they the strength and the vitality left in them to live and to develop themselves as a free nation? I personally hold the opinion that if a nation once loses its vitality, its inner vitality that existence will even if it does continue to exist after losing its vitality, that existence will have hardly any worth or value for mankind. The only reason why I stand for India's freedom and believe that as a free nation we shall have a glorious future is that I believe that we have sufficient vitality left in us to live as free men and to develop as a nation.

Now, if I have to answer this question as to whether sufficient vitality is left in us, I shall have to answer two questions: firstly has our nation any creative faculty and secondly, is it prepared to fight and to die in order to preserve its existence? These two tests have to be applied to India.

With regard to the first question, we have seen that in spite of the British in India, in spite of the innumerable restrictions and disadvantages which follow from foreign rule, we have been able during the century to give numerous proofs that in different departments of our national life we still have creative power.

The number of philosophers and thinkers produced in India under British rule, the number of writers and poets that enslaved India has produced, the artistic revival in India in spite of British rule, the scientific progress made by the Indian people in spite of so many difficulties in the way of their education, the standard already attained by our leading scientists as compared with scientists in different parts of the world, the industrial progress made by India as the result of the her own effort and inititative and, last but not least, the distinction which we have attained in the field of sport, all these go to show that in spite of being politically subjugated the vitality of the nation has remained intact.

If under foreign rule and in spite of the obstacles and restrictions that follow from foreign rule, we could give so much proof or our creative faculty, then it stands to reason that when India is free and when the masses of the Indian people are afforded educational facilities they will be able to give much better proof of their intellectual calibre and creative faculty in different walks of life.

I have just referred to the first test of a nation's vitality, namely, creative faculty. I shall now consider the second test, namely, as to whether the Indian people are able to fight and to die for the sake of freedom. On this point I should like to say, first of all, that, since the last great fight that they had with the British in 1857, the Indian people have not given up the struggle against the enemy, even for one day.

Unfortunately, owing to what I would call the folly of our forefathers, after our final defeat in 1857, the leaders in those days had allowed themselves to be disarmed. Whatever difficulty we have subsequently experienced in winning back our freedom has been due largely to our having been disarmed. But though owing to the mistake of the leaders the people were disarmed, nevertheless they continued to fight for their freedom in other ways.

I shall not take up your time unnecessarily by giving a description of all the methods that have been used in India against the British. I will only say this, that all the methods that have been tried by revolutionaries in different parts of the world for the achievement of their own independence have been tried in India.

At the beginning of this century, particularily after the victory of Japan over Russia in 1904 and 1905, the Freedom movements in India got a new impetus and since then, during the last 40 years, our revolutionaries have been studying very closely the methods of revolutionaries in the other countries and they have tried to adopt as many of their methods as possible.

They have tried also to manufacture secretly arms and explosives inside the country and to use those arms and explosives for the achievement of independence. As a development of this struggle for freedom. India tried a new experiment—Civil Disobedience or Passive Resistance—of which the best exponent was Mahatama Gandhi. Though personally I believe that this method will not succeed in bringing us complete independence, there is no doubt that it has greatly helped to rouse and unify the Indian people and also to keep up a movement of resistance against the foreign government. I should, therefore, say that the fact that in spite of all the difficulties that result from foreign rule, a nation can produce a new method and pracitce that method with a large measure of success is also a proof of that nation's vitality. It shows that, that nation does not accept enslavement as a settled fact and is determined to struggle against it and to work out new methods for achieving independence.

I have, as a revolutionary, made a very close study of the revolutionary movements in other countries, and I can say without any exaggeration that since 1857 we have used every possible method of revolutionary struggle. In the course of this struggle, tremendous sacrifices have been made and many have given their lives. There was, however, one method that still remained for us to take up and that was the organisation of a real modern national army.

That work we had not done up till recently because it was impossible to do that inside India under the eyes of the British army and the British police. But the moment this war gave the Indian people an opportunity of organising a modern Indian National Army outside Indian they at once seized it. As a result of that effort, and with the help of the Japanese Government and the armed forces of Japan, they have been able to build up this army.

So my point is that throughout our revolutionary struggle against the British Government and their armed forces we have shown sufficient initiative, creative power and vitality and have made tremendous sacrifices. We now hope that under the conditions, and with the advantages that this war has given us, we shall be able, after all, to fulfil our national aspirations and win freedom for India.

Having replied to the question regarding the vitality of the Indian people and their right to live as a free nation. I shall now attempt a sociological analysis of modern India. If you are to understand modern India, you have to take note of three important factors. The first factor is the ancient background, that is, the ancient culture and civilisation of India, of which the Indian people of today are conscious, and of which they feel of proud. The second factor is the struggle which has gone on without any break or interruption since we were finally overpowered by the British. And the third factor consists of certain influences which have come into India from outside.

Modern India is composed of this ancient background, the unbroken national struggle against Britain, and the impact of influences from abroad.

I shall now deal, in some detail, with the influences which have reacted on India from outside and which have been responsible, to some extent, in making modern Indian what it is today. Among these outside influences, the first factor is the influences of Western thought which was crustallised in Liberationism, Constitutionalism and Democracy.

In other words, since 1857, modern liberal and democratic thought has been influencing the intellectuals of India to a large extent.

From the beginning of the present century, a new factor came into operation. After the victory of Japan over Russia in 1904-1905, the eyes of the Indian people were opened to a new movement in Asia, the movement for the revival, not merely of Japan—but along with Japan—of other Asiatic countries. Since then Indian thought has been greatly interested in Asiatic revival. During the last 40 years we have been thinking not merely of what was happening inside India, but also of what was happening in other parts of Asia.

Another important factor which had influence— on our mind–consisted of the revolutionary struggles that have gone on in different parts of the world. Indian revolutionaries studied the Risorgimento Movement in Italy under the leadership of Mazzini and Garibaldi and the struggle of the Irish people against their British oppressors. In Russia, before the last World War, there was, as you know, a movement against the Czar called the Nihilist movement. That also was studied. And nearer India the new awakening in China under the leadership of Dr. Sun Yat-Sen was also studied very closely and with great interest by Indian revolutionaries.

Thus, Indian revolutionaries have been exceedingly receptive to the influences exerted by revolutionary struggles abroad. Then during the last World War, when the revloution broke out in Russia and, as a result of it, a new government—the Soviet Government—came into existence, the work of that Government was studied with great interest in our country.

People in India have not been interested so much in the Communist movement as in the work of reconstruciton in Soviet Russia—in the rapid industrialisation of that country and also in the way in which the Soviet Government solved the problem of minorities. It is this constructive achievement of the Soviet Government which was studied with great interest by people in our country. As a matter of fact, intellectual like our poet Tagore, who had no interest in Communism as such, were profoundly impressed when they visited Russia by the work of educational reconstruciton in that country. Then there is another influence which came to India from ourtside in more recent times—I mean, the new movement in Europe headed by Italy and Germany called Fascism or National Socialism. This movement was also studied by our revolutionaries.

I have just dealt with some of the influences that have reached India from different parts of the world, from England, France, Japan, China, Russia, Germany and so on. I will now take up another question viz., as to how we have reacted to these influences—how much we have accepted and how much we have rejected out of these outside influences.

In dealing with this question of our reaction to these outside influences, I must first point out that there is a big gulf between our generation and the last generation. As typical exponents of the last generation, I would like to mention Tagore and Gandhi. They represent for us the last generation, and between their thoughts and ideas of our generation there is a big gulf.

If you study the works of Tagore and Gandhi, you will find that all along there is a conflict in their minds as to what their reaction to Western influence should be. So far as Mahatama Gandhi is concerned, he has never givern us any clear solution of this problem. He has left people in doubt as to what his attitude is toward the acceptance of Western ideas. Generally speaking his attitude is one of antagonism. But in actual practice he has not always acted in accordance with his own ideas, the reason being that the rest of his countrymen do not share that inner hostility or antagonism which Mahatma Gandhi personally has towards Western ideas and conceptions.

You all know about Mahatma Gandhi's attitude on the question of violence or physical force. He does not advocate the use of arms, or the shedding of the blood of the enemy for gainning one's freedom. This attitude toward vilence or physical force is closely related to his general attitude toward foreign influence, particularly Western influence.

Our generation has followed Mahatma Gandhi as the leader of a political struggle, but has not accepted his ideas on all these questions. Therefore, it would be a mistake to take Mahatma Gandhi as the exponent of the thoughts and ideas of the present generation in India.

Gandhi is in some ways a complex personality, and I would like to analyse his personality, so that you may understand him better. In Gandhi, there are two aspects—Gandhi as a political leader and Gandhi as a philosopher. We have been following him in his capacity as a political leader, but we have not accepted his philosophy.

Now the question arises as to how we can separate the two aspects. Why, if we do not accept his philosophy, are we following him? Though Gandhi has his own philosophy of life, he is a practical politician and therefore, he does not force his own philosophy on the people. Consequently though we are following him in our political struggle, we are free to follow our own philosophy. If Gandhi had tried to thrust his philosophy on us, we would not have accepted him as a leader. But he has kept his philosophy separate from his political struggle.

I have mentioned as representatives and exponents of the last generation Tagore and Gandhi. Now let us compare their philosophies. There are some points on which they agree, but on some other points they do not. The points on which they agree are firstly, that they would like to see the national struggle being conducted without the use of arms. In other words on the question of physical force, they have the same views. On the question of the industrialisation of the country, they also have the same views. Both Tagore and Gandhi are against modern industrial civilisation, But in the realm of culture, their views are not the same. So far as thought, art and culture are concerned. Tagore is prepared to accept foreign influence. He believes that in the realm of culture there should be full cooperation between India and the rest of the world and there should be reciprocity. We should not be hostile of antagonistic to foreign influence. We must however, remember that Mahatma Gandhi has nowhere given a very clear exposition of his views. I am only referring to his general attitude on this question.

I have previously remarked that there is a big gulf between the fundamental thoughts and ideas of the last generation and of our generation. I will now explain what I meant thereby. As I have just said, this problem as to what our reaction should be toward foreign influence and toward industrial civilisation troubled the leaders of the old generation all their lives and we see proofs of it in their actions. But this problem does not exist for us. It does not exist for us, because our starting point is that we want a modern India based of course on the past. We do not believe that India can achieve freedom without use of arms. Now once you take up this attitude, that for winning freedom we have to fight and to use arms it follows that we must have modern industries to manufacture the arms. So we take our stand on modernism. We have to fight the enemy with modern methods and with modern arms—So we must have modern industries. What constituted the biggest problem for the old leaders constitutes our starting point. The problem for modern India is not our attitude toward modernism or foreign influence or industrialisation, but how we are to slove our present day problems.

I believe that modern Japan will understand our generation much better than modern Japan understood the last generation in India. Our stand is virtually the same. We want to build up a new and modern nation on the basis of our old culture and civilisation. For that we need modern industries, a modern army and all those things necessary to preserve our existence and our freedom under modern conditions.

Having dealt with this fundamental standpoint of my generation, I will go on to discuss some of the detailed problems. For the present, of course, the bigger problem is how to fight and win this war. But there is a problem of which you are aware from what you have read in the papers or heard over the radio. I will now consider some of the problems of Free India. The moment India is free, the most important problem will be the organising of our national defence in order to safeguard our freedom in the future. For that we shall have to build up modern war industries. So that we may produce the arms that we shall need for self-defence. This will mean a very big programme of industrialisation.

After satisfying the needs of our nation in the matter of self-defence, the next problem in the degree of importance will be that of poverty and unemployment. India today is one of the poorest countries in the world, but India was not poor before we came under British rule. In fact, it was the wealth of India which attracted the European nations to India. One cannot say that in the matter of national wealth or resources India is poor. We are rich in natural resources, but owing to British and foreign exploitation, the country has been impoverished. So our second most important problem will be how to give employment to the millions of unemployed in India and how to relieve the appalling poverty which now exists among the masses of the Indian people.

The third problem in Free India will be the problem of education. At present, under British rule, about 90 per cent of the people are illiterate. Our problem will be to give at least an elementary education to the Indian masses as soon as possible and along with that to give more facilities to the intellectual classes in the matter of higher education.

Connected with the question of education is another problem which is important for India and that is the question of script. In India there are principally two scripts in vogue. One is the script known as the Sanskrit (or Nagri) script and the other is the Arabic (or Persian) script. Up till today, in all national affairs and conferences we have been using both these scripts. I must add that in some provinces, there are scripts in vogue which are modification of the Sanskrit script. But fundamentally there are two scripts, and in all national affairs and conferences we have to use both these two scripts.

There is now a movement to solve this problem of scripts by using the Latin script. I personally am an advocate of the Latin script. Since we have to live in a modern world, we have to be in touch with other countries and, whether we like it or not, we have to learn the Latin script. If we could make the Latin script the medium of writing throughout the country, that would solve our problem. Anyway that is my own view and the view of my close friends and collaborators.

I have referred to three important problems in Free India national defence, how to remove poverty, and how to give education to the people. If we are to slove these three problems, how are we going to do it? Shall we leave it to private agency and private initiative or will the State take up the responsibility of solving these problems?

Well, at present, public opinion in India is that we cannot leave it to private initiative to solve these national problems, especially the economic problem. If we leave it to private initiative to solve the problem of poverty and unemployment, for instance, it will probably take centuries. Therefore, public opinion in India is in favour of some sort of socialist system, in which the initiative will not be left to private individuals, but the State will take over the responsibility for solving economic questions. Whether it is a question of industrialising the country or modernising agriculture, we want the State to step in and take over the responsibility and put through reform within a short period, so that the Indian people could be put on their legs at a very early date.

But in solving this problem, we want to work in our own way. We will, naturally, study experiments made in other countries—but, after all, we have to solve our problems in an Indian way and under Indian conditions. Therefore, the system to suit the needs of the Indian people.

Now if we do not tackle the economic question from the point of view of the masses, the majority of whom are poor, if we do not do that in India, we shall produce the same confusion or the same difficulties in our country, as we see in China today. You see in China today a split between the Kuomintang and the Chinese Communist Party. Personally I do not see why this should have occurred or why, if the Kuomintang Party has the interests of the Chinese masses at heart, there should be any need to have a separate pary like the Communist Party under foreign influence.

Having learnt from experience,. we do not want to repeat the mistake that China has made. We actually find today that because the nationalist movement in our generation has identified itself with the interest of the masses, that is, of the workers and the peasants who form more than 90 per cent of the people, because we have their interests at heart, there is no *raison d'etre* for a separate party like the Communist Party. If the nationalists in India did not have the interest of the masses at heart, then you would have seen the same phenomenon as you see in China today.

Now we come to another question—namely, the political system of the Government. If we are to have an economic structure of a socialistic character, then it follows that the political system must be such as to be able to carry out that economic programme in the best possible way. You cannot have a so-called democratic system, if that system has to put through economic reforms on a socialistic basis. Therefore, we must have a political system—a State—of an authoritarian character.

We have had some experience of democratic institutions in India and we have also studied the working of democratic institution in countries like France, England and United States of America. And we have come to the conclusion that with a democratic system we cannot solve the problems of Free India. Therefore, modern progressive thought in Indian is in favour of a State of an authoritarian character, which will work as an organ, or as the servant of the masses, and not of a clique or of a few rich individuals.

That is our idea with regard to the political institutions in Free India. We must have a government that will function as the servant of the people and will have full powers to put through new reforms concerning industry, education, defence etc. in Free India.

Before I pass on to the next problem, I should like to mention another point, namely, the attitude of Free India toward religion and caste. This is a question that is frequently asked. India has several religions. Consequenlty, the Government of Free India must have an absolutely neutral and impartial attitude toward all religions and leave it to the choice of every individual to profess or follow a particular religious faith.

With regard to caste, that is now no problem for us, because caste, as it existed in the old times, does not exist today. Now, what is the caste system? The caste system means that a community is divided into certain groups on a professional or vocational basis and marriage takes place within each group.

In modern India there is no such caste distinction. A member of one caste is free to take up any other profession. So, caste in that sense does not exist today. Then there remain the question of marriage. In the old times, it was the custom to marry within each caste. Nowadays, intermariage between the different castes takes place freely. Hence caste is fast disappearing. As a matter of fact, in the nationalist movement we never inquire as to what caste a man belongs to and we do not even know the caste of some of our closest collaborators, which shows that in our generation we do not think at all about caste. For Free India, therefore, caste is no problem at all.

In this connection, I should like to tell you that it was the British who created the impression throughout the world that we are a people quarrelling among ourselves, especially over religion. But that is an absolutely wrong picture of India. It may be that there are certain differences among the Indian people, but such differences you will find in every other country. If we take the so-called progressive countries of the world e.g., France before the outbreak of the present war, or Germany before Hitler and his Party came to power, you will find that there were acute differences among the people in these countries. Spain had even a first-class civil war.

But nobody ever says that, because the people in these countries had disputes and differences, they are not fit to rule themselves. It is only in the case of India that he British say that, because there are certain differences among Indian people therefore they are not fit to be free. Again, the fact is that whatever differences there are among the Indian people are largely the creation of the British Government. There are hundreds of examples to show you that throughout the history of British rule, the British have tried by every possible means to divide the Indian people. After having done so much to artificially create differences among the Indian people, the British turn around and say that we are not fit to be free.

I should also point out that if you take a modern Power like Soviet Russia and see how heterogeneous the composition of the Soviet Union is, you will realise that if, in spite of this heterogeneous character, so many different religious could be unified in one political system and become such a strong power, there is absolutely no reason why India which has much more homogeneity than the Soviet Union, should not be united as one nation. As a matter of fact, you will find that outside India, where there is no British influence, there are no differences among the Indian people. In the Indian Independence.Movement in East Asia and in the Indian National Army there is no question of religion or caste or class. It is just in India where the British have influence and control that you will find these differences.

On the question of national unity, I should like to give you a friendly warning that British propaganda tries to give the world the impression that the Muslims of India do not support the independence movement. This is wrong. Very often you read in the papers about certain organisations like the Muslims League or the Hindu Mahasabha. The British boost these organisations, because they are in their policy pro-British and are against the Indian National Congress, and they try to make that Muslim League represents the Muslims of India. But that is British propaganda. The fact is that the Muslim League and its leader, Mr. Jinnah, represent only a minority of the Indian Muslims. The majority of the Indian Muslims are nationalists and they support the independence movement as much as anyone else. The President of the Indian Naitonal Congress is a Muslim, and so are many other members of the Congress, many of whom are in prison today.

These facts are not known to the outside world and the outside world gets the impression that Mr. Jinnah represents all the Muslims of India, and that they are not supporting the nationalist movement. I would like to give out this warning about British propaganda.

I have already told you about the kind of economic and political system that we would like to have in Free India. Out of this, arises the problem as to what our political philosophy is. On this question, I gave my own views in a book I wrote about ten years ago called "The Indian Struggle." In that book I said that it would be our task in India to evolve a system that would be a synthesis of the system in vogue in different parts of the world. For instance, if you take the conflict between Fascism (or what you might call National Socialism) on the one side and Communism on the other, I see no reason why we cannot work out a synthesis of the two systems that will embody the good points of both. It would both foolish for any one to say that any one system represents the last stage in human progress. As students of philosophy, you will admit the human progress can never stop and out of the past experience of the world we have to produce a new system. Therefore, we in India will try to work our synthesis of the rival systems and try to embody the good points of both.

Now I would like to compare some of the good points of National Socialism and Communism. You will find some things common to both. Both are called anti-democratic or totalitarian. Both are anti-capitalistic. Nevertheless, in spite of these common points, they differ on other points. When we see National Socialism in Europe today, what do we find? National Socialism has been able to create national unity and solidarity and to improve the condition of the messes. But it has not been able to radically reform the prevailing economic system which was built up on a capitalistic basis.

On the other side, let us examine the Soviet experiment based on Communism. You will find one great achievement and that is planned economy. Where Communism is deficient is that it does not appreciate the value of national sentiment. What we in India would like to have is a progressive system which will fulfil the social needs.of the whole people and will be based on national sentiment. In other words, it will be a syntesis of Nationalism and Socialism. This is something which has not been achieved by the Naitonal Socialists in Germany today.

There are a few points in which India does not follow Soviet Russia. Firstly, class conflict is something that is quite unnecessary in India. If the Government of Free India begins to work as the organ of the masses then there is no need for class conflict. We can solve our problems by making the state the servant of the masses.

There is another point which has been overemphasised by Soviet Russia and that is the problem of the working classes. India being predominantly a country of peasants, the problem of the peasants will be more important than the problem of the working classes.

Another point on which we do not fully agree is that according to Marxism, too much importance is given to the economic factor in human life. We fully appreciate the importance of the economic factor which was formerly ignored, but it is not necessary to overemphasis it.

To repeat once again, our political philosophy should be a synthesis between National, Socialism and Communism. The conflict between thesis and antithesis has to be resolved in a higher synthesis. This is what the Law of Dialectic demands. If this is not done, then human progress will come to an end. India will, therefore, try to move to the next stage of political and social evolution. I will now pass on to the last point in my address, and that is our conception of an international order. On this point I have already spoken several times in Tokyo. I full support the steps that have been taken through the Joint Declaration to create a new order in East Asia on the right basis of freedom, justice and reciprocity. I have been personally greatly interested in international problems, having tried to work in several countries in order to get support for our movement and, in that connection. I also had the opportunity of studying the work of the League of Nations.

The experiment of the League of Nations has failed, and it is desirable and profitable for us to investigate as to why it failed. If I were to answer that I would say that it failed because the sponsor-nations were too selfish and short-sighted. The sponsor-nations were England, France and America. America dropped out of the League, so the Powers that controlled the League were England and France. Now these two leading Powers, instead of setting an example of unselfishness, tried to use the League of Nations for their selfish interests and for their own benefit. The only basis on which we can set up an international order is freedom, justice and reciprocity.Therefore, the work in East Asia has commenced on the right lines and on the right basis. The only task that remains for us is to see that in actual work the principles embodied in the Joint Declaration are put into effect. If they are so put into effect, then the experiment will be a success. If not, then it will again prove to be a failure. You must have seen in my speeches and press statements that I have been very enthusiastic about this Joint Declaration. There are several reasons. Firstly, it is on the right basis and on the right lines that the work has begun. Secondly, if you want to set up an international order, it has to have a beginning in a particular region. If we make it a success in one region, it can gradually be expanded all over the world.

It is very difficult to set up a world order suddenly out of nothing and make it a succss. But if you begin in one region where friendship and reciprocity between the nations can be developed, and if in that region you meet with success, then that example will be emulated by other nations in other parts of the world. So the method of setting up a regional order is the only way in which a world order can gradually be built up.

The third reason is that I have found that this idea or plan finds support among the mass of the people of this country, and especially among the youths. If I had found that this new order was being sponsored by a few politicains or leaders and that the rest of the nation was apathetic or indifferent, I should certainly not be optimistic. But it is because I have found that the people as a whole, and especially the youths are vitally interested in it and support it enthusiastically, that I believe that through the cooperation of the leaders and the people and the youths, it can be made a success.

I should like to repeat that this undertaking is for the Government and the people of this country a very great responsibility. As you know, your Government was responsible for sponsoring this idea, so you are the sponsor-nation. The League of Nations failed, because the sponsor-nation were selfish and short-sighted. This time if the nations that have joined together, and particularly the sponsor-nation, avoid a selfish and short-sighted policy and work on a moral basis, then I see no reason why the experiment should not be a success.

I should like to emphasise again the tremendous responsibility which Japan has undertaken by becoming the sponsor-nation in this task. And when I talk of the responsibility of the nation, I want also to stress the responsibility of the youths. The youths of today will be the nation and the leaders of tomorrow. An idea that is welcomed and supported by the youths will one day be supported by the whole nation. But an idea which does not find support among the youths will die an natural death. Therefore, the responsibility for making this new order a success devolves, in the last analysis, on the youths of this country. I hope and pray and trust that the youths and the students who are the future representatives of the nation will realise the tremendous moral responsibility which Japan has undertaken in initiating this new order.

There may be people who doubt whether a nation can rise to a high moral level, whether a nation can be farsighted and unselfish, to live one's life at a high moral level, I see no reason why an entire nation cannot also rise to that level. In the history of the world we have seen examples in which a revolution has changed the mentality of a whole nation and made it rise to a high level of morality. Therefore, if anybody has any doubt whether an entire nation can rise to that level, then I do not share that doubt.

I repeat, in conclusion, that the sponsor-nation should realise the tremendous responsibility that it has undertaken. This is a task not only for the leaders and the politicians, but for the whole nation and especially for those who are the hopes of the nation—the youths and the students.

5

Bose Press interview in Tokyo. Expresses his views on the future course of action against the British in India. (Extract)[1]

8 November, 1944

If one were impartially and objectively to select the twenty leaders of the nations of the world who are making history today, it would be difficult not to include. His Excellency Subhas Chandra Bose. He is the central and guilding force behind the movement of 15 million free Indians outside of their homeland, who are backed by 388-million of their countrymen at home and are pledged to regain independence for their country. He is the undisputed leader of these men and women. To a large extent India's eventual fate rests upon the success or failure of his military campaign.

Of the many leaders of the world, I have interviwed during the past twenty years, Netaji impresses me as the most earnest and determined as well as one of the most cordial and warm-hearted. He seems to be imbued with a magical power to win one over to his cause. And his charming personality gives one a delightful first impression, a feeling which keeps on growing as you talk with him. You seem to be at ease from the very moment he greets you, and you are drawn to him by his warmth even before the conversation gets well under way.

"You must be finding it cold here," I asked his Excellency as we shook hands.

"Why no," he answered. And before these words were uttered. I knew from the sunny smile on his dynamic face, from the manner in which he responded, that there was need to feel him out.

Netaji talks with glow and zeal, passionately but not fanatically and you soon understand why his supporters treat him worshipfully, why their accounts of his activities and pronouncement verge on the plastic. He instintively gives the feeling that he will not fail those who place their trust in him.

1. *Nippon Times*, 10 Nov, 1944.

One of the first questions I put to him was what, from his experience as the leader of the Free India Army, he could say to them the often trepeated British contention that the various sets and religious elements in India could never get together.

"Yes," he declared, "we have many religious elements in our National Army. Hindus, Mohammedans, Christian, and they are all fighting and cooperating together wholeheartedly. It is especially so in our Army since the Indians in East Asia, who constitute the soldiers of our Army, are widely varied as to religion. One could really say that the National Army is a picture of the whole of India, so we give the reply to British propaganda in actual practice and in our deeds.

"The British contention has been proved wrong even from this. As a matter of fact, the whole endeavour of the British is to attempt to divide Hindus and Mohammedans. In the last fight in 1857, after which the British conquered India, also the different religious elements were fighting side by sside, especially this talk of the religious difference in India is a creation of British in recent years.

"You see, that is the only arguement which the British can put forth to deny freedom to India. They couldn't very well say openly that they were dominating India for selfish reasons.

"Up to now we have given arugment for argument. We have replied by arugment. But now we are replying by action to show that we can live together, fight together and die together, for our country and to give the lie to the British contention."

Netaji is a heavy-set bulk-some man by Oriental standards. He is in the pink of condition, a thing which seems surprising in view of the arduous life he has led during the past year, much of it in malaria infested jugles on the fighting front in India, where the hardships must have ofen been extreme. The worry which naturally must have been entailed by the different military and political problems which confronted him, would have harried a less vigorous man.

For Mr. Bose the recent campaign on the Indo-Burmes border, in which his Free India Army has had to withdraw in a few sectors after practically getting into striking distance of Imphal, is not a frustrated effort. Rather he has found new strength in it, strength born of the knowledge of what his man are capable, and inversely of the weakness of the enemy.

We stand for full independence for India. Recently in a press report after, I came to Tokyo, it was stated that a number of leaders of the Indian

National Congress, who are not in prison, met and unanimously supported Gandhi in finally breaking the talks with Jinnah."

No one can talk with the Netaji for any length of time and not be moved by his sincerity, his patriotism and his fervent desire to see his country free.

The facial feature of this leaders of free Indians, cut him out as a persons who is interested in big things rather than in details. His fleshy checks, which jut out prominently, have a forcefulness in them that is striking and which do not fit in with the first impression one obtains of a mild, even jovial personality.

Netaji's well-modelled face is swarthy by Occidental standards bu unusually fair for an Indian. And as you talk to him, you'are moved by his masterful command of English Language, his emotionalism and his intense interest in the subject he is discussing.

Talking about he American penetration into India, he declared—

"I might say that the United states came into India during the course of this war with a double purpose. The first was, through India, to help Chungking, primarly on the military side, and also to give military help to the British in India. They have given in the British so far, mainly, apart from them aid to war materials, but they are not doing it unselfishly. Taking advantge of war, they are trying to penetrate economically also. They have also invested some capital, purchase some railways. In appears that they are showing more interest in their commercial ponetration in the Eastern side of India. They don't seem to have much interest in the Western part of India. The Eastern part of India is where British capital is still more influential. I mean where it is more influential than Indian capital. Around Bengal the British have developed their industries and therefore in that area British capital is more important.

"It may be that they want to take even the interests which the British capitalist controlled at one time. Another reason is, perhaps they think that from Eastern India it is possible to make a connection with China overland or by air. If they settle down commercially in the Eastern part, it will help their connection with Chungking, either by the land route, that is the Burma route or they might try the Ledo route. They can also make commercial contract with Chungking by air.

Months of hard fighting much of it in the rain, and all of it under condition which facored the enemy, have given the Netaji the conviction that his army can and will eventually march to New Delhi.

Regarding the much-talked of difference between Mahatama Gandhi and Jinnah, which some attribute to British machinations, the Netaji declared.

"There are in India certain organizations like Hindu Mahasabha and Muslim League that are following a pro-British policy, and such organization exist among members of all religions, for example, among the Hindus who are weak in their national feeling, among the Mohammedans. What the British are trying to do is to give these Pro-British organization as much importance as they can, in order to minimize the importance of the Nationalist Party. It has been particularly their policy all along to give as much prominence to the Muslim League.

"The majority of the Mohammedans also are nationalist and they want freedom. The Muslim League represents only a minority.

"Now take this Muslim League which has been showing a pro-British policy, not always but in recent years. It has recently adopted a plan, what they call the Pakistan Plan. Which aims to divide India into several States. Unfortunately the Muslim League has adopted this plan, which began origianlly as a British plan.

"This plan to divide India was first conceived by some British politicians in London. In Ireland they also tried it and put it into effect. They tried it in Palestine too, to divide it into Jewish and Arabian states, which could not be put through because of the war.

This policy of dividing a country is a policy followed by the British everywhere in the world, wherever they go and succeed in ruling. The only alternative left for them in India was to try to divide the country. The plan, as I have said, was conceived in London by some British politicians. Then leaders of some of the pro-British Mohammedans took it up, and recently, that is during this war, Mr. Jinnah adopted this plan.

"Now this is a plan which the Nationalists, whether Hindu or Muslim, can never accept. No one wants to see his country divided into a number of States? I myself think it a mistake for Mahatma Gandhi to have had the talks at all. It was so futile; there was no chance of coming to any agreement with Jinnah. But probably Gandhi was thinking of bringing Jinnah round to some agreement. He thought that if he had an agreement with Jinnah, he could face the British Govenment more strongly. But it was a mistake. The first mistake was that with Jinnah it is impossible to have an agreement Secondly, even if Jinnah agree in some sort of agreement, he will never join in the fight against Britain. He has been following a pro-British policy to recent years. As soon as I heard that the talks were going to take place. I said both through press statements and by boradcasts that it was à mistake, and that nothing will come of it.

"Unforunately, Gandhi started thinking that somehow he could bring Jinnah to an agreement. Now the talks have broken down and I am glad of it. We don't want any compromise with the British, for a compromise will mean that we have to give in, that we don't get complete independence. No, we aren't interested at all in any talk of compromise. I have always said that compromise with Britain will mean compromise with slavery.

6

Secretary, Assam Government asking Reports from Political Agent. Manipur about the Persons, who helped the Japanese[1]

13 November, 1944

I am vaguely aware that steps are being taken in Manipur to collect evidence against a number of persons—Manipuris, Kukis and others—who are known or suspected to have taken an active part on the side of the Japanese during the invasion of their territory.

It seem to me that there may be difficulties firstly in sifting the evidence which is being collected and secondly in finding an efficient prosecuting staff. As you know Profulla Das Gupta's services had to be utilised in the prosecution of certain murder cases although they at that moment were not strictly his line of country, but it is unlikely that he would again be available - if indeed it was contemplated by you that he should carry out the necessary preliminaries in these cases and I therefore write to ask if you would be requiring any assistance in the way of officers to this end. I should also be glad to hear if these trials are being, or are likely to be, undertaken by Military Courts.

I would have written to Edwards of this subject but I imagine he will have left by the time this letter reaches you.

1. Assam State Archiese, Special Branch Files, Dispur, Guwahati.

7

Report by E. T. D. Lamhert on the Hill People in the North-East Who Helped the Japanese and I.N.A.[1]

15 November, 1944

The men who joined the Japanese Hikari Kikan were employed in a somewhat similar manner to those employed by the British V. Force. They worked in connection both with military and civil affairs and their main duty was to report to the Japanese officer whatever they heard or came to know in their areas. They were given arm-bands with Japanese letters painted in black ink on a white background, and the following persons are noted as members of this organisation:—

1. Pakhai of Lakhan (SF 0565)
2. Yangrong, Headman of Yangmull
3. Yangkhongam of Maku (RK 9089)
4. Letkhothang of Yangmul
5. Tongkhothang of Chassad (RK 9963)

The following persons are also alleged to have assisted the Japanese:—

1. Pakhai of Lakhan (SF 0565)
2. Yandong of Lakhan (SF 0565)
3. Tongkhothang Headman of Chassad (RK 9963)

A secret report, dated 24.3.1944, stated that he arranged men to figth for the Japanese against the British. The same source again reported on 11.9.1944, that he was addressing people for siding with the Japanese. Another secret report, dated 19.8.1944, stated that he declared himself as Rajah (King) of Haokip according to the promise of the Japanese, held three meetings at Chassad, Maokot, and Nungse and urged people to supply food, men and guide to the Japs. He also asked people to arrest the

1. E. T. D. Lamhert was the Intelligence Officer. Assam State Archives, Special Branch Files, Dispur, Guwahati

men who helped the British and to inform the Japanese of such men. A secret report, dated 11.9.44, also states that this man was set up as a Rajah by the Japanese and was authorised to raise two gunmen from each village and to collect house taxes. Another secret report, dated 7. 9. 1944 stated that in November, 1943 he crossed the Chindwin in order to contact the Japs and to ask for 400 rifles for fighting the British which request was turned down. He took an oath of friendship with the Japs by biting the sword of a Japanese officer, and was given a gold ring by the Japs as a token of friendship. The Japs also took his photograph and distributed copies there of among army units. He is also reported to have been collecting abandoned arms for Kukis.

4. Onkhoram, 2nd Headman of Chassad (9963).
5. Khaingam of Chassad (RK 9963)..
6. Ngamahao of Gribang (RK 1761).
7. Paong of Maku (RK 9529).

The A. S. I. states that he has heard that the Japanese left behind some of their agents, and he gives a particular instance of a man. viz. Angdong of Lakhan (SF 0565) who is reported to have visited Thanan (SF 0649) in Burma on 15. 7. 1944 to give the Japanese information of British movements after the former had left Manipur state.

8

Assam Governor asking the Political Agent to Submit Latest Reports on Persons from Manipur, Who Joined the Japanese[1]

22 November, 1944

I am directed to invite a reference to the report encolsed in the Central Intelligence Officer's Memo. No. 21/Police (II) / 376– 80 FIB. dated the 2nd November 1944 and also the several reports which have come in from the F. I. B. and other sources in connection with alleged disloyal activities on the part of inhabitants of Manipur State and the Manipur Hills and to say that His Excellency who has been considering the whole position, would be glad of your considered opinion of the situation especially in regard to the Kukis.

His Excellency would be grateful for an assurance that vigorous action is being taken to deal with alleged fifth columnists and that you are also giving this matter your close and constant attention.

I am to request you to submit a complete list of all persons so far named in connection with disloyal acitivities together with a short note against each showing what action has already been taken and/or is being contemplated.

2. It is now hoped that Webster will be relieved in order to take over as Superintendent of Police, Manipur, by the first week in January.

1. Assam State Archives, Special Branch Files, Dispur, Guwahati.

9

Bose while Addressing a Mammoth gathering of Indians in Singapore; Referrs to the Events of the Past One Year and How the I.N.A. Performed on the Battle Front; Asks the People to be Ready for a Fresh War Against the British[1]

17 December 1944

We have achieved a lot during the past one year. The establishment of the Provisional Government last year in the month of October was the stepping stone for our success. When our Army of Liberation started from Syonan on their march to Delhi, Indians were thinking under what government we are going to fight and to whom our victories can be attributed. History records many instances of establishment of similar Provisional Governments. But the establishment of our Provisional Government was unique in that it was recognised by nine world Powers. No other revolutionary government has received so much esteem and respect as ours. India is no longer a slave country in the eyes of these nations. In the history of the world we have witnessed many revolutions. Let us take, for instance, Ireland. The Irish people established their Provisional Government. But the respect that our Provisional Government commands to-day was never commanded by Ireland. America had sympathies with the Irish cause. De Valera went to America to seek American assistance. He managed to get money, but not respect. He returned disappointed. The secret of respect commanded by us lies in the recognition of our Government by nine world powers. The Indian sisters and brothers in Malaya will have their honourable place in the history of India. It is here in Syonan that the Azad Hind Fauj was organised. It was here in Syonan that the Provisional Government of Azad Hind was established. It was from Syonan that the Azad Hind Fauj began its march to India. We expect ceaseless help and assistance from Syonan.

1. I.N.A. Relief and Enquiry Committee Paper, Darya Ganj, New Delhi. See also K.S. Giani, *op.cit.*, pp 135-139

While I was in Rangoon I learnt that the revolutionary spirit and enthusiasm of the people of Malai and Syonan is coming down. I have come here to see it for myself, If it is really true, I am sorry to say that it is a matter for regret. The war of independence for India is not a child's play. It is a matter of life and death for 38 crores of Indians. Either we will live like free men or we will embrace death.

I know there are British agents in Syonan, left by them when they retreated to spread false rumours and propaganda. But it does not concern us Indians. There is only one way left to us and that is the way to Delhi. There is no room for compromise. These enemy agents may be able to put obstacles in our path, but we have only one thought branded in our heart and soul and that is India and her Independence.

I have brought with me Divisional Commander Colonel M.Z. Kiani to furnish you with up-to-date information about the battles in the Arakan and Imphal. I could have brought other Commanders also with me. But it was not possible to bring all of them here.

Before I came here I went to Tokyo. My object in visiting Tokyo was to establish personal contact with the members of the new Cabinet and to discuss with the members of the Imperial Government and leaders of Army and Navy concerning future programme, both political, and military. We have settled all questions, both military and political amicably. As regards military questions, I cannot disclose them as they are military secrets. As regards political questions, diplomatic relations will be established very soon which will strengthen our position. That will enable us to work with close co-operation and prosecute the war successfully.

At the end of December last year I toured the Andamans. On the 30th December we hoisted our National Flag on the British Chief Commissioner's residence. I had talks with Nipponese authorities and it was agreed that the Provisional Government of Azad Hind should send a Commissioner there. So Colonal A.D. Loganathan was sent to Andamans as Chief Commissioner. In January I went to Rangoon and along with me Army and League Headquarters were shifted to Rangoon. On the 4th February, an offensive was launched in Arakan against the Anglo Americans. The Arakan fight was a minor struggle, but great important was attached to it. It was the first test to our Army of Liberation. Hitherto no one knew much about the Azad Hind Fauj. The world was amazed at the bravery and courage displayed by the Azad Hind Fauj. It was a wonder not for us but for those who had shades of doubt in the core of their heart. Before we began the offensive Nipponese Army authorities asked a question whether the Azad Hind Fauj will be able to undergo all hardships with Nippon forces. The commanders were instructed to ensure from their officers and men, before giving any definite answer. When the soldiers of the Azad Hind Fauj were questioned they all with one voice replied that they are capable of enduring as many hardships as the Nippon soldiers can endure and even more. They knew they were fighting the battle of India's independence. But in spite of this assurance, the Nipponese still had some doubts. But when it was proved that the Azad Hind Fauj is giving a bold show to the enemy, they were very much surprised.

This war is not waged by Nippon alone. It is a national war for India's liberation. We have to go to India and therefore will have to suffer more and more difficulties. Although the battle of Arakan was a minor struggle it was very important to us because it was the first test of our forces. On the 18th March the Provisional Government proclaimed that the Azad Hind Fauj crossed the Indo-Burma border and were fighting on Indian soil. In March our advance was so rapid that when our thrust into Imphal was delayed there were inquiries why Imphal was still standing against our assault. I was annoyed at persons asking such questions. These were persons who were not actually on the front line, but far behind in their homes. Those who know anything about fighting will not ask such questions. Only military observers realise the strategical importance of Imphal and Chittagong. If these cities had no military importance we would have caputred them earlier. The fortifications on the Eastern Front of India are like that of Maginot Line in France. So long as these fortifications are safe, the British are secure. When these fortifications are pierced through, our forces will easily make rapid advance towards Delhi.

In each and every battle there is a certain strategic point which will decide the course of the war. Those who are aware of the past history of India know well that Panipat always settled the fate of India. But in this war the fate of India will be settled somewhere in the jungles between Imphal and Chittagong. When once we smash enemy fortifications on the Eastern Frontier and reach the plains of Bengal and Assam then our road to Delhi will be clear. So the enemy will strive hard to hold these fortifications. In this war when the Maginot Line was pierced, France collapsed in a few weeks. So when the fate of Chittagong and Imphal is sealed there will be no war in the Bengal Province and our advance to Calcutta will be only a route march.

I have just now told you that the battle of Imphal and Chittagong will settle the fate of India. We will get hold of these important strategic points at all cost even if we have to attempt ten times or more. When we withdrew from Imphal people were disappointed. They asked for my opinion and I replied that there is no doubt for any such ground. We know our path and we will never waver until we reach our goal.

Friends, we should realise the importance of Imphal and Chittagong and be ready to make any sacrifice to occupy these cities. Once we take these strategical centres, our task will become easier for it will have wide repercussions throughout India. There is no Indian who likes the British. Every Indian hates the British and if a handful of them side with the British it is not out of love for the British but to achieve their self-interests. If the three hundred and eighty million Indians rose in revolt they could have annihilated the British with sticks and stones. Then there would have been no necessary for the Azad Hind Fauj. It is regrettables that they have not seen the destruction of the British with their own eyes as we Indians in East Asia have experienced. You are confident that the British Empire will be shattered. Now it is our duty to go into India and defeat the British so that the 380 million Indians could see the destruction of the British with their own eyes.

Friends, you perhaps remember that in August last year in the course of a speech at the Farrer Park I said that before the end of this year we will cross the Indo-Burma border and will stand on Indian soil. When I spole I thought we will be able to commence fighting in the month of December. But we were delayed on account of necessary military preparations. Our forces entered India in March and we were fighting on broad front from Akyab to Kohima. We defeated the enemy in every battle but due to transport difficulties we could not continue our advance. In the heavy rain we had only two courses open to us : either to stay in these jungles or to withdraw. The Nippon commander and our commanders considered over the matter and it was decided to withdraw because to stay in these jungles meant disaster to the army. When the enemy saw that we have withdrawn and the road was clear they occupied the place without resistance and proclaimed to the whole world by every weapon of propaganda that they have won a great victory. But our officers and men know the real reason for our withdrawal. we are confident that we can occupy all the lost ground in no time. I would once again stress the importance of Imphal and Chittagong and we will have to occupy these places at any cost. After six months of battle we have judged correctly our strength and the strength of our enemy.

When the Azad Hind Fauj was organised the enemy began to make propaganda that the Azad Hind Fauj was not an army but only a propaganda stunt. But when our 'army went into action the British propagandists changed their tune and began to give out that the Azad Hind Fauj was very poorly equipped. In reply I said that our army possessed everything except meat, rum, beer and whisky which were abundantly supplied to theBritish forces. Our army will fight in the face of hunger and thirst. There have been many revolutions in the world history, but you can never find a single example where the revolutionary army was better equipped than their opponents. They have succeeded not because of the strength of their weapon or of numbers but by the strength of their conviction that they are fighting for a sacred cause. Take the case of Ireland. She had 5,000 revolutionaries who had dedicated their lives for their country. The British sent 50,000 troops well equipped to crush the revolution. But they miserably failed in spite of their superiority in number and weapons. I know very well the strength of our enemies and I know what we are capable of doing. We will have to make great sacrifices. Even if every soldier and officer of the Azad Hind Fauj has to lay down his life for the liberation of 380 million Indians, we are prepared for that. Even if the three million Indians in East Asia turn destitutes, that is nothing. We are proud that we are given such a golden opportunity to serve our Motherland. We are thankful to God that we have got men and material needed for the liberation of India. Three million Indians have been united. Now we have to pay the price of our independence with our blood which is not a big price. Now the responsibility that lies on our shoulders is to strengthen our army and march across into India. There is only one way for us. We have to shed our blood. So many of our comrades laid down their lives in the first campaign; nobody can say how many of us will remain alive until the war of liberation comes to a successful conclusion. Officers and men who hesitate to lay down their lives have no place in this army. Side by side with the Army the nation has to make total sacrifices. The nation must be prepared for such a sacrifice. Last year in Bengal Province alone 20 lakhs of Indians perished due to starvation. 5 lakhs of Indians retreated along with the British from Burma and out of these more than one lakh lost their lives. If so many Indians had given up their lives for the independence of our Motherland, India to-day would have been a free country. If you are not willing to face death for the liberation of your country you have no right to call yourself an Indian. Some so-called Indians think that if India is freed they can go to India and if the British came back then also they can go back to India. I can assure these traitors that they will not go to India. We are not liberating India for them. They will have no place in a free India. We will pick up all those traitors and they will be at the mercy of the Free Government. The only favour they may expect from us will be a third class ticket to Britain.

Friends, we have to enhance our programme of total mobilisation. Preparations are being made for the next offensive and we are collecting materials for this campaign. Our well-to-do brothers who are lagging behind will have to come forward and make sacrifices. Those wealthy Indians who have amassed a great fortune and are afraid to lay down their lives will have to take a Habeeb mixture. Janab Habeeb is the first patriot who has sacrificed all his property, amounting to ten million and three thousand rupees. Those people who do not enjoy sleep thinking of their money may better take a dose of Habeeb mixture and cure themselves by contributing all their money for our funds. I tell you as long as the entire nation is not fully prepared to sacrifice everything our victory cannot be achieved. We must inspire and set an example to those who are obstructing our way. Fortunately their number is very small. Still they are doing harm to our movement. They think that we can only prattle and that we cannot suppress them. Now the entire nation has to come under military discipline. Those who are weak we will make them strong. And if we are forced to suppress these enemy agents disguised as Indians I know the whole nation will support us. Up to this time we entreated you with folded hands. In Nippon, Germany or in England, the Governments never request but order. I can sure you that not only Syonan but the whole world, except perhaps America, is suffering from food shortage. The reason for America not suffering from such food shortage is that war has not gone to American soil. If you are prepared to sacrifice everything then the food problem will not exist at all. We also need more volunteers for the Rani of Jhansi Regiment; so I have to appeal to our sisters to come forward and join the Regiment.

I would like to ask you a question. I want you to answer honestly. When I was in Rangoon I received a report that the revolutionary spirit and enthusiasm of Indians in Syonan are fading. Now tell me how many of you are willing to work with us, prepared to make any sacrifice and to fight shoulder to shoulder with us and, if need be, to die with us ?"

Immediately the whole audience got up and expressed their willingness to lay down their lives or make any sacrifice for the liberation of India. They shouted "Inqilab Zindabad," "Netaji ki Jai" and "Chalo Delhi."

10

Report by A. D. Loganadan on his activities in Andamans as Chief Commissioner[1]

23 December 1944

To the Head of State, Provisional Govt. of Azad Hind.

Jai Hind,

A short note on the work done at Port Blair by the staff of the Provisional Government of Azad Hind from 18th February 2604 to the date of my departure, 30th September 2604 is submitted. The problems in the Andamans are about the same as are common in all occupied territories with the exceptions that are peculiar to Islands that are far flung and form the front line of offence or defence. The defect in the quality and quantity of food is partially made good by the intense selfsufficiency programme to the extent possible locally. The increasing shortage of clothing has to remain unsolved as importation is impossible. The civilians have realised that while the War is on they have to put up with discomforts and inconveniences, go without even some of the essentials and should give their best for tthe final victory. It is pleasing to record that the maximum output consistent with health and fitness has been reached. But the local administration as judged by the standards of their own country may be less generous in their findings out this misconception is due to the exhibition by the civilians of depression and helplessness and the feeling of insecurity caused by the spy scare. It is astounding to note and I am ashamed to acknowledge that there should have been so many cases of spying by the Indians in these inaccessible but liberated Islands. Considering the smallness of population, the greatness of their illiteracy, the absence of intelligentsia, the definite anti British feeling amongst the ex-convicts and their pro-Japanese feeling on being released and made free citizens with the prospects of returning to their homes in India. I must confess that my comprehension is at a discount, not to discover the cause of spying. The table below shows the period covered and the number punished so far.

1. I.N.A. Trail Papers.

Case No.	*Date*	*Shot or hanged*	*Imprisoned for various terms.*
1.	March 2603	7	—
2.	January 2604	43	22
3.	April 2604	3	6
4.	May 2604	2	—
5.	June 2604	—	1
6.	September 2604	200 under arrest and investigation	—

A few of them are said to have died of illness developed while under arrest.

The table above does not include those that are arrested and detailed as witness. It is stated that in Port Blair there is not a single house one or two inmates of which have not suffered; as a rule the educated (which here means English knowing) are the chief victims. These were and are Ex and present Government servants of importance and influence and a scare amongst them leads to general stampede. The situation of spying in Andamans as with a small stationary population seems to be completely a contrast to that of the rest of the countries in the Far Eastern Asia where 22 million of Indians are scattered and live peacefully and actively with different nationalist under different and superimposed Government organisation with a few or no spics at all.

(a) Education— Taken over and nationalised by Major Alvi.

(b) Judiciary—Civil disputes—deal with by 2/Lt. Iqbal.

(c) Supplies—2/Lt. Suba Singh attached.

(d) Propaganda—All required by the Japanese administration are carried out especially on the montly Provisonal Government Day and assembly meetings. Any propaganda for the Independence movement is ineffective.

(e) Assembly of Andaman Adminstration Councillors—A Sleepy Council with self-imposed silence result of scare.

(f) The total amount of work done by staff is so little that their absence will not be missed.

   (a) The higher authorities say that we have been helpful but to what extent I cannot conceive.

   (b) The subordinates think and feel and show that we are a hindrance to their work. This is applicable chiefly to the Police Department.

(c) The public have lost confidence in us as we failed to lessen their sufferings.

(d) The public feel that withdrawal of Provisional Government may improve their lot as its intervention if any is likely to stiffen the attitude of the local authorities. The staff of the Provisional Government is composed of nationalist Indians who knowing the language, customs and habits of their own people, are best qualified to deal with all matters concering Indians. If the Nippon authorities have belief in the Indian Independence Movement and confidence in Netaji they must trust the staff to deal with all Police matters including spying without any reservation of military secrecies which is as much our concern as our allies.

Police is the first department that should be completely handed over without any interference later prior to considering transfer of other subjects which being of secondary importance may well wait for better times. The thoroughness with which the authorities had dealt with spy suspects during the past 18 months would, one would expect, have eliminated all vestige of spying. We will be rendering a very valuable service in total War efforts by relieving the local authorities of unnecessary anxieties and worries and thus let them concentrate on Military measures which are of prime importance.

"Jai Hind"

11

Persons from Manipur Who Helped the Japanese and I.N.A.[1]

28 December, 1944

I am submitting herewith the lists of local suspects. They have been classified in four different classes. The Security Police is always on the look out for the class of people known as "Traitors" and also collecting all possible evidence against them, but so far no clue of their being in the valley could be found. Moreover the Security section is making surprise check on the movement of local suspects from time to time.

No.	*Name and Address*	*Brief note of Being taken as traitor*	*Remark*
1.	Potsangbam Tomal Singh of Chingamakha	This man was a leading member in Manipuri Mahasabha and Praja Sanmeloni as well. He had closed connection with Irabot Singh, the Ex-President of Manipuri Mahasabha. During the stay of enemy at Moirang this man with Laisram Kanhai Singh a prominent man of the said Samitee proceeded to—Moirang via Thanga Karang by boat on the false pretext of being bought fish. At Sendra these men came in contact with Mairengham Koireng Singh of Moriang & joined the enemy party. One Thongam Munal Singh who had returned from the camp of these man said that they were living on the bank of Moirang Turel and had talked with Col. Malik through P/790 Naki Ahmad. From Private information it is clear that these people had gone with Jap on their retreat. No news about their being in the valley is found as yet.	

1. Special Branch Papers. Assam State Archieve, Dispur, Gawahati. See these records for more details about persons, who helped I.N.A.

No.	Name and Address	Brief note of Being taken as traitor	Remark
2.	Laisaram Kanhai Singh of Sagalambi.	Same as above.	
3.	Thokchom Angow Singh of Singjamei Thokchem Leikai	The man was sometimes a President of Manipuri Praja-Sanmilani. During last part of May 1944 he left home for Sendra to become a private tutor for certain boys of Moriang and Thanga. After a week or so ofhis departure from home rumour came to the effect that he had also joined the I.N.A. party at Moirang. On interrogation of Thangam Munal Singh who had escaped from the Japs campaign gave the story that he had seen this man with other Manipuri Jap helpers at a hut near Moirang Turel. Munal Singh said that he knew that this man definitely well. From information it is learnt that he with his compaions had gone back with Japs. No news has since been heard about him.	
4.	Longjam Bijoy Singh of Elang Leikai.	This man was Secreatry of Praja Sanmelony. He hd close relation with Irabet Singh, the ex-President. About the time when Thokchom Angow Singh had left home this man also left Imphal and went straight to Buri Bazar. He stayed some nights in the house of Wahengbam Jhaneswor Singh where he used to stay during evacuation from homes. He went to Moirang by the edge of Loktak lake and joined the others. He has not returned home since then. Thangam Munal Singh also gave his descripition fully. He is also said to have gone with his companions. His present whereabouts could not be ascertained.	

No.	*Name and Address*	*Brief note of Being taken as traitor*	*Remark*
5.	Wahengbam Jnaneshwor of Nambol	Jnaneswor Singh was a prominent member of Mahasabha. He sometimes worked as contractor. From information collected it is learnt that this man used to send news to Bijoy Singh and his friends through Mutum Amu Singh. About the beginning of July 1944 he along with his followers Amu Singh proceeded to Moirang via Loktak and joined the party. Thongam Munal Singh also knew them to be at Moirang with other Jap helpes. P/790 Naki Ahamad Choudhuri also stated their names vide interrogation report No. 137/163 D/29th July, 44. These two men also said to have gone with Japs. No news about them has since been heard.	
6.	Mutum Amu Singh of Nambol (Former-Resident Terakeithel).		
7.	Laisram Jatra Singh of Bishenpur.	This man is a notorious B.C. He escaped from Manipur State Jail while awaiting trial U/S 395 I.P.C. No approximate date or month could be ascertained as to how and when he joined the other Manipuri traitors. He used to go to Japs' camp. No information as to his presence in the velley could be had so far. It is stronggly suspected that he had also gone with other Jap helpers.	
8.	Kiyam Gopal Singh of Moirang.	These are men of Moirang village. During the evacuation of Moirang village, these people were staying at Thanga-Basti. From private information it is learnt that Gopal Singh gave food- stuff to the enemy at the first instance and also gave every possible assistance within his means. Ibohal Sing became a contractor who	
9.	Heman Ibohal Singh of Moirang.		
10.	M. Korieng Singh of Moirang.		

No.	*Name and Address*	*Brief note of Being taken as traitor*	*Remark*
		used to supply rice to the Jap and also let out his house to Jap as godown. Thongam Munal Singh saw his supplying food stuff to the enemy. M. Koireng Singh is the only English and Urdu speaking man at Moirang. He was employed by the Jap as interpreter. Amu Mia brother of Quazi Wali Ulla, Darbar Member in his statement stated that Koireng Singh took him to Moirang bazar and introduced to Col. Malik and Naki Ahamad Choudhuri. Since the Jap evacuated Moirang area, these three men also disappeared from Thanga. Military F.S.S. with Civil Police raided in their houses as soon as enemy had cleared, Moirang but no trace of them could be found. It is rumoured that they have been concealing themselves in some hill area near Wangoo but so far the probable resort could not be ascertained. Hope this may be done in near future.	
11.	Sarungbam Ibohal Singh of— Singjamei Makha Mayen gkhon gangn-khong.	He was a man of congress view. He was doing contract work between Chothe and Thinungei. During the evacuation of this area he stayed at Thinungei. Thongam Munal Singh stated that this man was arrested along with him by the enemy and taken to some where near Torbung Lamjao. They were detained for about 11/2 months. After many interrogation and warning being given they were removed at Moirang where other Manipuri traitors were. When	

No.	Name and Address	Brief note of Being taken as traitor	Remark
		he (Munal) escaped from there he remained with other Jap helpers. He is still absent from home. It is believed that he had gone with others. No information as to his valley could be found.	

List of locals who are untraced believed either to have gone with Japs or to have been killed.

1. Sinam Changh Singh of Sagolband.
2. Sinam Iboongoyaima Singh of Sagolband.
3. Sinam Iboongotombi Singh of Sagolband.
4. Meitam. K. N. Singh of Awang Sengmai
5. Konjengbam. Singh of Moirang Pansang.
6. Jogeshwar Singh of Thangmeinband.
7. Gandhar Singh of Thamnapokpi Moirang.
8. Loukrakpam Kalnjo Singh of Maibam Lokpaching.

List of Traitors at large

1. Totesangbam Tomal Singh of Chingamakha.
2. Tokchom Angow Singh of Singjamei Thokchom Leikai.
3. Leisram Kanbai Singh of Segalambi.
4. Longjam Bijoy Singh of Miangbam Leikai.
5. Wakengbam Gyanawar Singh of Mumbai.
6. Mutum Amu Singh of Nambol formerly of Teakeithel.
7. Laisram Jatra Singh of Bishenpur (Escaped H/T prisoner).
8. Kiyam Gopal Singh of Moirang.
9. Heman Ibohal Singh of Moirang.
10. M. Koireng Singh of Moirang.
11. Sarungham Ibohal Singh of Singjamel Makha Mayenghongnanghong.

12

Note by Military Intelligence on the Indian National Army[1]

31 December, 1944

1. This army was set up by the Japanese immediately after declaring war in the Pacific when a small nucleus of captured Indian officers, in both Malaya and Hongkong helped to suborn Indian troops. By January 1942 numbers of P. W. in the two colonies had joined. One of the very earliest traitors, Capt. Mohan Singh, 1/14 Punjab Regt,was proclaimed G.O.C. After the Bangkok conference in June 1942 the INA was placed on a "constitutional" basis.

2. After the fracas which resulted in the arrest of Capt. Mohan Singh, and the almost total disbandment of these forces in Dec. 1942, they were reconstituted and reformed in the first half of 1943 with insistence that enrolment of members should be voulntary and that various forme of "persuasion" which had been used in Mohan Singh's time be abolished. Some 15,000 volunteers (half of the target) came forward but it was not still the arrival of Subhas Chandra Bose in the Far East that a wide recruiting campaign began.

3. Bose's immediate action on taking over Supreme Command was to improve conditions for the rank and file and build up morale. In a high-powered publicity appreciable success, Recruiting was carried out among the P.W. and also among the Indian civilian population all over the Far East.

4. At this time the puppets were represented in Burma by a small advance the end of 1942. There were in addition personnel working in the forward areas, but they cannot be considered as "INA" proper on account of their purely.

5. Towards the end of 1943 the Special Groups (Bahadur, Intelligence and Reinforcement) began to move into Burma. The first unit of

---

1. W.O. 208/808. P.R.O.

Bose to be identified was "E" Coy of the Bahadur Group, specially forced in Burma for this purpose and later absorbed into Guerilla Regiment of 1 Div. The first unit to be identified in action in a fighting role was 1 Bn 1 Guerilla Regt in Arakan during the Feb 44. operations. When the Japanese crossed the Hind and began their advance into Manipur the remainder of the First, the Second and the Third Guerilla Regiments were identified in this area in quick seccession. The Fourth Regiment remained in reserve in the Mandalay area.

6. Alongside the regular Regiments, three composite units, those of 2/ Lt (Capt) Ajmer Singh, Capt (Major) Maghar Singh and Capt (Lt. Col.) S. A. Malik were identified. Those were largely independent units carrying out tasks similiar to those of the Bahadur and Intelligence Groups. 1 Div there were also, in Burma, "Command troops", such as M.T. Coys and Engineer Coys. It is estimated that some 12/15,000 troops had arrived in Burma by March 1944, of whom a third were committed in the forward areas.

7. While all was going well for the Japanese and their advance was maintained, the morale of the puppets was reported to be high, but with the halting of the advance and the eventual rout of the Japanese, the puppets sustained casualties and became considerably demoralised. They had been led to believe that our troops would welcome them but when they found that they were regardeds enemies and treated as such, this, coupled with hard conditions and disease, had its effect on their fighting capacity and will to fight. A great number were captured or deserted the "intake" of the period April-August was 715, the peak monthly intake being reached in July with 244. Including killed and wounded it may be said that almost a quarter of the forces engaged in these operations were put hores de combat. The result of the Japanese defeat was withdrawal of the INA into the back areas, which accounted for a sudden decrease in the "arrival" figures, those for September and October being almost negligible.

8. Meanwhile, Rear HQ, INA in Singapore was busy with the training of 2 and 3 Divs and more "Command troops." 2 Div is reported to be composed of P.W. and civilian recruits, though there are probably military officers and NCOs. Both Divs are approximately 7,000 strong. 2 Div was believed to be ready to move into Burma about the middle of 1944, but it was not until October that the first elements arrived in Rangoon. These parties belonged to 1 Inf Regiment, otherwise known

as 'the Field Force Bdn.' believed to number about 3,000. The remainder of 2 Div is reported to be enroute for Burma. 3 Div is believed to be still training in Singapore.

9. Preliminary training of civilian recruits is carried out in the Azad Hind Fauj Training Camps (formerly "Bharat Youth Training Centres"), from which trainees graduate to "Azad Schools" before posting to units.

10. In other territories in enemy occupation little is known of INA activities. In Hong Kong a certain number of P.W. are known to have vounteered and been sent to Singapore and Burma. In SIAM there is a Training Camp and a Special Recruiting Officer for that country.

11. Having failed in its main objective– that of marching victoriously into India – the INA now presents a problem to the Japanese (that is, unless the Japanese are still confident of final victory) for they have a body of men who have been allowed great freedom, have been vitiated with "brotherly Asiatic" propaganda and known the Japanese soldier intimately in the days of his success and failure, who may easily turn, perhaps not against, but certainly away from their present allies. The INA, therefore, has become for the Japanese, a problem child who has to be dealt with carefully and certainly very firmly.

12. The above summary is intended to give a short concise background to the INA activities for anyone who is new to this subject, and on which what follows can be devotailed without having to read laboriously through a lot of material which is irrelevent to what is required.

PART I

No. 1 Div

1. **Motar·Coy**—A Mortar Coy 100 strong organised into 6 dets, with one 3" mortar per det, was formed in Burma and last reported moving with Nehru Bde towards TAMU in June 1944. Probably the Coy remained with this Bde, which was detailed to move fwd but actually did not get very much further than Mandalaya. It formed a part of 1 Div and was put under this Bde's Comd as a supporting unit for impending operations.

2. **1. M. T. Coy:—**

(a) This Coy formed a part of Hind FD Force in the original I.N. A. organisation, but was transferred to Comd tps on the present reorganisation. It did not leave Singapore till January 1944. Towards the end of January, it left Singapore, and moving via Thailand, Moulmein and Martaban, arrived in Rangoon during the first week of March 1944, and was stationed at Mingaladon and Cushing High School.

During the 1944 operations in Northern Burma it was employed on tpt of tps and kit, etc of both I.N.A. and Japanese tps between Rangoon and Mandalay, and later up to Kalewa. It was earmarked for duties come up as far as North as Tamu. Its scheduled programme was to transport troops from Imphal to Dimapore, which it was never destined to perform. It was last reported in YE-U in the third week of July 1944, from where it withdraw to Mandalay. The Coy is composed entirely of PW, and has a mixed class composition, with Jats and Sikhs prodominating.

(b) **Strength and Armament**—Total strength of the Coy was 250 divided into five Seco. Drivers were armed with bayonets only (some sources report rifle and bayonets, but in view of the shortage of equipment it is probable that rifles, if issued at first, might have been withdrawn later to meet the demands of the combatant tps), and Havildars and above with pistols.

(c) **Transport**—Coy had 70 vehicles (40 3-ton lorries and 30 15-cwt trucks.)

(d) **Unit Signs**— According to captured documents this Coy was alloted a yellow circle as unit sign when it formed part of Hind FD Force, but judging from subsequent information it appears that (when the Coy moved to Burma as a comd unit), the above sign was changed for two blue circles side by side and touching each other.

3. **2 M.T. Coy**—This Coy was raised in Singapore in September 1943, and was not admissible as an I. N. A. unit as it would have been above the limit of 15,000 men set by the JAPS, so it moved to Burma as an independent unit. When the Japanese raised the limits of the I. N. A., this Coy became a normal I. N. A. unit and was absorbed into

the I. N. A. as comd tps. This Coy carried out similar duties to 1 Coy, and was last reported in YE-U in July 1944 with a det at Kaduma.

It is believed that 1 and 2 Coys had only 70 vehicles between them on charge, as mentioned under 1 Coy, because when 1 Coy was reported with transport, 2 Coy was reported without, and vice versa.

Strength, arms, and organisation. Same as 1 Coy.

4. **1 Eng Coy**—In June 1942, various elements of Eng units were collected at Neesoon Camp by Sub (Capt) N. B. Sindhe for fromation of an INA Eng Unit. In July 1942 the Coy was formed and joined the INA Field Force Gp at Bidadari. After Mohan Singh's debacle the Coy was incorportated in the new I. N. A.

The Coy want by rail to Penang and then by ship, arriving in Rangoon early in October 1943. After a week at the Staging Camp at Kushing High School, they moved to Mingladon. The strength then was 250.

In November 1943 they moved by rail to Indaw and then by M. T. arriving at Pinbon in mid December. There they came under comd of a Japanese HQ and were emplyed on road construction duties as follows :—

Near	Kynagle	15 Dec – 1 Jan 44
Near	Settaw	1 Jan –20 Jan
Near	Kywegawgyi	21 Jan – 14 Feb
Near	Sinlamaung	15 Feb – 27 Feb
Near	LE – U	29 Feb – 5 Nov

On 14th March, the Coy moved up the Chindwin and crossed the river on rafts at Mafthamyit and were again employed on rd construciton duties as follows:—

	Near Sedam	15 Mar – 20 Mar
Between	Tonhe and Thawan	22 Mar – 15 Apr
Between	Humine and Chassud	15 Apr -- 15 May

On 16th May the Coy went to Tamu to repair the Tamu-Palel road, but was called back again on 18th May to the Humine area to repair the damage on the road on that sector caused by heavy rains. The Coy stayed there maintaining the road until 9th July, when orders were received to move back to Kuntaweg. They were in Moreh by the end of the July and reported moving towards Kalewa on 1 August on their way to Mandalaya.

Strength, Armament, Organisation. Total strength 250(reduced to 150 by July 1944), organised into a Coy HQ and four Fls. All classes represented with Sikhs predominating. Men armed with pistols. Usual entrenching tools carried as techincal tools.

Unit Sign. A pick-axe on yellow cloth worn on left arm.

5. **2 ENG Coy**—This Coy was raised in Burma and was supposed to have relieved 1 Coy, but it appears to have arrived too late or have been employed else where. No information is available regarding its movements.

Strength and organisation reported to be same as 1 Coy.

6. **1 FD Park Salvage Coy**—This Coy arrived in Mingaladon in March 1944 and remained here for about 3 months, and then moved to Mandalaya in July 1944. Either the whole Coy or part of at is believed to have been in YE-U for some time.

Note—No. 2 FD Park Salvage Coy.

7. Captured documents mention 2 Fd Park Salvage Coy, but no mention is made of its whereabouts.

Part II

Bose Brigade (1 Guerilla Regt.)

1. **Early History**—This Brigade was raised at Taiping (Malaya) in August/ September 1943. It was formed by taking a Bn each of the three existing Bdes (i. e. Gandhi, Azad and Nehru Bdes) and renumbering them as folows:—

1Bn Gandhi Bde	– 1 Bn Bose Bde
1Bn Azad Bde	– 2 Bn Bose Bde
1Bn Nehru Bde	– 3 Bn Bose Bde

Formation of this Bde was to a large extent considered a matter of prestige for S. C. Bose. By attaching his name to this Bde, Bose probably wanted to impress the Japanese of its efficiency and fighting qualities which he, himself, was convinced of.

During its stay in Malaya the Bde underwent extensive training in jungle warfare which included patrolling, field firing, mountain climbing, etc.

2. **Move to Burma**—The Bde left TAIPING on 20th November 1943. and proceeded via Chumporn (Thailand) - Kao Fa Chi and thence by

sea to MERGUI and MOULMEN. From MARTBAN they entrained and reached Rangoon on 7th January 1944, and were sent to MINAGALADON camp. Here the Bde carried out further training mainly consisting of night marches.

3. Organisation—

Notes:

(a) Some Ordinance and Sappar personnel were included in the Bde HQ strength.

(b) The Bde had some M. T. (See under Tpt.) and probably an M. T. Section formed part of Bde. HQ.

(c) There appears to be a certain amount of controversy about MG Pls. Some sources report an MG Pl. in every Coy, in addition to 3 Rifle pls., While others suggest an MG Pl. and 2 Rifles Pls. per Coy. Probably the above was the original organisation but was later amended due to MG's with trained personnel not being available and possibly in some cases MG Pls. were temporarily replaced by Rifle Pls.

(d) Coys in 2nd and 3rd Bns were designated as follows:—

2nd Bn.	3rd Bn.
1 Coy .... Awal	1 Coy .... Dharam
2 Coy .... Bahadur	2 Coy .... Bhim
3 Coy .... Jangju	3 Coy .... Arjun
4 Coy .... Dipak	4 Coy .... Nakul
5 Coy .... Parwana	5 Coy .... Sahadev

4 **Strength**—Following is the strength of the Bde according to its war establishment dated February 1944 :—

	Lt. Col	Maj.	Capt.	Lt.	2/Lt.	SOI	SOII	Hav	Nk.	L/Nk.	Sep	Total.
Bn	-	1	7	18	*	2	6	28	61	76	783	984
Bde HQ	1	1	3	6	11	3	-	19	18	33	79	174
Total	1	4	24	60	11	9	18	103	201	261	2434	3126

According to the strength statement of Regt. dated April 1944, there were 302/Lts. It is probable that the above establishment which was in existence in February 1944, was amended as far as 2/Lts were concerned.

5. **Arms and Equipment**—The following table shows arms and equipment per Bn working on a basis of 3 rifle Pls per Coy :—(Ref. para 3, note 3.)

	Mg	lmg	Tommy Gun	A/tk Rifles	Pistol	Rifle	Swords
Pl.	2	3	3	1 or 2	4 or 5	32 far	
Coy.	2	9	9	9	All Offr	Ors not not carry-ing	All Goy Comds and above
Bn.	10	50	60	50		MG or Bren gun	

Note:

(a) 1 Bn has one 3" Mortar (See para 17 (a) (ii))

(b) 2 Bn had its A/TK rifles withdrawn at KALEMYO in March 1944. Probably this was a temporary measure.

(c) In the MG Pl., 1 & 2 Secs carry an MG each, while 3 & 4 Secs carry spare ammunition and their own rifles. (an unconfirmed report states that there were 4 MMGs per Pl., i.e., one MMG per Sec.)

6. **Ammunition.**

Bren Gun	......	1000 rds per gun
A/Tk Rifle	......	50 rds per rifle
Rifle	......	150 rds per rifle
Revolver	......	36 rds per revolver
T.S.M.G.	......	300 rds per gun
Grenades	......	1 per man
A/Tk Mines	......	6 A/Tk magnetic mines + 6 Demolitia mines per Bn.

Note: Arms and Ammunition in all cases are British.

7. **Transport.**

(a) **M. T.** In july 1944 the Bde had twelve 3 ton lorries. 1 bn had one 3 ton lorry.

(b) **A. T.** In July the Bde had 2,500 bullocks. 2 & 3 Bns had 150 bullocks each, half of which had died by 1st July. 1Bn had 4 mules carts.

Note: 12 lorries and 2,500 bullocks referred to in (a) and (b) above were probably temporarily attached to the Bde because no prior or subsequent information confirms this.

8. **Intercommunications**—A nucleus of 22 Signals personnel was posted to Bde HQ while the Bde was in Malaya and before leaving for Burma it consisted of 30/40 sig. personnel organised as shown in the diagram in para 3.

The wireless section had 4 Battery Sets (British-type not known) but they were never used during ops in Northern Burma as no facilities for charging batteries existed. (According to another source the Japanese would not trust them with serviceable sets.)

During the Bde's stay in Haka — Falam area, main telephone lines Falam — Haka — Kalemyo — Natchaung were used.

Flags and runners were the only other means of communication. No motor cycles were available for the D/R Sec. and they were used a runners.

9. **Class Composition**—

1Bn.	1 Coy	–	Dogras and Sikhs
	2 Coy	–	Jats, Gujars and Madrassis
	3 Coy	–	Gujars
	4 Coy	–	Jats and Ahirs
	5 Coy	–	Jats and Ahirs
	6 Coy	–	Dogras, Sikhs, Jats, Gujars, Madrassis all mixed.

Note: 6 Coy was formed from the other 5 Coys of this Bn in Kaladan area and had mixed class composition.

2 Bn:	1, 4 & 5 Coy	–	Jats, Punjabis, Musalmans and Sikhs, mixed predominating
	2 Coy	–	All Jats
	3 Coy	–	Mainly Musalmans

3 Bn. All Garhwalis, except 1 coy which is Kumaonis.

10. **Brigade Signs**—

(a) **Bde Signs**. An orange and green strip worn side on sleeves starting from shoulder seam and extending for about one inch-green to the rear.

(b) **Bn & Bde HQ**. In addition to the above Regt sign, Bn & Bde HQ wore the following Bn signs:

(i) Bde HQ.—A diamond split vertically in Bde colours (Orange and Green)

(ii) 1 Bn.—A Circle split vertically in Bde colours.

(iii) 2 Bn.—A triangle split vertically in Bde colours and worn with point to the top.

(iv) 3 Bn.—A square split vertically in Bde colours.

(c) **I. N. A. Signs.** In addition to the above Bde & Brigade all ranks wore the following I. N. A. signs:—

(i) Congress tricolour in cloth worn on the left sleeve and a metal one on the chest.

(ii) Hindustan Badge—A brass badge with the words I.N.A. and outline map of India worn on the left side of the cap or Pagri. (This is reported to be obsolete now).

Note: Congress tri-colour is orange, white and green.

11. **I. N. A. Numbers**—Personnel from Btns of various other Bdes (See para 1) which were drawn to form this Bde, retained their original I. N. A. numbers allotted to them by their repective Bdes. There is no evidence of this Bde having been allotted any separate block of I. N. A. numbers. The following blocks are used by Bns of this Bde:—

1Bn: 20,000 to 24,000 (This being the block used by Gandhi Bde where this Bn originally came from).

2 Bn: 30,000 to 34,000 (Azad Bde Block)

3 Bn: 40,000 to 44, 000 (Nehru Bde Block)

Attached Bahadur group., 54,000 to ? (1 Bahadur Group Block)

Note: Due to inter-Bn transfere it is not uncommon to find personnel of 1 Bn in 3Bn and vice versa, hence the mixture of various blocks, though the majority of the Bns conform to the above blocks of number.

12. **Badges of Rank**—See part IV para 2.

13. **Pay**—See part IV para 5.

14. **Clothing**—See part IV para 7.

15. **Rations**—See part IV para 6.

16. **Medical**—Each Bn had a Medical Staff of 2 Officers , 2 Nos and 28 Qrs. no. 1 bn detailed 5 ORs per Coy and balance remained with Bn

HQ. Similar arrangements are believed to have been made in other Bns of this Bde. (See para IV para 11.)

17. Move Forward Of Rangoon—

(a) 1 Bn.

(i) 1 Bn with its attached personnel of Bahadur Gp (25) left Rangoon on the 4th February 1944 for Kaladan. It moved by rail to Prome and the no Khaungdok via Taungup and Myohaung, arriving there towards the end of Mar. 44 29th March 1944, 4 Coy under Lt. Nathu Singh was detailed to attack Br positions at Khabaw. The Coy was accompanied by a party of S. S. Gp personnel under Japanese Lt. Matsumoto. On arrival at Khabaw on 30th March, two of the S. S. personnel were sent in civilian clothes to locate Br positions towards the evening they ran into a Br patrol. One of them was captured the other one, though wounded, got away, and reported to Khabaw the same evening.

On the 31st March, 2, 3 & 5 Coy also arrived at Khabaw and were sent the same day to contact the enemy. 5 Coy took up a position North of Khabaw, and was attacked by Br troops on 1 April. On the 2nd April, the Coy's position was shelled and the Coy withdraw South after suffering 7 killed and about wounded.

(ii) The Coy was then ordered to take up the following positions:—

(a) Coy —which was left behind at Myohaung came to Khaungdauk towards the end of April and want to Paletwa arriving there on 26 May 44.

(b) Coy— Kyauktaw Town area

(c) Coy— South of Paletwa

(d) Coy— Est of Khaungdauk village

(e) Coy—Alegyun area – in junglo 50 yds from the bank of the river.

(f) Coy—This Coy was formed at Khaungkauk on arrival of a 3" Mortar and 4 mules on 22nd May 1944, by drawing men from the other 5 Coys. It was stationed about 200 S. E. of Khaungdauk.

Bn. HQ – In the middle of a Mugh village about 250 N. E. of Khaungdok Pagoda.

(iii) At the end of June 1944, a composite party of 50 I. N. A. mon consisting of 25 specially selected mon of this Bn and 25 attached Bahadur Gp personnel, left Khaungkauk under Lt. Amanullah (Bahadur Group) to establish a post at Mowdok. Mowdok was reahced on 4th July 1944 and the party took up a position close to a Japanese post about 60 strong, and was employed on normal duties.

(iv) Towards the end of July 1944, 1 Coy was ordered to preceed to Mowdok on arrival in early August 1944 the Coy took up the following positions and carried out routine patrols:–

1 Pl less 1 Sec	–	Kwebo
1 Sec 1 Pl	–	Area Frontier Hill (PG 6332). Frowarding sups brought by coolies from Labawa to Mowdok and Lalaroa.
2 Pl.	–	Lalaroa
3 Pl.	–	Mowdok
Attached S. S.		
Gp personnel	–	Lalaroa
Coy HQ	–	Mowdok

The rest of the Bn remained at Khaungdauk doing garrison duties, except one Coy, which was sent to Wama in June/July 1944.

(v) Towards the beginning of October 1944 the Bn started a gradual withdrawal and parties were seen passing through Taungup at the end of October and early November 1944, on their way possibly to Prome or even Rangoon.

(vi) Athough no confimation of the withdrawal of attached S. S. Gp personnel of this Bn has been received, but in view of the arrival of a fresh Intelligence Gp in Kaladan, it is considered likely that the attached personnel of this Gp also withdrawal with the Bn.

(b) **Bde less 1 Bn**—Bde left Rangoon about 7th Feb 1944, and moved to Haka-Falam area vis Mandalay-YE-U and Falam.

(i) **2 Bn**—Arrived Falam on 5th March 1944 and was disposed as follows :—

Bn HQ with Rear Bde HQ at Natchaung

Awal Coy with Adv. Bde HQ at Falam.

Parwara Coy at Haka

Dipak, Jangju and Bahadur Coys spread in Gps over a front of six miles per Coy for carrying rations between Natchaung and Falam.

Note: All Coy QM. Hav's with 6 men from each Coy were left behind at Kalewa to look after Bn's heavy baggage which was dumped here, and also to assist in forwarding rations to Coys when called upon to do so. A similar party is believed to have been left by 3 Bn at Kalewa.

(ii) **3 Bn**—Arrived at Kalewa end of February and stayed there till mid-March 1944. Two coys were sent to Pakokku from Mandalaya to bring up rations for the Regt. on bullocks.

Two Coys with Bn HQ were sent on road construction to widen the road between 2 and 3 Stockados.

Fifth Coy was posted in area between Kalemyo and Natchung to keep watch on expected landings by Br Paratroops.

(c) **1st encounter with Br Troops**—On 18th March 1944, Lt. Sikandar Khan, Awal Coy Comd (Falam) was called by the Jap L. O. (Major) who was with the Coy and instructed to go with his Coy and suborn 7/14 P. R. Regt which was identified in the Semual area.

At about 1800 hrs on 20th March, accompanied by the JAP L. O., the Coy left Falam. About 0800 hrs next morning they saw 22 Chin levies near a Chaung close to Zemaul and challenged them. The Chins mistook them for our own troops and told them that they belonged to Major Manning's patrol. In the meanwhile Sikandar Khan surrounded these people and ordered them to lay down, their arms, which they did. Major Manning, who was in the Chaung below was approached by Sikandar Khan and ordered to put his hands up, but he emptied his Sten gun in Sikandar Khan's direction who also fired three pistol shots at him, but missed him. Major Manning then got away, and the remainder of his patrol were taken prisoner.

(d) Alterations in Locations, April/ May, 1944—

(i) Adv. Bde HQ and Adv. HQ 2 Bn moved to Haka, Jangju Coy moved to Haka and Bahadur and Dipak Coys were called back to Natchung, as it was decided that bullocks and coolies would be utilised for carrying rations.

(e) Object of this concentration at Haka and attack on Klanglang—By May 1944 the following were concentrated at Haka with a view to the imponding attack on Klanglang—

Adv. Bde HQ.
Adv. HQ 2 Bn.
Parawana and Jangju Coy, 2 Bn.
One Coy, 3 Bn.
There were two reasons for attacking Klanglang —

(i) To obtain rations from Br post at Klanglang as it was hard to procure any supplies locally from Haka.

(ii) As the intention was to leave only one Coy at Haka, this attacking in force would bluff the British into overestimating the strength in Haka and thus keep them from harassing the Haka Coy.

As Col. Shah Nawaz (Bde Comd.) was called away to JAP HQ to discuss the move of Bde to the Kohima area, he instructed Major Khan (Bde Adj.) to carry out the attack.

The above force under Major Maboob Khan attacked Klanglang on 15th May 1944. Two adv. posts were captured without opposition. Some blankets, cigarettes, milk tins and matches etc. in small quantities were found in the position. The force withdraw towards Haka on 16th May 1944.

Dipak Coy came from Natchaung to garrison Haka and the above forces withdraw to Natchaung.

Awal Coy which was still at Falam want to Myitha Haka on 22nd May. In the meanwhile information was received that some Assam Rifle troops were advancing towards Falam so it was decided to leave a Coy there. Sick and weak personnel of this withdrawing force were organised into one Coy and left at Falam.

18. **Move to Kohima Area**—Orders were received that Bde should got ready to move forward to the Kohima front. Move was to be completed by 31st May 1944. Japs with M. T. arrived to help speed up the move.

Rear Bde HQ remained at Natchaung while the following left for Ukhrul:—

Adv. Bde HQ.

HQ 2 and 3 Bns.

2, 3 and 5 Coys 2 Bn.

3 and 4 Coys 3 Bn.

This force was rushed up to Ukhrul but arriving there too late to be committed, due to the turn of events in the Kohima sector, was hastily withdrawn again to Tamu. In the meanwhile 2 Coy 3 Bn the above force.

19. **Withdrawal**—

(a) Tamu was evacuated by about the middle of July 1944, and this force moved down towards Kalewa on route to Mandalaya:

14 July – 17 July .... Halt at Indaing to purchase rice.

18 July – 20 July .... Halt in jungle West of YU River as no boats were available for crossing the river.

21 July – 24 July .... Reached Ahlaw and started by batches for Mawlaik. Last batch left Ahlaw on 24th July.

Kalewa was reached in the first week of August. The original orders of a halt at Kalemyo were cancelled as the ration dump there had been destroyed by Allied bombing and the Bde could not be supplied there.

(b) Towards the end of the August 1944, the Haka - Falam garrisons which were disposed as under, were ordered to concentrate at MONYWA :—

Rear Bde HQ .... MS 18, Kalemyo - Natchaung Rd.

*AWAL Coy 2 Bn .... Myitha Haka

*DIPAK Coy 2 Bn .... Haka

1 & 5 Coys 3 Bn .... Natchaung.

(one of those Coys was employed on transporting rations from Gangam to Nagapa).

Night and day posts at Haka manned by this Coy were taken over by the Japs and this Coy was put under strict surveillance due to the large number of desertion from this garrison.

They started concentrating at Natchaung and the moved by batches towards Namhka, starting on the 20th October 1944.

(c) On 6th August the Q. M. Party at Kalewa (Note, para 17 (b) (i)) was also ordered to withdraw to Monywa.

20. No information as to Bdes move further South is available and in view of the infromation supplied by 2 Bahadur Group personnel, who surrendered in Arakan in December 1944, and who were in Rangoon in October 1944, it is presumed that the Bde is either still in the Mandalay area or has moved southwards. 3 Bn was identified at Mandalay in October 1944.

13

Address of Subhas Chandra Bose to the I.N.A. Soldiers[1]

1 January, 1945

Comrades of the Azad Hind Fauj!

On this auspicious New Year's Day, I want you, first of all, to look back on your achievement and on your progress since the formation of the Azad Hind Fauj. There can be no doubt whatsoever that in spite of many difficulties and drawbacks, your achievement and progress may have been truly remarkable. This has been possible because of the passionate desire for freedom which inspires the Indian people today, the many-sided assistance rendered by our countrymen in East Asia, the valuable aid offered by our Allies, and, above all, the hard work and sacrifice that you yourselves have put in.

Before the end of 1943, units of the Azad Hind Fauj began moving in the direction of the Indo-Burma frontier. On the 4th February, 1944, India's War of Independence was launched in the Arakan region of Burma. On 21st March, 1944, we were able to proclaim to the whole world that the Azad Hind Fauj had crossed the eastern frontier of India and was fighting on the sacred soil of India. Since then, the fight has been going on and in the course of that campaign, many of our comrades, while fighting heroically, have laid down their lives on the field of battle.

The heroism and self-sacrifice of the officers and men of the Azad Hind Fauj in India's War of Independence have already become a priceless heritage for the India of tomorrow—while for the Azad Hind Fauj itself, they have become a glorious and undying tradition which will serve as an inspiration for all time.

Comrades! On this auspicious day, I want you all to pay a silent homage to our immortal heroes and to renew your solemn pledge to continue the fight until complete victory is achieved. India is calling you. The souls of your comrades are urging you on to still braver deeds.

1. 601/7378/H.S.

Therefore, gird up your lions for the hard battle that lies ahead. There can be no rest and no pause for us, until our tricolour national flag is hoisted over India's metropolis.

Comrades! Our immortal heroes have paid for India's liberty with their own blood. We are proud of them. But we too must be ready for that supreme sacrifice. The Azad Hind Fauj can justify its name and fulfil its task only if it is ready to fight and die to the last man. We have to give our blood and take the blood of our enemies. Therefore, let your slogan—your battle-cry-for the year 1945 be 'Blood, blood and blood'.

14

Operation Order No. 2 for the Deployment of I.N.A.[1]

24 February, 1945

1. **Information**

   (a) **Enemy**—Enemy Infantry and armoured troops have captured Pyinbin and elements of the same have been reported in Seiktein and Legy and Kyank Padaung Myingyan road. But this report is not confirmed.

   (b) **Own Tps**—Our Bn. of the Khajo Botai has taken up position Kyauk Padaung Myingyan road in Gyaingywa. One Bn. of the same unit is going to take up the defence of KYAUK PADAUNG. Unit No. 205 A.H.F. is preparing Popa defences and strengthening up the same, apart from patrol activities in its front and flanks.

2. **Intention**—No. 170 unit will carry our intensive Grla. warfare and patrolling against the enemy in the areas marked in the attached map.

3. **Method**

   (a) No. 2 Bn. with Kyauk Padaung as base will operate in No. 1 area and will also send a fighting patrol along the route marked on the Map to find out the type, location and activities of enemy. The patrol on finding out will report straight back to No. 251 unit.

   (b) No. 1 Bn. will form a Guerrilla Company, No. 3 Bn. will also form a Guerrilla Company. These Companies with Popa as base will operate in areas 2 and 3.

   (c) Regimental Headquarters and rest of the unequipped strength of 1 and 3 Bns. will also move to Popa and will help in preparation of defences there.

---

1. I.N.A. Trial Paper

4. **Administration**—Seven days ration will be taken by the outgoing parties. Each Guerrilla party will be accompanied by orderlies, who will carry with them necessary medicine. A.Q.M. will have hundred Grenades from 265 unit Rs. 1000 will be taken by each party for purchase of fresh rations or to meet any unforeseen necessities, and issue fifty each to No. 1 to 3 Bns.

5. **Inter-Communication**—Under all circumstances during the absence front parties will send back necessary information at least once a day or more, if needed.

(Sd.) G.S. Dhilkon,
Major, Commander 170 Unit.

15

Activities of I.N.A. on thc Burma Front[1]

3 March, 1945

Intelligence Summary No. 3

Reference : Map Sheet No. 840, 84 K and 84 P Scale 1"4 miles or 1 = 2,50,000.

28th February 1945 : Enemy was reported to be advancing towards Kyauk, Padaung by Pyinbin, Letpanbin road. An attack was put up by certain Japanese units but it was found out afterwards that there was no enemy.

Undermentioned officers with their batmen went on exercise with all Div. Ancillary Units. Units came back safely with the officers and their batmen did not. It appears that either they have been captured or have gone over to the enemy side:–

Major Mohammad Riaz Khan, Major P.J. Madan, Major S.N. Day, Major Mohammad Sarwar and Lt. Mohammad Bakhsh.

1st March 1945 : Nothing much happened during these days. Patrol activity from our side continued. Enemy tried to encircle the Guerrilla party in the vicinity of Tibu, but failed. Our Patrols went up to Sektien and Welaung and got information that enemy has gone towords Taungtha. The enemy strength was 12 tanks, and five hundred lorries. No enemy could be seen on the roads between Taungtha, Welaung and Seikten. Neither a Telephone line. Most of the civilians are pro-Americans as they are given rice,

1. I.N.A. Trial Papers

milk, cigarettes, P.T. Shoes and clothes by the enemy OYE parties had to pretend that they were on the American's side in order to get information from the civilians. It was also found out that the enemy is strong in medium and light tanks as well as carriers.

Following forms the enemy :-

Americans-Not much.

Indians, Gurkhas, Negros, Chinese and Kachins.

One of our parties was very heavily bombed at a place about six miles from Popa in the Northernly direction. Our losses were the following :-

Rifles	6	Equipment	8
Bayonets	6	Rounds 303" ball 500	
Grenades	2	Blankets	9
Ration Tins	11	Pay books	8
Ground Sheets	11		

Only one man was slightly wounded.

3rd March 1945 : Reference—Intelligence Summary No. 1 of 25th February 1945.

The enemy which had gone from Pyinbin towards East and Taungtha has now been reported to have gone partly to putting up an offensive from Myingyan towards south from Meiktila towards Tauongtha from Popa towards Pyinbin, while A.H.F. Troops are going to attack from Kyauk parading towards Nayaungu.

(Sd.) G.S. Dhillon,

Major "C"

16

Dhillon's Report about I.N.A. Units Fighting at Different Place[1]

4 March, 1945

Reference— Map Sheet No. 84 0, 84 K and 84 P Scale 1" 4 Miles or 1" 250000.

3rd March 1945.— Eenmy about 300 strong. Nationality Indian, was located digging near Kaungnyo. On Kyaune Padaung, Nyaungu road, four carriers were seen 13 miles from Eyank Padaung. Later on towards the evening at about 2000 hrs. some enemy estimated about 500 was also found about eight miles from Kyaunk Padaung on the same road.

A recce patrol of the enemy came about two miles from Pozu at 1800 hrs. They were fired at by a Japanese post thus making them run away.

It has been found that the villagers round about Taung Zin area give information to both sides. They have told the enemy that Azad Hind Fauj is located in most of those villages. The result is that the enemy is very cautious. The enemy tactics are very much dependent on tanks, armoured cars and carriers. Usually they do not send out a party less than about a hundred. The vehicles carrying these parties are escorted infront and in the rear by A.F.Vs. on reaching a place where they need stopping, they fix their M.Gs. and Mortars before disbursing the troops.

(Sd.) G.S. DHILLON,
Major "C'

1. Ibid

17

Instruction on Safety and Security for the I.N.A. Units[1]

5 March, 1945

It has been noticed that many new foot paths have been made in the camp. As the enemy is superior in air, these paths give out exact positions of our location. Unit commanders and officers must always keep their men warned against this danger.

Still, sentries are found at night challenging very loudly or making enquiries from approachers in a very loud tone. An enemy spy near about can get much information which may cause us many lives and apart from that give enemy a tactical advantage. May unit commanders please take steps to check and rectify this common mistake.

(Sd.) G.S. Dhillon,
Major "C"

1. Ibid

18

Operation Order No. 2. for No. 501 Unit A.H.F. Fighting on Burma Front[1]

5 March, 1945

1. **Information**—On 5th the enemy patrol composed of 4 tanks and about 500 infantry were seen operating in the area Daungle on Popaywa Pyinbin road and after making contact with patrol of 515 unit the enemy is reported to have withdrawn back from that area. No enemy reported on Popaywa Taungtha road. On Kyauk Padaung Taungozin road at a distance of 9 miles from Kyauk Padaung 200 enemy infantry with 7 lorries and 3 carriers are reported to be digging in. This enemy mainly consisted of Americans and Indians.

   On Kyauk Padaung Meiktila road small forces of enemy supported by tanks have been reported near Taungywa.

   Own troops—Kaungjo Unit of Nippon Army is attacking the enemy along on Popaywa Taughtha Road and Popaywa Pinbin Road.

   One Company of Japanese Engineers in the area Nyaun Gan on Kyauk Padaung Meiktila Road. Dispositions of 515 and 420 Units is as before.

2. **Intention**—Units under command of 501 unit will :-

   (a) Occupy defensive positions round Popa Hill Kyauk Padaung and Nyaunggan area and stop and annihilate any enemy approaching these defences.

   (b) Keep Popaywa Yenangaung Road clear.

   (c) Cooperate with the attacking Nippon units to annihilate the enemy which has crossed over the East of Irrawaddy.

3. **Method**—No. 420 unit will undertake the defence of Kyauk Padaung and Nyaunggan areas. Commander 420 unit will liaise with Commander Nippon Engineering unit in Nyaunggan area to get

1. *Ibid*

detailed information about the defensive positions in that area. Commander 420 unit will occupy these positions in sufficient strength to check any enemy advance in that direction and with the remainder of his forces he will undertake active Guerrilla operations on Kyauk Padaung Meiktila and Kyauk Padaung Taunglin Road. All units of 420 unit in Popa area will move to their new positions on the night of 6th/7th March 1945.

No. 515 unit with two platoons of 510 unit under Command will undertake the defence of Popa. He will also carry out active patrolling in front of his defensive positions.

Anti-Tank defence—Commanders 420 and 515 units will arrange to erect anti-tank obstacles and lay anti-tank mines at suitable points. No. 352 unit under directions of D.A.G. 501 unit will under-take all duties in the camp area and will form a general reserve in the hand of Commander 501 unit.

4. **Administration**—'Q' 501 unit will arrange to provide transport for the move of 420 unit so that the move will be completed on the night of 6th/7th March 1945. He will also make arrangements to issue extra rations to make up the scale of Dhall 100 grammes and Oil 20 grammes per day.

5. **Communication**—Commander 529 unit will arrange to send a D/R to 420 unit every night starting Popaya at 2100 hrs. with effect from 7th March 1945. He will also arrange to get a motor cycle, put into working order and attach it with 420 unit for duty.

6. **Acknowledge**

(Sd.) G. S. Dhillon,
Major 'G'

19

I.N.A. on the Burma Front. Intelligence Summary No. 5 by No. 501. Unit Azad Hind Fauj (A.H.F.)[1]

7 March, 1945

Ref.—My Sheet No. 840 84 K, and 84 P Scale 1" 4 miles or 1" 250000.

4th March 1945—A fighting patrol of about 20 men, under command of S. Abdullah Khan No. 516 unit A.H.F. was reconnoitring the area of Daungle village on 4th March 1945 at 1700 hrs. when the patrol was informed about the arrival of an enemy patrol in the area 014558 Map Sheet No. 84/P1 by a Burmese. The enemy patrol consisted of 15 British soldiers carried in three Jeep cars. On receiving the news about the enemy our patrol approached the enemy patrol and opened fire on them. The enemy patrol who had been caught by surprise replied the fire of our patrol, but they could not stand up against the accurate and concentrated fire of our patrol. The enemy fled leaving two dead bodies and 2 Jeep Cars behind. It was confirmed from the Burmese that all the other numbers of the enemy patrol had also been wounded before they fled.

Following arms, ammunitions, equipment and vehicles were captured from the enemy :—

Cars (Jeep)	3	Gas checks	3
Bren Gun	1	Binoculars	2
Sten Gun	1	Compasses	1
Rifles	2	Shorts	2
Discharger Cup	1	Blankets	8
Grenades	8	Web Equipment sets	6
Ammunition Rounds	400	Map sheets 84 1/13	1
Wireless sets	1	Bren Gun Magazines	6
Sten Gun Magazine	8	Tools for 3 Cars	3
		Some quantity of Toilet material.	

1. I.N.A. Trial Papers.

On examination it was ascertained that the enemy dead were British and from the documents captured it was confirmed that they belonged to 2nd Lancaster Regiment.

The documents which were captured from the enemy will be sent in due course. The Map sheet which was captured from the enemy is sent to you.

Our losses were one slightly wounded.

From the documents found in the cars it appears that upto the end of Nov. 44 2nd Bn. S. Lancer were in Kohima and in Dec. they moved to Palel and the Bn. has now arrived in this sector from Palel.

On same date enemy with 7 lorries 3 carriers strength about 200 mostly Indians and few Americans were seen 9 miles from Kyauk Padaung on Kyauk Padaung Taun^gfin road. When they saw our patrol, they showed a white flag but when our patrol called them they tried to open fire. Patrol being weak in numbers came back.

5th March 1945—Outposts and forward patrols of No. 515 unit saw an enemy composed of 4 tanks and about 500 infantry operating in Daungle area. As a result of some fire from both sides the enemy withdrew.

Patrols of 420 units found some enemy about 9 miles from Kyauk Padaung on Kyauk Padaung Taungzin road near a village Dhatsi. They were digging. This appears to be a permanent position.

On Kyauk Padaung Meiktila road small forces of enemy supported by tanks have also been reported by 420 unit.

6th March 1945—Nothing unusual.

(Sd.) G.S. Dhillion
Major G8.

20

Bose to Dhillon Praising his Work and the I.N.A. Soldiers Under Him[1]

12 March, 1945

Major G.S. Dhillion
Jai Hind,

I have been following the work of your Regiment and of yourself with the closest interest and I want to congratulate you on the manner in which you have stood up to face bravely the situation that is difficult. I want to express my complete confidence in you and in all those who are standing by you in the present crisis.

Whatever happens to us individually in the course of this historic struggle, there is no power on earth that can keep India enslaved any longer. Whether we live and work, or whether we die fighting; we must, under all circumstances, have complete confidence that the cause for which we are striving is bound to triumph. It is the finger of God that is pointing the way towards India's freedom. We have only to do our duty and to pay the price of India's liberty. Our hearts are with you and with all who are with you in the present struggle which is paving the way to our national salvation. Please convey my warmest greetings to all the Officers and men under you and accept same yourself. May God bless you and crown your efforts with success.

"Jai Hind"

(Sd.)
Subhas Chandra Bose

1. I.N.A. Trial Papers. The above letter was personnely given to Dhillion by Shah Nawaz when he came to visit him on the Forefront. Dhillion was commander Nehru Brigade.

21

Special Order of the day by Bose for Dealing with Desertion in the I.N.A.[1]

13 March, 1945

To

All Officers And Men of the Azad Hind Fauj

Comrades,

In order to express our indignation, disgust and hatred, against cowardice and treachery, a special observance will be held in every camp of the Azad Hind Fauj on a day to be previously fixed for the purpose. All officers and other ranks must take part in the observance.

With regard to the details of the observance, each camp will be free to draw up its own programme with a view to making the observance a complete success. Directions in broad outlines are, however, being given herewith.

(a) Poems or articles may be written and read, expressing hatred and disgust against cowardice and treachery.

(b) Dreamas may be improvised and acted for expressing abhorrence against cowardice and treachery.

(c) Effigies of the traitors (Riaz, Madan, Sarwary, Roy, Mohammad Bakhsh and others) in carboard or straw or clay or any other suitable material, either in human or in animal form, should be prepared and every member of the camp should give full vent to his disgust and hatred against the traitors.

(d) Lectures should be delivered praising Indian heroes of the past and lauding the brave deeds of the members of the Azad Hind Fauj in the course of the present War of Liberation.

---

1. I.N.A. Trial Papers.

(e) The day's observance should end with the singing of the National Anthem and collective shouting of slogans.

Special reward will be given to the camp that can put up the best show.

(Sd.) Subhas Chandra Bose,
Supreme Commander,
Azad Hind Fauj.

22

Special Order of the day by Bose Dealing with the Deserters in the I.N.A.[1]

13 March, 1945

To

All Officers and men of the Azad Hind Army

Comrades,

As you all know, the positive achievements of the Officers and men of the Azad Hind Fauj last year on the field of battle and the victories that they scored over the enemy through their patriotism, bravery and self-sacrifice, were marred to some extent by the cowardice and treachery of a few officers and men. We were hoping that with the advent of the New Year all traces of cowardice and treachery would be wiped out, and that in this year's operations the Azad Hind Fauj would be able to put up an unsullied record of heroism and self-sacrifice. But that was not to be. The recent treachery of five officers of the H.Q. of the 2nd Division has come as an eye-opener to us that all is not well within our ranks and that the seeds of cowardice and treachery have yet to be wiped out. If we now succeed in exterminating cowardice and treachery once for all, this shameful and despicable incident may, through God's grace, ultimately prove to be a blessing in disguise. I am, therefore, determined to take all possible measures necessary for the purification of our Army. I am confident that in this I shall have your full and unstinted support.

In order to destroy completely the germs of cowardice and treachery, the following measures will have to be adopted :-

1. Every member of the Azad Hind Fauj, Officer, N.C.O. or Sepoy will, in future, be entitled to arrest any other member of the Azad Hind Fauj,

1. I.N.A. Trial Papers.

no matter what his rank may be, if he behaves in a cowardly manner or to shoot him if he acts in a treacherous manner.

2. I am giving an opportunity to all members of the Azad Hind Fauj who may not feel inclined to work dutifully or fight courageously in future to leave the ranks of the Azad Hind Fauj. This offer will be open for one week from the time of its communication.

3. In addition to giving an opportunity to unwilling elements to leave voluntarily the ranks of the Azad Hind Fauj, I want to carry out thorough purge of our army. During the course of this purge, all those will be removed against whom there is suspicion that they may fail us, or betray us, at the critical moment. In order to carry out this purge successfully I want your fullest cooperation and I want you, therefore, give to me and my trusted officers all available information about any cowardly or treacherous elements that may still exist in our Army.

4. It will not be enough to carry out a thorough purge now. In future, also, vigilance will have to continue. It will, therefore, be the duty of every member of the Azad Hind Fauj, in future, to keep his eyes and ears open in order to detect in good time any tendency towards cowardice or treachery. In future, if any member of the Azad Hind Fauj detects any tendency towards cowardice or treachery, he should report at once, either orally or in writing, either to me or to the officers who may be within reach. In other words, from now on and for all times, every member of the Azad Hind Fauj should regard himself as the custodian of the honour and reputation of the Azad Hind Fauj and of the Indian Nation.

5. After the purge has been carried out and unwilling elements have been given an opportunity of leaving our Army, if there is any case of cowardice or treachery, the punishment will be death.

6. In order to create within our army a moral bulwark against cowardice and treachery, we have to create an intense hatred against cowardice and treachery in any form. A strong feeling has to be created in the mind of every member of this army that for a member of a revolutionary army, there is no crime more heinous and despicable than to be a coward or a traitor. Instructions are being issued separately as to how we can create such an intense hatred against cowardice and treachery so that there will be no more cowards or traitors within our ranks.

7. After the purge has been carried out, every member of the Azad Hind Fauj will be required to renew his oath to fight on bravely and courageously until the emancipation of our dear motherland is achieved. Instructions regarding the form and manner of this oath will be issued separately.

8. Special rewards will be given to those who give information regarding cowardly and treacherous elements or who arrest or shoot at the front cowardly and treacherous elements.

(Sd.)
Subhas Chandra Bose,
Supreme Commander,
Azad Hind Fauj.

23

Report by Dhillon on I.N.A. Fighting on the Burma Front[1]

18 March, 1945

Subject :—*Battle Report No. 4*

As per operation Order No.8 of 14th March 1945 of Unit No. 450 timed 2037 hours Unit No. 451 was occupying a defensive position on 11th March 1945 as under:-

A Company commanded by Lieut. Kartar Singh in Nglaing vicinity and 'B' Coy. commanded by 2/Lt. Gian Singh on North-East of Kanzaung, with Bn. Headquarters South of 'B' Coy. near a Nippon Coy. commanded by Capt. Midori Kawa.

At 100 hrs. enemy artillery from North-Western direction started shelling heavily these positions. At that time a patrol from 'A' Coy. commanded by Hav. Nazar Singh, was out in the direction of Nyaungu about one mile ahead of Coy. Headquarters. This patrol was fired at by an enemy about a platoon strong coming from Nyaungu direction on the Western side of the main road.

Our Patrol took up position at point 'A' and exchanged fire, thereby killing seven of the enemy. A message from this patrol was sent back to Coy. Headquarters as to the enemy advance. 'A' Coy. commander sent forward another party of 10 men under 2/Lt. Dittu Ram to check the advance of that platoon, 2/Lt. Dittu Ram went forward and took up a position between the road and 'A' point, i.e., point 'B'. He was also engaged and the enemy was held up.

At about 12:30 hours 15 enemy tanks, 11 armoured cars and ten trucks came advancing by the main road, and started shelling and firing at point 'A'. Our men replied this fire with rifle and a Bren Gun. The enemy column changed its direction towards 'B' Coy. and directed itself into two

1. I.N.A. Trial Papers

halves. One went towards 'B' Coy. and the other towards 'B' Coy. and then to 'A' Coy.

'B' Coy. was given warning by the Bn. Headquarter through a runner. Soon the Coy. gained contact as the enemy A.F.Vs. came right into the Coy. locality and wanted to crush our men in the trenches. They started shelling and throwing hand grenades into the trenches from inside their vehicles. The Coy. fell helpless against the superiorly equipped enemy. Two mines which were with the Coy. were use but unluckily both went missed. No. 5 and 6 platoons got out of the trenches and with Bayonets fixed charged on to the A.F. Vs. with shouting slogans of Neta Ji Ki Jai ! Inqilab Zindabad ! and Chalo Delhi. The A.F. Vs. came to a stand still, enemy jumped out of them and the trucks and a hand to hand fighting began which lasted for over one hour. 2/Lt. Gian Singh, Coy. Comdr. amidst men, was charging and inspiring them. No. 5 platoon Commander his 2/Lt. Mangu Ram was killed and only about one-tenth of the two platoons were left when 2/Lt. Gian Singh called for No. 4 platoon Commander 2/Lt. Ram Singh, and was issuing orders for a withdrawal from a standing position, when a bullet hit him in the head and he fell down. His death caused a little bit disturbance but 2/Lt. Ram Singh got hold of the situation by withdrawing the remnants of the Coy. to a rear position. At the same time the enemy also got into their vehicles after collecting weapons of the dead and withdrew. This engagement lasted from 1400 hours to 1600 hours approximately. The enemy lost about 50 killed and many wounded. We lost about 40 killed. Some of the seriously wounded—about ten—were captured by the enemy and taken back.

The enemy which has come towards A Coy. side, started first by shelling the village and then approached the Coy. position. The A.F. Vs. entered the village. Enemy automatic from the ground also opened fire. Fire was also opened from our Coy. At about 1800 hrs. the enemy charged with bayonets and tommy guns. The Japanese set the village on fire thus making it a tank obstacle. The tanks could not approach and the enemy had to withdraw leaving back three dead. 'A' Coy. also lost three killed.

Towards the dark Taungzin was still in our hands and the enemy withdrew. 'B' unit 551 then came back to a position near Kwebyok for reorganisation.

Only following articles were captured from the enemy

Mag. bren Gun	3
Hand Grenades	8
Amm 303" Res.	100

Boot ankle Prs.	3
Trousers Prs.	3
Pay book	1 (attd. herewith)

Note—One L.M.G., one Tommy Gun and a Rifle fell to Japaneses lot.

Our losses were :—

Killed in Action

2/Lt. Gian Singh ,, Mangu Ram	Regarding these two officers, I strongly recommend for a posthumous reward and decoration. Their bravery is unparalleled in the history of War. Attacking of tanks and A.F.Vs. may seem impossible, had these heroes preferred to die fighting than to handup or show their backs.

Other ranks killed

Number about 50.	A separate list is being submitted.

Wounded in actions and thus captured about ten wounded brought back six.

The arms of our killed could not be collected as the enemy collected it and took back.

(Sd.) G. S. Dhillon
Maj. Comdr. No. 450 Unit.

24

Dhillon to Bose Thanking Him For the Appreciation[1]

20 March, 1945

Beloved Netaji,

Jai Hind.

I have received your letter of 12th March 1945. Not words, only tears could express my feelings.

I thank you with all my heart for expressing your complete confidence in me and in those who are with me. I assure you, our Netaji, on behalf of the Regiment that does not matter what may come our way, we will continue the struggle according to your ideals, and wishes to earn our Motherland's Freedom as long as a single soldier of this regiment is alive.

As for myself, my last words to you at Rangoon, "Main ap ki ankhen kisi ke samne nichi na hone dunga," have been ringing in my ears ever since I left you, and spcially so after I have come back from NYAUNGU. I fully realize that in spite of reasons which may be produced I have not only failed to do what I voluntarily promised, but have been the only regimental Commander to bring humiliation to you and to the AZAD HIND FAUJ. I have no face to promise against, only my actions will do so.

Your letter has put a new spirit into us.

All the officers and men present here, and I humble and with warmest hearts have accepted your greetings. We are confident that with God's grace annd your blessings it will not be difficult to achieve success.

We all pray for your long life and health to guide us through this Holy War.

Jai Hind

Your Excellency's
Obediently
(Sd.) G. S. Dhillon

1. I.N.A. Trial Papers

25

Note by British Military Intelligence on Subhas Chandra Bose's Activities in the Far East During the Period May 43 to Dec. 44[1]

22 March, 1945

1. Introduction. This note presents an account of Subhas Chandra Bose's activities in the Far East from the time of his arrival in May 43, when he assumed the leadership of the Indian Independence Movement there, to the end of Dec. 44. It is divided into an account of his more interesting movements and connected activities, the part played by him in conducting for the Japanese their intelligence offensive against India, and Japanese estimation of him.

Bose's movements in the Far East, 1943

2. The exact date of Bose's arrival in the Far East from Europe is not known, but it is believed to have been on or about the 10 May 43. It was not until the 14 June that a public announcement was made from Tokyo concerning his presence there and that he had conferred with the Premier and Foreign Minister of Japan and attended the 82 Extraordinary Imperial Diet Session. He himself confirmed his presence by Press interviews and a series of broadcasts directed to Germany, Italy and India, and to the Japanese. It was then that his intentions of raising the standard of active revolt on enemy soil, and his view that as far as he was concerned the Indian Freedom Movement could dispense completely with any idea of continuing Gandhian passive resistance, were made clear the active assistance of Japan, he proclaimed, was essential.

3. At the beginning of July he made his way to Singapore accompanied by Rash Behari Bose, the Head of the Indian Independence Movement in the Far East. Within two days of his arrival he was

---

1. F. No. 601/7868/H.S.

unanimously elected as the leader of both the Japanese and German sponsored Indian Independence Movements. His official titles include "President of the Indian Independence League" and "Commander of the Indian National Army." He arrived in Rangoon at the end of July. By 11 Aug he had returned to Singapore, visiting Bangkok, Saigon, Ipoh and Kuala Lumpur on the way. It was on his return to Singapore that he made his first big propaganda gesture by offering unlimited quantities of rice for the relief of Bengal, provided the Japanese ships that were to carry it were granted safe conduct.

4. His task now was to assert his leadership of the Indian Independence Movement in the Far East and to this end he spent the next six weeks touring South East Asia addressing meetings and carrying out a recruiting campaign. The whole theme of his pronouncements at this time was designed to secure the support of the Indian community and assure them of the benefits of joining wholeheartedly in the Japanese Co-Prosperity Sphere. Burma, he pointed out, had received her independence: so had the Filipinos, and in the same way Indian could rest assured that under the patronge of Japan she could be certain of achieving her complete freedom.

5. Bose concluded his campaign on a trimumphant note, with the announcement on 21 Oct of the establishment of the Provisional Government of Free India. Having thrown out his challenge to the Allies and he hoped, focussed on himself the attention of India, he returned at the end of October to Japan to attend the Greater East Asia National Assembly as an observer and representative of Free India, though not yet a formal delegate, since India was not regarded as a full member of the privileged circle of Greater East Asia nations. Further interviews followed ranging from the Emperor himself to high Japanese government officials. He returned on 25 Nov to Singapore having visited Nanking, Shanghai, Manila and Saigon *enroute*.

6. To serve the purpose of the I.N.A. he inaugurated a new broadcasting station on 5 Dec which was to prove as the Indian National Army Headquarters Broadcasting Station. After attending the graduation ceremony of cadets specially trained as administrators of "liberated" areas of India, he took off on a flying visit to Sumatra, Java and Borneo, which he followed up by a visit to the Andamans and Nicobar

Islands, the re-naming of which to *Shahid* and *Swaraj* respectively he had announced earlier.

7. Having made his new year's speech in Singapore expressing his determination to bring the war to a satisfactory and in celebration with his Axis Allies, Bose next appeared in Rangoon of 7 Jan. On the afternoon of the same day Bose officially announced the formal removal of the Headquarters of the Provisional Government of Free India and that of the whole of the Indian independence Movement to Burma.

8. On 15 Feb. Bose announced the institution of the observances of the 21 of each month as "Provisional Government Day" on which rallies and meetings would be held to keep up enthusiasm among the Indians in the Far East for his Independences Movement.

9. He left Rangoon and spent between the 4 and 14 of Mar in Maymyo and declared later in a Press interview that he had conducted an extensive tour of the frontlines and had been considerably impressed by the valour and enthusiasm of his troops. On 27 Mar he attended the opening ceremony of the I.N.A. Officer's Training School in Rangoon and in his address to the cadets he again reiterated his objectives of overthrowing Britain and the United States and his further expansion of the I.N.A.

10. In order further to enthuse his public Bose organised the celebration of 6 to 13 April as a "National Week" and appealed for appropriate celebrations. An exchange of personal messages between Bose and Yoki Kazao, Japanese Minister of Greater East Asiatic Affairs, took place in the first week of Apr with mutual congratulations and felicitations on the progress of the war, with special reference to the entry into India of the I.N.A. on the 23 Apr he was pleased to announce the capture of Kohima, a statement he did not extract despite its falseness. At the end of the War he was at one time reported have set foot on the end of war he was at one time reported to have set foot on the Indian soil during an inspection tour of the Indo-Burma front.

11. Little more is heard of him until the 4 July when "Netaji week" began. During the celebrations he held several Press conferences and inaugurated anew series of talks over the I. N. A. broadcasting station, taking the opportunity to make an attack on All Indian Radio. The week's celebrations also included a large military parade at which he decorated several of his "heroes".

12. He remained in Burma until the end of Oct when he left for Tokyo, arriving on 2 Nov. On arrival he was received by the new Japanese Premier Koiso, and had conferences withe the Chiefs also received by the Emperor and spent several days visiting Japanese colleges and institution and banqueting with the Foreign Minister.

13. On 14 Dec. he returned to Singapore and declared that whatever the present state of affairs on the fighting fronts the emphasis was on offensive action and that final victory was sure to be his. At the same time, he once again called for total mobilisation. He spent the remainder of Dec visiting the Principal cities in Malaya.

The part played by Subhas Chandra Bose in the Japanese intelligence offensive against India.

14. In order to obtain a clear picture of Bose's achievement while working for the Japanese this subject is treated under J.I.F.C. headings rather than as a chronological account of his doings from the time he came under the Japanese aegis.

15. **Radio Campaign.** From the time of S.C. Bose's arrival the enemy radio intensified its propaganda campaign based on the Indian puppet movement in Far Eastern occupied territories. As might have been expected, Bose himself took a prominent part in this campaign with speeches directed to India. These speeches may be said to have contained three salient feature:—

(a) Efforts to boost the J.I.F.C. This feature was presented from two angles, namely, telling Indians in India and the world at large of the extent and growth of the movement and more important, impressing upon Indians outside India the wonderful opportunity presented to them by the Japanese to fight to 'liberate' their Mother country. This angle was, of course, intermixed with appeals which, incidentally, often became threats for more recruits, more money and more effort on the part of the 3 Million Indians in the Far East.

(b) Reactions to political events within India. This was probably the most important feature of Bose's radio campaign and one which was dictated solely by the fear that Government and nationalist/subversive parties within India would reach a settlement. Throughout, this broadcasts contained four main clues to his conception of the problem with which he was confronted by the Indian situation. During thelatter half of 1943 and up to the time of the releases of the correspondence between the Viceroy and Gandhi, in 1944, Bose constantly acknowledged Gandhi's supreme leadeship and understanding of the Indian people which, however, he many times tried to offset by claiming that an important part of political India and the greater part of the Indian masses supported Bose and the Forward Bloc. He repeated many times the uselessness of nonviolence as a positive revolutionary weapon and the necessity for replacing it by armed violence. These two lines were plugged fairly constantly, and it was not until a compromise between Gandhi and Government appeared imminent that he began accusing Gandhi of founding his whole policy on compromise with Britain, against which he put his own steadfast refusal even to consider coming to terms with India's enemy. this accusation was chiefly actuated by the dread that Bose shared at that time with the Japanese that Gandhi would succeed in effecting a settlement, and the realisation that once this happened the J. I. F. C. game was up. The same dread was apparent in his broadcasts relating to the meeting between Gandhi and Jinnah in Sep. 44. Even as late as Oct 44, he intermixed defence of the I. N. A., a propos of its withdrawal with the Japanese army from Manipur, with accusations against wavering nationalists in India." who were in favour of a settlement with Britain.

(c) **Instructions to Indians in India to work for the Japanese.** Such broadcasts were featured from time to time and included in some cases detailed instructions to subversive elements within India to spread pro-Bose and anti–British propaganda, to assaisinate government and military officials, to commit sabotage and generally to foment strife within India, the signal to be given by Bose himself.

16. Subsidiary features of his radio campaign were his appeals to Ceylon to unite with Indians in their "battle for freedom", to Chungking and Communist, China to sink their differences, unite with Nanking and cease fighting their Japanese "benefactors", and those broadcasts designed to impair inter allied relations.

The I. N. A.

17. While it cannot be said that the conception of this force was Bose's it has been proved beyond doubt that since Bose's arrival in the Far East it owes its position as a major factor in the J.I.F.C. to him. Very soon after becoming "Commander-in-Chief" he launched a huge recruiting campaign, chiefly through the agency of the administrative organ of the J.I.F.C., the I.I.L. This campaign entailed suborning Indian P. W. from their oath of allegiance and, by indirect methods, subverting civilian Indians. Later he succeeded in obtaining recognition of this force as an allied army by the Axis and affiliated quislings. By the beginning of 1944 the I.N.A. had been organised into some sambliance of a military force, and during the Japanese advance into and withdrawal from Manipur and, of course, the Arakan the I.N.A. was committed once a number of occasions to taking up arms in actual combat against Allied forces. The Japanese might have taken this action even if Bose had not been present, but it is considered that the process of organising them into instructions capable of use by the enemy was hastened by Bose, who saw in its success his most powerful propaganda backing. Reliable evidence indicates the effect on considerable numbers of this force of Bose's personal influence, which has done a great deal to produce an anti-British frame of mind and willingness to fight (for the Japanese). In the balance must also be considered the state of hopelessness which must latterly have been created in the members of this force, and for which Bose is responsible since he has not scrupled to deceive them as necessity demanded.

The I. I. L.

18. When Bose arrived in Singapore the I. I. L. was established in all the large towns in Burma and Malaya and also another Japanese occupied territories. But it was only through Bose's personal intervention that it became powerful and was dreaded by non-collaborating Indians, since the measure of authority delegated to it by Bose and allowed by the Japanese knew no bounds. Many more branches were set up and the I.I.L. began a campaign of enrolment of all Indians as members. Its methods, condoned by Bose, to subvert loyal British subjects were not altogether in keeping with the ideology of "freedom" which it was plugging daily over the radio.

19. By the beginning of 1944 this organ of the J. I. F. C. was all-important and throughout 1944 it expanded in size and strengthened its grip on Indians in E. O. T. Its function is ostensibly the administration of the Indian community. In reality it is to harness the community to the Japanese war efforts. It is the structure around which Bose has built his plans and on which he is dependent. Its charter includes recruiting for the Indian National Army and for all aspects of overt and secret intelligence warfare. Since the authority vested in gives it the power of life and death over all Indians it is not surprising that this Fascist party of Bose's has met with some successs. It must not be forgotten, however, that it owes a large part of its success to Bose's personal prestige with Indians.

The Provisional Government

20. In late 1943 Bose announced the formation of a Provisional Government, which is the executive and paramount body of the J. I. F. C. Little need be said about this important aspect of the J. I. F. C. The move forward of the Government from Singapore to Rangoon in the beginning of 44 foreshadowed J. I. F. C. events of some importance, and was evidence of the great expectations held by Bose and the Japanese at that time. Bose has stated that once in India it was to be disbanded and its place taken by a Government of elected representatives of the people.

Secret Warfare

21. The fifth column weapon composed of Indians, which has been used by the Japanese to carry out secret warfare against India, was welded together prior to Bose's arrival in the Far East. There is reason to believe, however, that he took a close personal interest in its tempering and proper use, and to some extent he has been largely responsible for the conduct of clandestine warfare through Indian agents.

22. At the end of 1943 Bose was sending tactical agents to the Burma front to work in the vicinity of our Indian troops at collecting information, spreading propaganda, and trying to cause desertions. Other enemy agents were detailed to the strategic intelligence front, which included contacting political organisatons and giving assistance to revolutionary and terrorist groups to assist in some way the invasion by the Japanese and Indian National Armies.

These plans did not meet with any appreciable success but this was apparently no deterrent to Bose.

23. Tacticial warfare increased in intensity as the Japanese military offensive gained momentum, but with the general withdrawal from Manipur and in Central Burma it faded away almost entirely. This was probably due to the lack of opportunity for the employing intelligence agents effectively on tactical work during a prolonged retreat. Events in Burma did not however affect the planning of the strategic secret warfare and throughout 1944 spy training schools in Burma and Malaya continued their efforts to turn out suitable Indian agents prepared to carry out Bose's work inside India.

24. Since the beginning of the war many agents have been sent to this country, including individual fully equipped to collect intelligence, spread anti-government propaganda, incite subversive elements to contact members of the Forward Bloc, to transmit information to the Japanese by W/T and to carry out other traitorous activities.

25. It is believed that Bose takes a personal interest in the training and instructions given to agents. It is true to say that after his arrival the morale of those Bengalis known to be collaborating with the Japanese was considerably improved by the presence in their midst of a Bengali of such "repute". Bengalis of an Intelligence Group in Burma were at one period asked to dedicate their lives even at the risk of death to protect the life of Subhas Chandra Bose.

26. The facts presented here, though necessarily brief, justify the conclusion that Bose is largely responsible for the conduct of Japan's secret warfare against this country and that his plans are dictated not only by his own will but by the enemy's military interests.

Japanese estimation of Subhas Chandra Bose

27. In any examination of the part Bose has played, and is still playing, in conducting this traitorous offensive against India the subject of Japanese estimation of him is of value. It is natural to assume that Japanese estimation of Bose is based firstly on his standing with subversive elements within India, and secondly on his achievements as head of the J.I.F.C.

28. Regarding the former it is clear from captured documents that the Japanese seem to have believed (till recently at any rate) that Bose's supporters in India outnumber those of Gandhi and that the efforts

of his "Secret Warfare Department" in India to stir up a revolution would result in a great rising as soon as the Japanese Army struck its blow inside India. Regarding the latter, official Japanese documents reveal the confidence the Japs have in Bose's ability to unify all Indians outside India and to direct their activities into one channel, i.e. assisting Japanese military operations accorded the most considerate treatment and received the greatest possible amount of publicity.

29. But it must not be overlooked that, despite Japanese propaganda on Bose as a co-belligerent and leader of an independent nation, the fact remains that Bose is in an unenviable position. He is carefully tended and observed by Japanese "advisers", and he and his puppets are in the grip of the enemy. It is clear that any propaganda pretensions to being master of his own destiny and deliverer of India, which Bose may put out over the enemy radio, are falsified by the facts. However, the conclusion is that the Japanese see in Bose their most useful Indian quisling and one whom they would be unlikely to abandon at short notice, since his value lies in facilitating their military designs.

26

Report by Dhillon onI.N.A. Fighting on the Burma Front[1]

25 March, 1945

Battle Report No. 5.

Since the submission of the last report No. 4 of 18th March 45 nothing of importance has happened, though the patrol activities on both sides have been on the increase. Some of the points noticed are reported below for the sake of interest and training:-

1. During these days we have been sharing the occupation of most of the places in our area with the enemy. We would occupy during the night and they during the day as if a definite settlement existed between the two.

2. Many a places we have attacked during the night only to find that there was no enemy.

3. Many a time our patrols were seen by the enemy patrols or vice-versa and firing started on both sides mostly from long range.

   One day, i.e., 20th March 05 at about 1600 hrs. an enemy patrol about fifty strong came in front of the dispositions of "A" coy 452 unit. Timely warning was given by the forward listening posts and our Coy. Comdr. Lt. Ram Nath sent forward two platoons to encircle this enemy. Before this could be done the enemy started running back. Our men ran after him for about two miles as if chasing a game during peace time. The Coy and Pl. Comdrs. tried their best to collect the two platoons, but men would not listen. Most of these men were civilian recruits from Malaya. The enemy was firing back at our men, but our men would not take to the ground instead they said "Oe, bat to sun jao". It was after about two hours that our Commanders could collect all the men. When told that you should not do like this and must make use of the ground.....our men said, 'Sahib ham kia

1. I.N.A. Trial Papers

karen, dushman to rukta hi nahin hai, bhage chala jata hai". This story shows a grand spirit, but poor training.

4. It was learnt from the Japanese M.P. that the villagers round about PONGOBIN informed that on the day following our attacks on Hill 1860, the enemy took back full lorry loads of the dead. Of course wounded must be more.

5. It has also been learnt that the enemy troops take away women from the nearby villages West of Taungin Hills by force, keep them for a day or so and then send them back. Rape cases being so frequent that the villagers are getting anti-British. This is another point where the enemy cannot defeat us for he may give them food stuffs, but honour cannot be compensated by anything and the Burmese people are very touchy as far as self-respect is concerned.

6. On 21st March 05.

Our positions of Unit No. 453 were disclosed to the enemy by a Burma Spy and thus were heavily shelled, bombed, mortar fired and machine gunned, foı about four hours during the afternoon. The result was one man L/NK Sudarshan was so slightly wounded that even his evacuation was not necessary. This is a proof of taking to the cover.

7. Pooling the necessity of more training, it is being arranged by these H.Qrs. to issue "Training Notes During war" upto platoons within this unit. A copy of Note No.1 is attached herewith.

As a result of this race, we got three 2" Mortar, bombs and one rifle magazine with nine rounds which the enemy had to leave back to lighten the load or due to nervousness.

(Sd.) G.S. Dhillion
Major,
Commander No. 450 Unit A. H. F.

Operation Order No. 2. for the I.N.A. Fighting on the Burma Fronts[1]

27 March, 1945

1. **Information**

(a) **The enemy**—An enemy mechanized column estimated to be approximately one Bde. that infiltrated into Meiktila late last month, is still there. It is being reinforced by the enemy who has formed strong bridge-heads at Nyangu and Pakokku. The strength of the enemy at these bridge-heads is estimated to be approx. 2 Bdes.

It is also learnt that the enemy has recently occupied Pyinbin with 10 tanks, 10 armoured cars and approx. one Bn. of Infantry.

At Thedaw approx. 12 miles N.E. of Pyinbin enemy's reserves for Taungtha front are located. Strong detachment of enemy are also known to be in the vicinity of Myingyan, Taungtha and Mahlaing.

(b) **Own and Allied Troops**—Powerful Japanese forces are fiercely attacking Meiktila and have managed to push the enemy out of the town to west side of the lake.

On our front one fresh Heidan has arrived at Seiktan 10 Miles S. E. of Pyinbin.

Khanjo units are at Setsetyo 4 miles south of Pyinbin. Further west on Kayauk Padang-Nayangu Road, one fresh Butai has taken over the defence of Taungzin and Mayaukye Negalaine from No. 459 Unit. The advance of Kantetsu on both sides of the Irrawaddy is progressing satisfactorily.

2. **Intention**

No. 531 Unit will attack, in co-operation with Khanjo, and annihilate the enemy garrison in Pyinbin on the night of March 30/31st.

3. Method

As a preliminary to the attack units from their present locations will concentrate in the areas on dates shown below :-

	Unit	Place	Date
(a)	No. 545 Unit	Seiktein	Night 29/30 March
(b)	(i) Khanjo Units	Oyin (2 Miles S.E. Pyinbin) Taungdaw 5 Miles South of Pyinbin.	
	(ii) No. 450 Unit and Hosokawa Units.	Cross Roads 6 Miles S.W. of Pyinbin.	Do

On the night 30/31 March Khanjo and No. 450 Unit will move forward from their concentration areas and carry out the assault on PYINBIN at 0100 hrs. and annihilate the enemy.

No. 545 Unit will send forward strong detachment to cut off from the East Roads (I) Pyinbin-Tada

(II) Pyinbin-Thabyewa

(III) Pyinbin-Kama

These detachments will be in position by 2300 hours on the night 30/31st March.

During the attack on Pyinbin by No. 450 Unit and Khanjo, No. 545 Unit will step and annihilate any enemy that tries to escape from Pyinbinby these Roads and also to stop any reinforcements from coming into Pyinbin from East and N.E.

No. 531 Unit Operation Order No. 2.

They will carry sufficient mines to effectively block all roads against enemy tanks.

Heavy artillery will support the attack from the direction of Oyin.

Action after the Attack—On completion of the attack, all units of No. 531 Unit will fall back on their original starting lines before day break.

During the day the troops will be well-dispersed and every precaution will be taken against losses from enemy aeroplanes and A.F.Vs.

4. Administration

Supply routes for units will be as under:—

(a) No. 450 Unit—Popaywa-Daungie—Cress Roads (S.W. of Pyinbin).

(b) No. 545 Unit—Popaywa-Seiktein.

As many bullock carts as are necessary will be commandered locally by units and on termination of the attack will be returned to the owners.

Ration, Water and othe Supplies. All unit demand will be submitted to D.Q.M.G. Popaywa, who will do his best to comply with them. A minimum of seven days dry rations will be dumped in forward areas under unit arrangements.

S.A.A. A very small reserve of .303" S.A.A. Ball is available with D.Q.M.G. Units are requested to exercise utmost economy in the use of ammunition.

A/Tk. Mines. A very limited number are available. These are being sent with trained engineers to assist units.

Medical. All casualties will be evacuated to Popaywa.

A small quantity of bleeching powder for use in case where water cannot be boiled is being supplied to Units.

Intercommunications

No. 450 Unit—No. 531 Unit will be by wireless through Hosokawa Unit.

No. 545 Unit—No. 531 Unit by Wireless.

Battle H.Q. 531 Unit will move from Popaywa to vicinity of Seiktein on night 29/30 March.

Main H.Q. 531 Unit remain at Popaywa under command of Major Ram Sarup.

Special Instructions of Units

(a) Attack on Pyinbin is more in the nature of a surprise guerrilla raid with the intention of causing as much damage to the enemy as possible and then clearing out of it.

Comds. must use the troops very cautiously and avoid all unnecessary casualties.

(b) Where possible some live prisoners will be brought back.

(c) All papers, other documents and any unit distinguishing badges found in enemy camp will be brought back.

28

Note on the I.N.A. by the Military Intelligence Based on Information Given by Two Staff Officers of H.Q. 2 I.N.A. Division who Recently Surrendered[1]

30 March, 1945

Order of Battle

1. The believed Order of Battle of the I.N.A. is shown at Annexure 1.[2]

2. Comments—Although not obvious from the Annexure, certain reorganisations have occurred since the Manipur campaign. These were expected in view of the fade out of the major combatant element of 1 Div after the retreat from Manipur, and the urgency of scraping together a semblance of an organised formation with which Bose could press his demands for another showing for the I.N.A. Subsequent paragraphs show to some extent the nature of these demands and their reception by the Japanese.

Strength

3. The total number "on the strength" is computed at 35,000 composed of 10/15,000 Indian Army personnel and the remainder civilian Tamils domiciled and recruited in Malaya. It is emphasised that the 35,000 are on the strength and not under 'arms'.

4. The 35,000 are believed to be disposed as follows—
   (a) **Burma**—About 4,500 of No. 1 Div at Pyinmana about 150 miles North of Rangoon, on the Irrawaddy plus about 1,000 in hospital in Rangoon. About 10,000 of No. 2 Div most of which are probably forward of Rangoon. About 4,000 Command troops concentrated mainly in Rangoon. Total approx. 20,000.
   (b) **Malaya**—About 2,000 of No. 2 Div. About 10,000 of No. 3 Div. About 3,000 Command troops concentrated in Singapore. Total approx 15,000.

1. F. No. 601/7378/H.S.
2. Not Printed.

5. In Burma the largest concentration is in the Mount Popa-Kyaukpadaung area. No. 1 Div., which featured in the Manipur operations, is no longer regarded (by I.N.A. officers) as a combatant formation; 1,000 are hospitalised in Rangoon; some more are also in Pyinmana where the main force is resting. Newcomers to Burma who visit these 1 Div units at Pyinmana, apparently listen to a lot of "eyewash" about the glorious part played by No. 1 Div in the Manipur campaign.

6. The strengths quoted above do not include the Training Schools potential which is difficult to assess since reliable information is lacking.

7. All sources are in accord with the statements that furthermoves into Burma are out of the question due, *inter alia*, mainly to lack of transport, arms and equipment. Even moves forward of Rangoon are being retarded through lack of proper transport facilities.

8. *Comments*—20,000 in Burma by the beginning of this year expected. It was also appreciated that No. 3 Div would be ready move into Burma but it is still in Malaya where it is likely to remain until the Allied forces arrive driving the Japanese before them. By this time the Japanese and Bose will probably plug.

General Morale

9. The main source under interrogation, while indicating his inability to give a clearly defined picture of I.N.A. morale, in view of the conflicting factors involved, expressed his opinion as follows—

10. I.N.A. officers fall into two categories—

    (a) the few who are sincerely behind the "Movement" and completely "in" with Bose,

    (b) the majority who are waiting for an opportunity to come over to us. This category is further subdivided into:—

        (i) those who see in the "movement" only a propaganda weapon, and

        (ii) those who are quite definitely anti-I.N.A. and Bose and everything he stands for.

    It is on category (a) that Bose depends to infuse into the I.N.A. his own enthusiasm and beliefs.

11. Although category (b) is the larger it is incapable of doing anything to negative the actions of the first. This is entirely due to the attitude of mind "one false move and I'm a dead man" which is prevalent. Confidences are only exchanged with those of similar caste. Even then it is only with very close friends that an officer would begin to discuss escape plans. There are apparently quite a number who are now under "observation" due to having disclosed their feelings and/or intentions and having been betrayed by "traitors". Naturally these "traitors" are encouraged in their work by Bose and the Japanese. The tension which this creates is only lessened by the common detestation of the Japanese.

12. If mutual trust is extremely difficult between officers it is completely out of the question for the officers in "gain the minds" of the other ranks. This is reflected in the attitude of those "loyal" officers who are selected to lead parties. They generally do not know the feelings of the men and so their actions during the patrol are dominated by the fear of making a false move; to fail in an attempt to surrender to our troops would mean arrest on return since it is practically certain that somebody would report what happened.

13. Regarding these guerrilla patrols, most of them are composed of very specially selected pro- I.N.A. personnel. Just before it sets out a patrol listens to a propaganda "pep" talk which is usually very well put across and apparently has the desired effect of stimualating the men. Their first pre-patrol pep talk comes after several years of feeding on Japanese and I.I.L. propaganda which is normally cleverly twisted. The lectures on No. 1 Division participation in the Manipur campaign have had a marked effect on 2 Div. This effect has been heightened by the "tall yarns" told by members of No. 1 Div of the actions they fought in during the campaign.

14. But the men are not "told everything"; for instance, with the exception of those in the immediate vicinity very few know of the voluntary mass surrender of part of IV Guerrilla Regiment in India but they are informed very quickly when anything occurs in India by which either certain internal or foreign press agencies attempt to discredit the Government. But it is only the P.W. element who think about conditions in India since 60/70 per cent of the civilian element (South Indians) have never been to India and do not rightly know the meaning of their one word of Hindustani "Azadi". These men have no

knowledge of war and thoughtful moments of a violated oath of allegiance are not theirs. They are genuinely shocked when they see war at close quarters.

15. **Comments.** These paragraphs reveal the tension existing among the officer class for fear of betrayal of confidences exchanged, the impossibility of officers getting to know what the men think and, finally, the attempts made to "conditions" the men prior to going out on patrol. The latter would seem to have effect since Jif patrols still fight even though many surrender afterwards. This tendency to fight despite their muddled state of mind is discussed under "Conclusions" below. The impression is also given that Bose depends solely on that top layer of former Indian Army officers who are completely in with him. It is these officers whom he will undoubtedly try to protect when things go wrong, in the same way possibly that the Japanese (Copying the Nazis) will protect those Indian elements who are pro-Japanese e.g., by faking their arrests. This is a possibility which Security authorities should watch.

Events Leading up to the Surrender of the Five Staff Officers

16. After the withdrawal of the remnants of Div. from Manipur there was only IV Guerrilla Regt. available to operate in the front line. This was put under command of 2 Div which by this time was arriving in Burma and was moving to the Central Irrawaddy front. Div H.Q., however, did not move forward until the end of February but staff officers had been sent out previously on and liaison visits. But it appears that the role of the Div was not finally settled until the latter half of February when a series of conferences was held between the Japanese and the I.N.A. Supreme Command in Rangoon and in the forward areas. The former were represented by Lt. Gen. Isoda Sabura head of the Hikari Kikan, and the latter by I.N.A. officers and at the "big" conference in Rangoon by Bose himself. At one of them Major Gen. Iwakuro Hideo, former head of the Iwakuro Kikan now C of S 23 Army was present since 2 Div was eventually to operate under his control.

17. The main points of these discussions were demands by Bose for:—

(a) Personal control of the I.N.A. in operations and for this reason the allotment of W/T frequencies,

(b) the allotment of an independent sector in the Popa-Kyaukpadaung area,

(c) the distribution and dispositions of troops to I.N.A. commanders, the supply of artillery and air support, the allotment of W/T sets, telephones, motor cycles etc; more transport, hand grenades. TK mines, magnetic mines, L.M.Gs, Tommy guns, pistols, entrenching tools, compasses, binoculars, range finders, maps, demolition materials and medical supplies,

(d) suitable ration arrangements.

The general answer by the Japanese was that they would "do their best to fulfil them".

18. On the important question of direct operational control by Bose the Japanese quite firmly refused to allow Bose any say in operations although he could remain in "general touch" with his division.

19. Regarding the allotment of an independent sector the Japanese at first opposed this demand on the grounds that I.N.A. desertions had cost the Japanese the Imphal campaign but eventually they agreed and as a result 2 Div began taking up positions in the area enclosed by the Irawaaddy-Popa-Kyaukpadaung.

20. Their tasks were—

(a) to guard against Allied crossings of the Irawaddy,

(b) to make strong points in the Popa and Kyaukpadaung areas,

(c) to make arrangements to guard against attack by airborne troops.

(d) to patrol the upper reaches of the Irawaddy.

The senior I.N.A. officer in the area received his orders from H.Q. 28 Army through the Japanese regimental commander on his flank because he had no W/T communication with Army H.Q. At first there were no Japaneses units in the sector but immediately Allied troops crossed the river a Japanese Regiment(?) moved into it to counter attack them. Even after this with Japanese on both flanks the I.N.A. commander is reported to hold an independent command.

21. **Comment**—The outstanding items are firstly the firm refusal of the Japanese to allow Bose to have operational control and secondly the allotment of an independent sector to the I.N.A. in an important sector of the front.

22. The Japanese apparently laid down an initial W.E.T. for the I.N.A. of 15,000. This was passed some time ago and since then the shortage of arms, ammunition and all types of equipment has been growing steadily more acute. The balance was partly restored by the issue of Dutch Rifles (0.275), M.M.Gs and mortars (81 mm). But now all British and Dutch stocks have been exhausted. 3 Div in Malaya posses very few arms. The Japanese are well aware of this acute shortage of equipment, vide the demands made at the Rangoon and Irrawaddy conferences, yet they will not issue the I.N.A. with Japanese arms.

23. **Comment**—Early in 1944 attention was drawn to the inevitable shortage of arms and equipment and the effect it would have on I.N.A. dispositions and also to the fact that the Japanese will not arm the I.N.A with their own weapons for reasons not difficult to guess.

Sidelights on Bose

24. The main source states that Bose is anti-Japanese because he knows they will not trust him nor members of his movement. But despite his aversion there is no indication of Bose's repudiating his present alliance with them. The source also states that Bose believes that the split will occur between Britain and the U.S.S.R. When this happens Japan will certainly ally herself with the U.S.S.R. and thus Bose will finally be on the winning side.

26. Just before source left Rangoon Bose impressed upon him the necessity for preventing desertions, saying that the death penalty must be adopted as a preventive measure. When Bose was informed of the mass defection of IV Guerrilla Regt., he became excited and left Rangoon hurriedly and arrived at Maikila with the intention of taking over command of the remnants of the Regiment and personally directing operations. A wireless message, however, from the Japanese G.H.Q. resulted in his being prevented from proceeding to the front.

I.N.A. Relations with the Japanese

27. Refusal to give the I.N.A. adequate arms and equipment, refusal to let Bose have a say in operations, and the delay in agreeing to allot an independent sector of the front to the I.N.A. all indicate Japanese distrust to I.N.A. All recent sources confirm this and add that the Japanese no longer believe in the I.N.A. as a military force and are

willing to put the blame for the Manipur debacle on the I.N.A.'s shoulders. The distrust is mutual but it has not yet found open expression.

Summary and Conclusions

28. This information confirms previous appreciations and contains the following major items—

(a) 1 Div is no longer a combatant force.

(b) 2 Div. the Jifs at present opposing us on the central Irawaddy, is still incomplete, part of it being still in Malaya.

(c) The I.N.A. in Burma numbers about 20,000 and in Malaya about 15,000. Of the total of 35,000 about 15,000 are suborned soliders of the Indian Army and the remainder are civilians.

(d) Transport difficulties and lack of arms and equipment are likely to restrict any appreciable reinforcement of the I.N.A. in Burma for some considerable time.

(e) The reliance placed on the top layer of Pro-Bose officers and the mist of suspicion in which most I.N.A. soldiers live.

(f) Almost everyone, including Bose, professes to be anti-Japanese. The mutual distrust between the Japanese and the I.N.A. results mainly in Japanese refusal to equip and arm the I.N.A. properly, the refusal to allow Bose operational control and the lack of cooperation between both forces.

29. In addition two important questions must be asked—

(a) Why did the Japanese give the I.N.A. an independent sector and

(b) Why, if Jifs hate the Japanese, and are poorly clad, inadequately equipped in a muddled frame of mind and of low morale, do they fight our forces, especially their brother Indian troops?

30. The answer to the first question may be that pressure from the top forced this decision. It may be that the Japanese cannot now handle the "Indian problem" as ruthlessly as they did in 1942. For instance, if they have projected long-term policy which involes a post-war Pan-Asiatic approach, it might be that they feel compelled to accede to many of Bose's demands. On the ther hand shortage of Japanese manpower has also been suggested as the explanation. All suggestions, however, are highly speculative: the fact remain that

whatever the reason, the I.N.A. still holds an independent sector through now it is linked very closely with Japanese forces, and recent clashes have been with mixed Japanese and I.N.A. patrols.

31. The answer to the second question as given by Jifs themselves is, firstly, fear of Japanese reprisals if escape plans go awry and, secondly, fear of being shot by the Allies if they succeed. This explanation cannot be entirely accepted, since many sources now report that our "surrender" literature is being seen and is generally having a good effect; some surrenders in the past few weeks have occurred as a result of reading our leaflets. Whatever version is accepted, the solution would appear to be firstly to remove the confused state of mind of these Jifs and secondly to weaken the Japanese hold over them. Our psychological warfare attends to the first, while our military oeperations have the effect of achieving the second by dispersing Jif concentrations and so freeing numbers of them from Japanese surveillance.

Operation Order No. 6 for the INA Fighting on the Burma Front[1]

6 April, 1945

1. **Information.** Unit No. 599 has been allotted new role and its responsibility will be as under:-

   (a) Anti Parachute work.

   (b) Guarding the L.O.C.

   (c) Establishing law and order in areas where I.N.A troops are stationed.

   In connection with para. (b) and (c) above, the troops of B.D.A have rebelled and have formed bands of dacoits, who are looting the villages and also harassing the main L of C of the INA and the Japanese Forces. Our activities will mainly be against them.

2. **Intention.** In order to carry out their role, formations of Unit No. 599, will move into the areas as shown below:-

   (a) Unit No. 603. In its present area of Magwe-Mainbu. Unit No. 606 on being relieved will rejoin Unit No. 603 at Magwe.

   (b) Unit No. 747. In the area of Natmauk-Taungdwingyi.

   (c) Unit No. 801. In the area of Minhala. (approx. 15-20 miles S.S.E. of Magwe) to Sinbaungwa.

   (d) H.Q. Unit No. 599 will move to a locality in Magwe area-Exact location will be intimated later.

3. **Method.**

   (a) Units will start moving independently from the evening of 10th April 1945. The move will be completed as soon as possible. All units will submit to these H. Qrs. a detailed programme of their move from this station.

1. I.N.A. Trail Papers.

(b) Routes.

(i) Marching columns of:-

Unit No. 599.

Unit No. 801.

will use cart track running through the following villages:-

Kyauk Padadaung-ywala-Yezon-Okshitton Wetmasut-Mawge.

(ii) Unit No. 747 will use cart tract:-

Kyauk Padaug-Kyatkun-Sangon-Magyigon Yamun-Natmauk-Taungdwingyi.

4. **Administration**

(a) Tpt. As far as possible, Units will make their own arrangements for transportation of their heavy baggage party to be left behind with the baggage, which will be transported, if and when the transport is available.

(b) Rations

(i) All parties except the Unit going to Natmauk will carry enough rations for the journey, plus 3 days reserve.

(ii) Unit bound for Natmauk will carry a minimum of 7 days reserve rations.

All ration that was issued as one month's reserve to Units in this area will be returned to D.Q.M.G. Details to Units in this will be issued to Units separately by D.Q.M.G.

As on their charge, units will return exact quantities of Reserve Rations espcially rice and salt to the D.Q.M.S.

(c) Medical—Medical Air Party Hospital closed here on 9th April 1945, patients and stores will be evacuated in accordance with the instructions issued separately by the A.D.M.S.

Special instructions in relation to the move of Formations of this Unit No. 599 have been issued separately. These will be strictly complied with.

5. **Information.** Immediately on their arrival at their destination, all Units will submit their All correct (or otherwise) reports to H.Q. Unit No. 599.

6. Acknowledge

(Sd.) Shah Nawaz Khan,
Colonel.
Commander No. 599 Unit.

30

Report by P.K. Sahgal on I.N.A. Fighting on the Burma Front[1]

6 April, 1945

Sub : Legyi Operations

In continuation of this office report forwarded under No. S/25/17/G, dated 2nd April 1945, a report called for under your No. 2/XX/G, dated 6th April 1945, is forwarded herewith:-

Ist April 1945—A Nippon platoon stationed on hill feature 1395 astride Seiktin-Welaung road sent the following report about the enemy movements:-

1. At 1130 hrs. 10 enemy tanks with 50 men were seen going towards Legyi from Welaung.
2. At 1530 hrs. 18 lorries. 2 tanks, I armoured car, 2 motor cycles and 2 guns were seen moving towards Legyi from Welaung. Out of these 11 lorries were loaded with stores and 7 lorries carried approximately 80 men.
3. At 1600 hrs. 1 tank was seen moving towards Legyi.

   All the tanks in the above-mentioned enemy force were medium tanks. This force was seen passing the road Nullah junction Pt. 1062 south of Seiktin map sheet 840/8 but no enemy was observed in the vicinity of Legyi and it was not clear whether the enemy were contemplating an attack on Legyi or whether he intended to go through Seiktin towards Kabyu.

   A fighting patrol under S.O Abdullah khan of 546 unit was sent to Seiktin Area. This patrol contacted one small enemy fighting patrol in the vicinity of Seiktin, but no enemy formation was seen in Seiktin area. The patrol returned to the base at 0400 hrs. on 2nd april 1945.

1. I.N.A. Trial Paper. Sahgal fell into the hands of the Allied forces soon ofter the battle.

One Recce patrol under S.O Ram Dutt of 546 unit was sent to Tada to bring back information about the enemy in that area. This patrol did not return by day-break on 2nd April 1945.

2/Lt. Gharib Singh, Mortar Platoon commander of 546 unit deserted during the night.

There was no enemy activity during the night.

2nd April 1945— (i) An enemy force between 500 to 1000 strong was seen in the vicinity of the cross road on the.

11.30 hrs 25 mile stone, Welaung-Seiktin road. There were a few lorries and a few motor cycles with this force.

(ii) Another enemy force about 1000 strong and some tanks were seen in the vicinity of the Nullah North East of the cross road at the 25 mile stone Welaung Seiktin road. This enemy force was seen digging in.

13.10 hrs. 13 enemy planes heavily bombed and machine gunned Legyi for about 40 minutes. The whole of the village was set on fire and some damage was done to our positions on the left of the road, but our casualties were only slight. As soon as the air raid was over, enemy artillery opened harassing fire on our positions. This harassing fire was continued until 2105 hrs.

1600 hrs. (iii) 3 enemy tanks were seen passing Thanbin village and 3 lorries, 1 gun and 40 men were seen under the palm trees in the vicinity of Thanbin. It appeared that the enemy was carrying out a recee of that area.

1700 hrs. (iv) An enemy force in 5 lorries supported by tanks moved towards Sciktin and Legyi. In front of this force were some dismounted men who advanced forward pretending to be gathering something from the fields on either side of the road. When the enemy came within range, 1 section of machine gun opened fire. A number of the enemy were seen falling down and the remainder disappeared into the Nullah. The tanks and the lorries fled towards the cross road on the 25 mile stone Welaung road. One of our machine guns was fired personally by Lt. Yasin khan the M.G. Coy. Commander. During the day no other enemy force approached Legyi. The enemy force that had moved towards Thanbin, also returned towards the cross road.

2200 hrs. (v) Lt. Yasin Khan, Lt. Mohd. Sadiq, S.O. Abdul Hakim with some N.C. OS. and men deserted.

2330 hrs. (iv) S.O. Ram Dutt and his men who had gone on patrol duty to Tada area, the previous day, returned and reported that there was no enemy in Tada area and that Seiktin was also clear of the enemy.

(vii) It was quite apparent that the enemy, during the day, had been reconnoitring and feeling our positions and that a full scale attack was imminent the next day, therefore I Coy. from 548 unit under the command of 2/Lt. Kanwal Singh was brought up and put into position on the right flank.

3rd April 1945— A great deal of alarm and despondency was observed among the officers and men, owing to the desertion of Lt. Yasin Khan and his companions on the previous night. Every body appeared to feel that the enemy had full information about our dispositions and as they had such overwhelming strength, our case was hopeless. Lt. Khazin Shah was also in a very bad state of nerve, I realised that he was not fit to command the battalion any more, therefore, I sent him to keep an eye on A Coy. Commander whose movements were also suspicious and I personally took over the direction of the battle.

1130 hrs. (i) An enemy force, composed as under, was seen moving towards Tasbaukkon and his forward elements had already reached Thanbin:-

Medium tanks	13
Light tanks	30
Lorries	60
Guns, more than	10
Infantry	1000

(ii) This report was given by a Nippon O.P. which was in Legyi village area and it was confirmed by Commander C Coy. which was the left forward Coy. of 546 unit. Later a part of this force was seen to be returning towards Seiktin and a large number of troops were seen debussing in the Nullah, North-East of Seiktin. A group of officers was observed carrying out recce and issuing orders under a palm-grove on the right of the road, about 2 miles in front of our positions.

1200 hrs. (iii) Enemy artillery opened harassing fire on our positions.

1300 hrs. (iv) An enemy force consisting as under, was seen advancing along the road towards Legyi:

Medium tanks	11
Armoured cars	30
Lorries	60

This force halted about 1000 yards in front of our position and deployed.

1330 hrs. (v) A small force of the enemy went round our right flank and attacked our 'B' Echelon. This was a complete surprise and our men were caught cooking food or carrying ammunition, rations and water. The casualties on our side were very heavy. The enemy occupied that area and was joined by some enemy tanks which moved round our left flank. No information of the action was received in the H. Qrs. until 1900 hrs.

1345 hrs. (vi) Heavy shelling on the right flank followed by an enemy attack by approximately one Battalion on the position occupied by one Coy. of 548 unit. The place was gallantly defended by the coy. and the enemy was pushed back after suffering heavy casualties.

1400 hrs. (vii) Approximately 1 platoon of the enemy opened light automatic and mortar fire in our position from the high ground astride the road in our rear. This fire was returned and the enemy was dislocated from his position.

By this time enemy artillery and mortars were shelling us from the front and our right rear and left rear.

1600 hrs. (viii) Enemy artillery opened rapid fire on the right flank and continued the fire for approximately 10 minutes. This was followed by an attack by approx. One enemy battalion on 1 Coy. of 548 unit. This coy. once again defended their position most gallantly and drove the enemy back, who, after suffering heavy casualties, fled in disorder.

During the whole of this operation 2/Lt. Kanwal Singh, the Coy, Commander. and Havl. Abdul Manan, one of the Platoon Commanders stood on top of 2 hills and directed the fire of their units. These two brave officers did not stir from their command posts, even when the enemy small arms fire was concentrated on them. It was due mainly to the gallant action of these 2 officers that the enemy was beaten off.

By now it was apparent that the enemy was determined to make a break-through on my right flank. Therefore I decided to withdraw back into reserve C Coy. of 546 Unit which was on the left of the road. Accordingly I approached the Nippon Coy. Commander in that area and requested him to assume the responsibility of stopping an enemy penetration from that side and linking up with B Coy. of 546 unit which was covering our left flank. This plan was agreed to and I ordered C Coy. Commander to withdraw his Coy. back and put one platoon astride the road south of Legyi and the remainder of the Coy. to be in reserve, prepared to counter-attack in any direction where the enemy may penetrate.

1900 hrs. (ix) Report-received about the enemy attack on our B Echelon and the enemy occupation of that area. Orders issued for C Coy. to attack and drive the enemy away from that area, When these orders were issued, Lt. Khazin Shah reported to me that there was only one Platoon of C Coy. available. The other two platoons under their commanders, S.S.O. Barfi Ram and Hav. Baldev Singh came running towards them and after a short conversation with the two platoon Commanders, these 2 platoons and one mortar platoon went over to the enemy. This matter was reported to Lt. Khazin Shah by a Tamil soldier, who managed to get back.

I issued orders to withdraw one platoon from A Coy., and 2 sections from 2/Lt. Kanwal Singh's Coy., this together with one platoon of C.Coy., under command of Lt. Ganga Singh was to immediately attack the enemy in our B Echelon area. I ordered 2/Lt. Bhopal Singh, Regimently. Intellegence Officer to accompany Lt. Ganga Singh. Lt Khazin Shah was in the meantime, to look after A Coy. in the absence of Lt. Ganga Singh. The attack was supported by 2/Lt. Kanwal Singh's Coy. Two section of 2/Lt. Kanwal Singh's Coy. did not arrive in time but the attack was launched by two Platoon at 2100 hrs. and was completely successful. The enemy after suffering heavy casualties fled in disorder.

1930 hrs. (x) Heavy artillery fire on our right flank and rear and 2/Lt. Kanwal Singh's Coy. was attacked for the third time and once again the attack was beaten off.

2100 hrs. (xi) An enemy force about two Coys. strong accompanied by tanks moved towards the left flank of B. Coy. of 546 unit which was covering our left flank but this force was pushed back after a short skirmish.

2130 hrs. (xii) Report received that the enemy had been completely cleared from B Echelon area and that the attacking groop under Lt. Ganga Singh had occupied a position on the hills astride the road south of Legyi.

(xiii) Report received that Lt. Khazin Shah with whole of his Bn. H.Q. and one platoon of A Coy. under S.O. Abdullah Khan had deserted. This matter was intimated to 531 unit and it was requested that reinforcement should be despatched immediately. Major A. B. Singh from 531 unit informed me that one Coy. of 548 unit under Major B.S. Negi was moving to reinforce Legyi.

(xiv) Report received that Lt. Ganga Singh, 2/Lt. Aya Singh and 2/Lt. Narindar Singh had deserted. Ordered 2/Lt. Bhopal Singh to take command of A Coy. By now whole of the Bn. H.Q. and all the five Coy. Commanders with about 200 men including the whole of the mortar Coy. with their mortars had gone over to the enemy side. The remainder of 546 unit could not be trusted.

One Coy. of 548 unit had fought most gallantly the whole day and by now was completely exhausted. The men had lived on biscuits and one w/bottle of water for 24 hours and were completely overcome by thirst and fatigue and were not in a position to stand another onslaught by the enemy.

4th April 1945— 0300 hrs.

1. 1 Coy. of 548 unit with 1 section of M.Gs. under Major B.S. Negi arrived. They had left the road well clear off Legyi and approached our position from the east. They were heavily fired on by the enemy, but luckily suffered no casualties.

I now appreciated the situation as follows:-

(a) Our position was completely surrounded and the enemy was overwhelmingly superior in numbers and armaments.

(b) The morale of 546 unit was very low and it was most likely that some of them may possibly go over to the enemy.

(c) All the officers and men were completely exhausted and unable to face another attack by the enemy.

Therefore, I sent for the Nippon Coy. Commander to consult him about our future action. He reported to me that another Bn. of his Regiment was moving up to occupy that position.

I decided to withdraw my tps. on the arrival of Nippon Bn. and I rang up 531 unit to ask the Commander 531 unit for orders, but as the Commander 531 unit was not available I decided to act on my own initiative.

(ii) I issued orders that on arrival of the Nippon Bn. the I.N.A. unit in Legyi area were to fight their way eastwards. Soon after I issued these orders, I discovered that the enemy had left the road and that the road between Legyi and

Popa was clear. Therefore, I altered the original orders and issued instructions to withdraw along the road.

0430 hrs. (iii) I received the information that the Nippon Bn.had arrived.

0500 hrs. (iv) Withdrawal was commenced and carried out without any casualties.

Special Notes Regarding Desertions

The three most salient features re. : these desertions from No. 546 units are:-

(a) All the officers who have deserted, had here worked most sincerly and considered very outstanding. Specially noteworthy among them were, Lt. Khazin Shah, Lt. Yasin Khan, Lt. Ganga Singh, 2/Lt. Chain Singh, 2/Lt. Balwant Singh, S.O. Barfi Ram, S.O. Abdullah Khan, S.O. Abdul Hakim, and Hav. Baldev Singh. On many occasions these officers had proved their devotion to the cause, and fought bravely and I had no occasion whatsoever to doubt their loyalty.

(b) None of the officers who have gone over, ever showed cowardice, and right up to the time they went over they fought most courageously.

On the 2nd when the enemy approached our positions, Lt. Yasin Khan personally manned a M. Gun and opened fire on the enemy and throughout the action, under heavy enemy artillery fire, he was going from post to post keeping up the morale of the men. On the night of the 29th when my party had been ambushed, 2/Lt. Balwant Singh, S.O. Barfi Ram and Hav. Baldev Singh showed complete disregard for their personal safety and fought most bravely.

S.O. Abdullah Khan had already distinguished himself for which he had been recommended for the award of Veere-Hind and he and S.O. Abdul Hakim were always singled out for the most difficult patrols.

On the night of 3rd. Lt. Ganga. Singh with about 45 men attacked and drove away a much superior force of the enemy.

(c) Not a single person ever showed cowardice in the face of the enemy. Our positions were attacked by very superior numbers, but not a single person ever left his post. We, with small units, attacked the enemy much superior in numbers and in armaments, but not a single soldier ever wavered. There were no desertions from a unit as long as the unit was in contact with the enemy, on the countrary, when in contact with the enemy, the units fought with unrivalled determination and utmost bravery. Lt. Inuzuka, the Hikari Kikan Liaison Officer, was so impressed by the brave fight put up by these Officers and men that he told me that was the biggest battle ever fought by the INA against such overwhelming numbers of the enemy. He felt that the manner in which the unit had fought surpassed even the Nippon tps. He conveyed these expressions to H.Q. 531 unit with a request to pass them on to H.E Netaji Subhas Chandra Bose, the Supreme Commander, Azad Hind Fauj.

After a very careful study of these points and the circumstances under which the unit fought, I am of the opinion that these desertions were mainly due to the following causes:-

(i) Turkey's alignment alongside the anti-axis powers has had a very adverse effect on certain Muslim Officers. In spite of our efforts to explain to them the circumstances under which Turkey has been forced to join the War, the officers feel that by fighting against powers that are allied with the Turks, they are being disloyal to Islam.

(ii) In the minds of a number of officers and men there is a lack of faith in our final Victory. They are in their own minds convinced that the Anglo-Americans are going to win the war and it is futile to carry on the struggle.

(iii) In this particular operation, after the desertion of Lt. Yasin Khan and his companions, there was a general feeling among the officers and men of the unit that it was unless to continue fighting against the enemy, so superior in numbers and armaments and helped by the traitors, who had gone over to his side. Majority of these officers, under normal circumstances, would never have done anything treacherous, but finding themselves overwhelmed, they did not have the moral strength to continue the struggle and decided to save themselves by going over to the enemy.

Before I conclude this report, I feel it my duty to pay a tribute to the steadfastness, devotion to duty and bravery of those of the officers and men (although some of them turned traitors afterwards), who fought most courageously and deperately against heavy odds and checked the enemy from penetrating our positions. Thinned in numbers, exhausted by hunger and thirst, weary both in mind and body, these brave soldiers of the A.H.F. tenaciously hung on to their posts until the arrival of the Nippon force. There were many cases of individuals whose actions deserve merit, these are being investigated and a fuller report will be submitted about them when these investigations have been completed.

(Sd.) P.K. Sahgal,
Lt. Col.,
Commander No. 747 Unit A.H.F

After writing this report, another important fact has come to light. In majority of the cases, when officers were going over to the enemy, they ordered the N.C. OS. and men under their commands to move with them under the pretext of either changing their dispositions or of attacking the enemy. Enquiries are being made into such cases and attempts are being made to separate the names of those persons who have gone to the enemy of their own accord and those who have been taken away under false pretences.

(Sd.) P.K. Sahgal
Lt. Col.

31

Special Order of the Day by Lieut. Colonel P. K. Sahgal, Offg. Comd. No. 2 Div A.H.F

8 April, 1945

21. In a special message addressed to the Commander of No. 2 Div. AHF. His Excellency Netaji Subhas Chandra Bose, the Supreme Commander of the AHF. has called upon all Officers and men of No. 2 Div. to make every sacrifice and to exert all their efforts to defeat the enemies of India.

Sathio, we have the privilege of fighting in the foremost ranks of AHF. so it behoves every one of us to be prepared to make the supreme sacrifice to uphold the honour and glory of Free India.

Enemies of India have managed to cross over to the left bank of the Irrawadi and our valiant allies, the Nipponese, are fighting grimly to defeat and annihilate this enemy.

Owing to the heavy losses suffered by the enemy, their morale has gone very low. They are entirely depending upon their air support to carry on fighting, but whenever they have been attacked by our forces, they have always fled from the battlefield.

In the name of thousands of martyrs who have patiently suffered for the cause of Free India and in the name of the heroes of the AHF. who have sacrificed their lives at the altar of India's Independence, I call upon all the officers and men of No. 2 Div. Azad Hind Fauj, to hunt for the enemies of India and destroy them wherever they may be found.

JAI HIND.

(Sd.) P.K. SAHGAL
Lt. Col.
Offg. Comd. No. 2 Div. AHF.

1. I.N.A. Trial Papers.

32

Decription by G.S. Dhillon of INA Glorious Fighting on the Burma Front[1]

9 April, 1945

The Charge of the Immortals[2]

It was a Flat Stretch of land without any cover either from view or from fire, except a shallow dry pond near which three Roads of great tactical importance met. Four miles North-West of this point was a Hill 1423 feet high behind which the enemy Artillery was located so as to cover the road junction and the area south of it, the occupation of which would effect the entire plan of operations.

At a key point like this was placed a company of Azad Hind Fauj under the command of 2/Lt. Gian Singh Bisht trained at the Officers Training School, Azad Hind Fauj. The Company was only Ninety-eight strong. They had no Machine Guns or even Light Machine Guns. Goods old Rifles were their only weapon of defence or offence apart from two A/Tk. Mines. Their orders were to check any enemy advance at all costs.

They remained in that position for two days, but the enemy dare not advance. Then on 16th of March, 1945 starting early morning hostile Fighting Planes bombed and machine gunned their positions until about 11 A.M. Having got rid of all the load they had, aeroplanes went away. Then the enemy Guns from behind the Hill started registering, and behind this barrage of Artillery fire advanced a column of Motorised Infantry consisting of 13 tanks, 11 armoured cars and 10 trucks. Half of this column made its way straight towards the Pond where two Forward Platoons of the Company were in position. Lead and explosives were being thrown out of the Armoured Fighting Vehicles, but this would not Frighten our

1. I.N.A. Trial Papers.
2 This battle was fought under the command of Lieut. Gian Singh Bhist.

boys, they waited in their trenches for the infantry to debuss. Tanks and Armoured Care like steel monsters creating hell with their fire power approached so close that they started charging on to our trenches so as to crush and cripple our men under their heavy weight. Two mines were thrown in their way which unluckily did not burst, but they caused monsters to stop which having stopped became stationery pill boxes oozing out most inhuman forms of killing materials.

There was no communication between this Post and the Battalion H. Qrs. When 2/Lieut. Gian Singh appreciated, that their Rifles Fire was no match to the enemy's Mortars, Machine Guns, Light Automatics and Hand Grenades and their staying in trenches meant certain death or captivity with no loss to the enemy, he ordered " ChargeE". Leading the assault he shouted slogans of "NETAJI KI JAI" "INQALAB ZINDABAD", "AZAD HINDUSTAN ZINDABAD" and "CHALO DELHI". All the men responded to slogans which echoed above the enemy fire. This was the only support which these heroes had against the superior armament of the enemy. In the name of India and Indian Independence they charged into the Enemy trucks. The enemy immediately debursed. Hand to hand fighting ensued which lasted for full two hours, but our heroes would not give in, forty of them sacrificed their lives after killing more than their equal number of the enemy. Their unconquerable spirit harassed the enemy so much that he started retreating.

Just then 2/Lieut. Gian Singh called forward his Third Platoon Commander 2/Lieut. Ram Singh and was giving out orders when a bullet struck on his head and he fell down never to give out orders again. 2/Lieut. Ram Singh then collected the remnants of the company and re-organised.

2/Lieut. Gian Singh Bisht used to tell his men that he would die with them. He fulfilled his promise and remained their comrade in life and death. This was a glorious deed of which the History will remain witness as long as there is world. 2/Lieut. Gian Singh and his men lived up to the ideals of our Great Leader—the Netaji— and have laid down their lives fighting by their posts to build up a tradition for us to follow. In Free India the spirit of these Heroes who knew no defeat will be worshipped for generations to come and will inspire the future Sons of India to live up to such high ideals.

(Sd) G. S. Dhillon,
Lt. Col.
Commander 801 Unit

33

Extract from the Diary of Capt. P.K. Sahgal (2/10 Baluch Regt.) for the Year 1945[1]

10 April, 1945

Jan. 24— Went to the range in the morning and fired the new Mortar it is a very accurate weapon, but the ammunition situation is not very satisfactory. Very busy carrying out the re-organisation of the Regiment. In the evening received orders that 29th has been finally fixed as the date for my move.

Jan. 27— The whole day very busy getting my first Battalion ready to move.

Jan. 31— Issued orders and instructions regarding the move of the Div. from Prome to Kyauk Padaung.

Feb. 4— New promotions have been published and there was a ceremony at Netaji's banglow when Zaman was presented with Major General badges rank. Saw Netaji for short time about the move of my Regiment.

Feb. 8— Got the news that my Role is going to be defence of Popa Hill.

Feb. 13— Left Rangoón at 0700 hrs by car...... spent the day at Sako Buta H. Q. Rest House....... Had a long discussion with Major General Iwakuro about the employment of No. 2 Div.

Feb. 17— Arrived at Yenang Yaung early in the morning. Recd. reports that enemy had already crossed the Irrawaddy river. Met Maj. Gen. Yamanoto and discussed the situation with his Staff Officers.

1. I.N.A. Trail Papers.

Feb. 18— Arrived at Popa early in the morning and met Dhillon who had arrived the previous day. Dhillon told me the crossing took place on his right flank where Japanese troops were guarding the crossing. He also told me that Capt. Hari Ram with a number of Officers and men had gone over. One of his Coys and one Pl. refused to go over to the enemy. Capt. Chander Bhan's Battalion fought most gallantly and at the end managed to extricate themselves. He expected within the next 2/3 days he will be able to gather nearly 500 men. This is good news.

Feb. 19— Dhillon is very despondent about the condition of the Regt. There is no discipline left and the morale is gone. They are a source of nuisance to me also because they wander about and give away my positions also.

Feb. 22— Col. Shah Nawaz and Boobi arrived early this morning. Col. S. N. is taking over the Tempy. Command of the Div. until Col. Aziz gets well. Spent the day explaining the current situation to Col. S.N. Comd. in preparing the defences of Popa came to call on Col. S.N. He seems to be a decent sort.

Feb. 23— Climbed up Pt. 2640 with Col. S.N. to explain to him the defences of Popa. An order from Saku Army was received to the effect that the INA. units should carry out Guerilla activities help the Nippon units attacking the enemy. S.N. decided to form 4 coys out of No. 4 Guerilla Regiment for this job. Went with S. N. to see Dhillon, who agreed to S. N. plan. S.N. left to report the situation to Netaji.

February. 24— Early morning received information that the enemy tanks have broken through to Seiktin. One Battalion of Kanju unit has taken up a defensive position of Kyauk Padaung-Myingyian road. My Regiment. takes over the responsibility for Popa Pyinbin road. Sending out a recee patrol to find out the situation on this road. I may have to employ one of Dhillon's Coys to carry out Guerilla warfare in Pyinbin area.

February. 27— Late last night report came thro' that some enemy had gone to Pozu near Kyauk Padaung and it was confirmed that it was only a fighting patrol supported by tanks and carriers. I am convinced that we must attack Meyne immediately, but I have no force available for the task. I requested the Kanjo unit to either take up a defensive position in my area for a day and relieve my forces for an offensive or to lend me a couple of Cys., to cooperate with my attacking units. I hope the Commander will agree with either of the 2 suggestions.

February. 28— Information from Nippon source that some enemy lorries have been seen going towards Kyauk Padaung from Pyinbin. I do not consider the Inf. trustworthy. Kanju Butai is going to attack the enemy to-night. I've promised to block the road behind the enemy to cut off his retreat.

March 1— I had to sentence an officer to death this morning for refusing to go to the front. What a pity, it is such a waste of human life. Information received that Majors Riaz, Madan, Sarwar, Dey and Lt. Mohammed Bux who went on an exercise last night have not so far returned. I am terribly worried about them. I do hope that they have not gone over to the enemy.

March 2— Those officers have not returned so far. I am certain they have gone over to the enemy—the treacherous swines. From now on I am going to be absolutely ruthless. I have already replaced one Battalion Commander. I have issued orders that any one making a suspicious movement is to be shot immediately. I wish Shah Nawaz would come back soon and take charge of his Division, then I can devote more attention to my own Regt.

March 3— News from Khanjo Butai that they are going to start an offensive w.e.f. to-night. I have promised to protect their left flank during the attack, but I am very keen that at least some of our own forces should participate in the offensive. I hope the Nippon side will agree to my suggestion.

March 4— Commander of Kanjo Butai came to have dinner with me while we were having dinner, news came there that my patrol had captured 3 cars and put to flight an American patrol who left 3 dead bodies behind.

March 5— Managed to bring back 2 of the Jeep cars and the captured arms and ammunition and one wireless Set. About 1200 hrs. got the report that an enemy force about 500 strong with tanks and guns were advancing towards No. 1 Bn's position, I rushed to Battalion area where I got the news that the enemy had burned Daungle and was around there. I had 2 platoons out, one of which kept on harrassing the enemy who moved off towards my right flank. Got the news that the Japanese Bn. on my right had moved forward and that my right flank was in the air. Rushed up one Coy. to 4 Guerilla and 2 platoons of No. 1 Inf. to fill up the gap.

March 6— A quiet to-day. The enemy force that came yesterday did not stay to fight. Enemy threat on the Kyauk Padaung Meiktilla road getting to be dangerous. Ordered No. 4 Guerilla Regt, to take up a defensive position around Kyauk Pandaung to meet any enemy advance from Meiktilla or Pagan side. Kawabara told me that it was most likely that my Regiment would carry out an offensive along the Kyauk Padaung Pagan Road. I hope it will be so, because I am confident my Regiment, would give a very good account of themselves in such an action.

March 7— Bulk of my Regiment has not so far arrived and as we have to get a Regiment ready to undertake the attack by the 10th. Much against my will, I had to detail No. 4 Guerilla Regiment for the attack. In the afternoon received a message that an enemy patrol is in a village 3 miles from Daungle. I have told Khazim Shah to carry out a raid. I hope it will be successful. Went to look for 2nd Division parties, found one on the way. Discovered that they had been delayed owing to a heavy air raid.

March 8— One party of the 2nd Division arrived to-day. One S.O. and Sep. had been killed owing to enemy air raid and two person had been wounded. In spite of every thing, the moral and spirit of the men is very high. Enemy aeroplanes dropped pamphlets specially addressed to the officers and men of my Regiment. These pamphlets were signed by Maj. Mohammad Sarwar, the dirty swine.

March 11— 2 Lt. Ali Hussain with one S. O. and two other men went over to the enemy to-day. They tried to take one of my Sepoy with them, but he escaped from them and came back. I have taken into custody all the officers and men whose movements are suspicious.

Dhillon has gone into attack to-day. I hope he will do something really good. We need to, to wash off the disgrace that has been caused by these traitors.

March 13— Dhillon must have gone into attack last night, but no news of the result as yet.

March 14— News that PYNBIN has been re-occupied by the Japanese and others are only about 500 enemy in Taungoon. I must attack them immediately. The enemy, I believe, is on the retreat. Dhillon attacked Taungoon last night, but there was no enemy. I have made up my mind to move out to-night with two companies of Banta Singh's Battalion and attack the enemy.

March 15— Marched off from Popa last night at 2300 hrs and arrived in Setsatyo at 0600 hrs. Marching thr' the sand very hard indeed Bullock carts carrying water could not reach us, nor could my car and the motor cycle. Had to buy water locally. Liaised with the Nippon Coy. Commander who said that he knew everything about the enemy dispositions. Decided to attack to-night with one platoon of the Japanese Cooperating. I had a severe attack of Diahorrea-feeling very weak.

March 16— Left Sestyo at 2130 hrs. on the 15th. Arrived Myene at 2330 hrs.Met no enemy on the way. Took up a position at Myene with 2 pls. Attacked from the left flank with one coy. under 2/Lt. Joginder Singh and made a faint from the right flank with one Platoon under Amar Chand. Two sections of the Japanese accompanied J. S. and one S.C.A.C. J.S. attacked 4 lines of the enemy trenches, but met no enemy.

March 17— The Japanese were reluctant to go forward after the first line, but J.S. had to beat them to take forward. A.C. met a small patrol of the enemy who opened fire on him.

A.C. replied by throwing grenades. Casualties enemy about 8 to 10 killed. Our side one killed and one missing. Retired to Setstyo in the morning and spent the day there. Left Setstyo at night and marched back and arrived Popaywa in the morning of the 17th.

March 19— News from Dhillon. His fellows are putting up a brave show; they attack a hill 3 times and eventually captured it and killed about 300 enemy; his casualties have been pretty heavy too.

March 20— Khango unit has been ordered to prepare themselves to go into attack. I have to take over the defence of the whole of Popa and Kyauk Padaung area. Moved Banta Singh's Battalion to cover Kyauk Padaung—Meiktila road. No definite information about the enemy in Meiktila area. I have ordered B. S. to send a patrol in that area to find out. Shah Nawaz has told the Japanese that we must be given a share in the offensive. I quite agree with him, but do not think will get a chance to.

March 23— Last night went to Kyauk Padaung and in the morning went round Banta Singh's position —a hot and tiring business. Japanese patrol returned from Meiktila area. After receipt of the information I am convinced that we should attack Meiktila from our side. Of course we must have more detailed information about the general situation before we can undertake such an attack and must co-ordinate it with the Japanese attacks.

March 26— Our milk goat died in the morning, so from now on we shall be in milk less Coffee. Conference with the Khanjo Commander about the coming operations and sent out patrols to recce the area in which I shall be operating. I do not like the task that has been allotted to Dhillon. Both our resource in tpt. we shall never be able to keep him supplied with water. I suggested to Shah Nawaz that he should be withdrawn from that area.

March 27— I have been reading Stonewall Jackson, there is little doubt that he was a great General. Still he is so little heard of. I put up my plan to Shah Nawaz and he has approved of it. It is a simple one. I am going to put a Battalion astride and in the high ground in the right of Sektein Welong Road and basing one Battalion N.W. of Perktien. Carry out harassing attacks against enemy in Pynbin from Tada area.

March 28--- The Nippon Haidan which was expected to be in Sektein area has not arrived so far. So my plan of action is, I think, a very sound one. Elaborated it and issued orders. One to be due to move tonight. Shah Nawaz sent for me at about 19–30 hrs. he is very worried, because he has no reserve at hand in case the enemy counter-attacks along Pynbin-Ovin Road. I do not think it is likely. I consider an enemy counter-stroke from Welong side more likely, still S. N. persisted, so I had to alter my plans. I will put only one Coy. to defend Welong Sektien Road and leave the remainder of the Battalion Popaya area until the arrival of Dhillon's Commander when I may expect them to join me.

34

Special Order by Subhas Chandra Bose on the Eve of his Departure from Burma[1]

24 April, 1945

It is with a very heavy heart that I am leaving Burma the scene of the many heroic battles that you have fought since February 1944 and are still fighting. In Imphal and Burma, we have suffered a reverse in the first round in our fight for Independence. But it is only the first round. We have many more rounds to fight. I am a born optimist and I shall not admit defeat under any circumstances. Your brave deeds in the battle against the enemy on the plains of Imphal, the hills and jungles of Arakan and the oil field area and other localities in Burma will live in the history of our struggle for Independence for all time.

Comrades: At this critical hour, I have only one word of command to give you, and that is that if you have to go down temporarily, then go down fighting with the National Tricolour held aloft; go down as heroes; go down upholding the highest code of honour and discipline. The future generations of Indians who will be born, not as slaves but as free men, because of your colossal sacrifice, will bless your names and proudly proclaim to the world that you, their forbears, fought and suffered reverses in the battle in Manipur, Assam and Burma, but through temporary failure you paved the way to ultimate success and glory.

My unshakable faith in India's liberation remains unaltered. I am leaving in your safe hands our National Tricolour, our national honour, and the best traditions of Indian warriors. I have no doubt whatsoever that you, the vanguard of India's Army of Liberation, will sacrifice everything even life itself, to uphold India's National Honour, so that your comrades who will continue the fight eslewhere may have before them your shining example to inspire them at all times.

If I had my own way, I would have preferred to stay with you in adversity and share with you the sorrow of temporary defeat. But on the

1. F. No. 601/7378/H.S.

advice of my Ministers and high ranking officers, I have to leave Burma in order to continue the struggle for emancipation. Knowing my countrymen in East Asia and inside India, I can assure you that they will continue the fight under all circumstances and that all your suffering and sacrifice will not be in vain. So far as I am concerned. I shall steadfastly adhere to the pledge that I took on the 21st October, 1943, to do all in my power to serve the interests of thirtyeight crores of my countrymen and fight for their liberation. I appeal to you, in conclusion, to cherish the same optimism as myself and to believe like myself, that the darkest hour always precedes the dawn. India shall be free and before long.

May God bless you!
Inqilab Zindabad
Azad Hind Zindabad
'Jai Hind'

35

Interrogation Report of P.K. Sahgal Regarding the Japanese Supply to the Indian National Army[1]

16 May, 1945

Foreward—The following report has been rendered by Staff Sergeant Arthur R. Lauson, MC. It is the result of an interview he conducted with a Lt. Col. P. K. Sahgal, a Prisoner of War of the British, at Magwe Central Burma. The report is dated 8 May 1945 from HQ 33rd Indian Corps, British 14th Army.

The Report—Colonel Sahgal was captured by the Japanese at Singapore in February 1942, and joined the INA in August 1942. He was among a group of 500 INA members, who gave themselves up at Wagyigan, 12 miles north if Allanmyo, 28 April 1945. While with the INA he was Military Secretary to Headquarters INA for approximately one year. In January 1944 Colonel Saghal assumed Command of the 2nd INA Infantry Regiment.

The following is a list of the questions asked and answers received.

Q. Who handled the administration for your Unit?

A. All administration was handled solely by us.

Q. Who issued food and clothing for your Unit?

A. All my requisitions had to go direct to Singapore for authority, where the INA had direct link with the Japanese. In the case of clothing, it was issued from the Intendence Department. In the case of food, money was sent direct to my Unit, and food was locally purchased/ (It might be noted there was no clash between the INA and the Japanese in purchasing meat, as the Japanese do not like mutton very much and the Indians do not eat beef.)

1. Office of Strategic Service. U.S. National Archieves Maryland. F. No. N.N.D. 730013. Record group 226.

Q. To what extent was food and clothing issued?

A. The Japanese did not furnish us with much clothing or equipment. The clothing and equipment issued was captured from British, Dutch, and some Japanese.

Q. What Japanese items were issued?

A. Mess Kits, canteens; some shoes, socks, trousers (Tropical, 10,000 lately), shelter halfs, puttees, shirts and very few packs. Very limited amounts of these items were available to us.

Q. How did the Japanese shoes wear?

A. Japanese shoes, made in Japan, were very good, but local made shoes were very bad. Some were out after a one days hike.

Q. Did the Japanese go without shoes frequently?

A. No, I don't believe I saw any without footwear of some sort.

Q. How did the Japanese socks wear?

A. Socks were very poor and we wore two pair at one time. We had a lot of trouble with blistered feet.

Q. Did the Japanese have the same trouble?

A. No. They wore but one pair too. The Japanese sort of slide their feet when walking, which might have some thing to do with it.

Note. I showed him the 26-oz oval canteen with same type previously sent in, that we believed to have been chinese (Sea East IBT Report 33)

Q. Is this a chinese canteen?

A. It is a local make, and I believe it is produced in Thailand. The Japanese ran short of canteens and these were furnished.

Note. I showed him a copy of our photograph QM 205 of a helmet believed to be Netherlands.

Q. Have you ever seen this type of helmet before? Has it any connection with the INA ?

A. It is a Dutch helmet. There were very few of these helmets issued to us. We wore only British and Dutch helmets.

Q. Was it worn by all ranks?

A. Yes.

Q. Were you, as an Officer, issued a sword?

A. I was not issued a sword, but they were available to Officers. I never wore a sword before and had no desire to.

Q. Did you wear British or Japanese rank insignia?

A. No, an entirely different insignia.

Q. Were Japanese arms issued the INA ?

A. No, we used British and some Dutch.

Q. Were you, as an Officer, issued Japanese clothing and equipment?

A. No, I wore my British uniform. A mixed uniform was worn by all ranks a large part of the time.

Q. Did the Japanese appear to be short of any item or material?

A. Canteens for a short period, and leather seemed to be very scarce.

Q. What reason did the Japanese give for not issuing the INA much Japanese clothing and equipment?

A. The Japanese stated priority was being given to the Pacific, and transportation. It is very hard to fit an Indian soldier with the existing Japanese sizes.

Q. Do you think one reason might be that the Japanese were not very much interested in the INA ?

A. No, they were very much interested in the INA.

Q. Was the Japanese soldier's morale high?

A. Yes, as long as a Jap has rice, salt, and curry sauce he is content.

Q. Was the Japanese soldier satisfied with his clothing?

A. Yes, A Jap will put clean underclothes on and wear a filthy uniform. This applies to Officers too.

Q. Can you give any outstanding characteristics of the Japanese soldier relative to clothing and equipment?

A. Yes, he takes exceptionally good care of his clothing, repairing his own clothing in most cases. The Jap does not live luxuriously even when possible. They can live on the land better than any other race of people I know.

36

Note by Military Intelligence on the activites of I.N.A in Burma during 1945[1]

22 May, 1945

Introduction

1. Referring to the I.N.A. in Burma para 15 of W.S.D.S dated Nov 44 stated:-

   "The tendency has been one of withdrawal which may indicate reorganisation and reinforcement for the next operation or complete exclusion of the I.N.A. from Japanese plans. however, cannot be accepted without strong evidence....................Events in Burma during 1945 have confirmed this appreciation for Bose army has, during the last few months featured to some extent in Japanese plans.

2. By late 1944 the forces which had taken part in the advance to and withdrawal from Manipur, comprising 1 Div and "Command Troops" had mostly withdrawn. 1 Div had suffered very considerable battle and sick casualties and the remnants were recuperating in the "back nursing. The only unit believed fit to operate in the front line was IV guerilla Regiment which had not been committed in the Manipur campaign. This was transferred to 2 Div., elements of which by this time had arrived in Burma.

3. The composite parties of "Command Troops" in Arakan, which were mainly new to the forward areas, were in a surrendering mood until they were withdrawn towards Taungup in face of the allied advance through Arakan. Since then they have not featured at all and little is known of their subsequent movements. They presumably withdrew right through to Rangoon.

Events of the "Pre-battle" Period

4. In Jan. elements of II Inf Regt. of 2 Div were moving up to the central Irrawaddy area to reinforce IV Guerrilla Regiment which was mainly

1. F. No. 601/7378/H.S.

along the Irrawaddy in the areas Myitche-Pakokku-Myingan. I Inf Regt. in Rangoon was also preparing to move into this area. The officers of HQ 2 Div.were visiting the battle area, carrying out recces, and liaison with Japanese and I.N.A units in preparation for their move forward in Feburary. Further East elements of 1 Div were reported in the Mandalay area as also was a M.T. Coy. During this month reports concerning I.N.A. units and their movements in the central area were few and vague.

5. It was not until the first week in Feburary that more definite information was received. During the first half of the month many Japanese patrols with men of IV Guerrilla Regiment were reported along the river.

6. These patrols were carrying out one of the tasks which had been allotted to 2 Div forces in the area as a result of conferences between the Japanese and Bose and his military advisers. The main points of these conferences had been demands by Bose for:-

(a) Personal control of the I.N.A. in operations and for this reason the allotment of W/T frequencies.

(b) The allotment of an independent sector.

(c) The distribution and dispositions of troops to be left to I.N.A. commanders; the supply of artillery and air support, the allotment of W/T sets, telephones, motor cycles, etc. more transport, more hand grenades, A/Tk mines, magnetie mines, L.M.Gs, Tommy guns, pistols, entrenching tools, compasses, binoculars, range finders, maps, demolition materials and medical supplies.

(d) Suitable ration arrangements.

The usual answer by the Japanese was that they would do their best to fulfil them; but subsequent events proved that they took no steps to meet any of Bose's demands with the exception of the allotments of an independent sector.

7. The initial refusal to grant requests was believed to be due to memories of the Manipur campaign which had left the Japanese in no doubt regarding the unreliability of I.N.A. units in a battle area. Eventually, however, it was agreed that a sector would be allotted to 2 Div: this was the area enclosed by Popa-Kyaukpadaung-the Irrawaddy. The tasks of the forces here were:-

(a) To guard against British crossings of the river,

(b) To make strong points in the Popa and Kyaukpadaung areas,

(c) To make arrangement to guard against attack by British airborne troops, and

(d) To patrol the upper reaches of the Irrawaddy.

8. Reports by forward troops during the first half of Feburary indicated that these patrols were mixed Japanese-Jifs and not all as would be expected as a result of the independent sector allotted to 2 Div. The I.N.A. commander's scope for independent action was further limited in that he was forced to communicate with (Japanese) Army by wireless through units on the flanks. Control of the I.N.A was ostensibly direct from Army HQ but in effect by the Japanese unit flank which was naturally the 'safety plug' if the I.N.A. were liked to jeopardise operations.

The Battle Period

9. The "Battle Period" proper may be said to have begun on about 15 February when British troops established a bridgehead across the river in the area Nyaungu-Pagan. During the two days following this operation more than 280 of IV Guerrilla Regiment surrendered voluntarily to our troops.

10. Japanese troops were immediately ordered into the I.N.A's "independent sector" and the remainder of IV Guerrilla Regiment with in a somewhat disorderly manner to the Popa-Kyaukpadaung area. Along the area at this time was half of II Inf Regt. the other half being located further South on its way to Kyaukpadaung. I Inf Reft. was also on its way from Rangoon.

11. During the second half of Feburary two action against Jifs was fought, one in the Seikpyu area and the other near Kyaukpadaung. Adv HQ 2 Div also arrived and opened up about 22 Feb. The mass surrender in the middle of the month had produced considerable reecessions in Rangoon. Bose left Rangoon hurriedly by car on 22 Feburary intending to assume personal control of his forces. On arrival at Meiktila on 24 Feb, he was "persuaded" by the Japanese not to proceed further.

12. Further disaster overtook the I.N.A on 1 March when the whole Adv. HQ. 2 Div includidng four Indian Army officers surrendered

voluntarily to our troops. In the battle area during the first half of our patrols encountered several parties of Jifs and Japs-cum-Jifs. The Jifs who took part in these clashes showed more fighting spirit on previous occasions. These actions were, however, accompanied by more surrenders.

13. The most important developments, or rather counter measures, during the first half of March took place in Rangoon. The mass surrender of IV Guerrilla Regiment, followed by the officers of HQ. 2. Div, staggered Bose so much that, according to his own account he was unable to rise from his bed for two days. He also stated that if any more "deserted" he would commit suicide. He took drastic steps in an attempt to restore morale. He interned some Indian Army officers in Rangoon and issued two Special Orders of the Day. One of these orders admitted that there were "cowardice and treachery" during Manipur campaign of 1944 and that their seeds still remained Intentiory for rooting them out were given in great detail. The most able of these instructions was the entitlement of any member "To arrest any other member ofthe I.N.A. ....if in a cowardly manner or to shoot him if he acts in a treacherous way. This instruction cut away any roots of military discipline which I.N.A might have had proviously and, although one of the immedint effects may have been to prevent further desertions, it undoubtedly intensified the state of distrust and fear which pervaded the I.N.A. Another instruction of the same order allowed a period of one week grace for unwilling volunteers to leave the Army. The second order dealt specifically with the five staff officers and called for action in the shape of "spiritual lectures" and public burning of the effigies.

14. Bose was not content with taking internal measures to hold Army together for, on 11 March, Rangoon radio broadcast a statement by him to the effect that in order to atone for the "crime" other "higher officers had volunteered to take over the vacant posts (new officers personalities did in fact appear in the battle areas). The broadcast went on to say that "a sense of sorrowful anguish is pervading the camp of the I.N.A at the treachery of the deserters". It closed with a statement that the morale of the troops had been maintained.

15. It was probably due to Bose's instructions that, in several clashes during the second half of March notably those in the Popa, Kyaukpadaung, Taungzin, Kazaung and Setsetyo areas, Jifs fought

more determinedly and inflicted casualties on our troops. At the end of the month the notorious commander of II Inf Regt. escaped from an ambush and Jifs were reported in the Meiktila zone for the first time. Surrenders during this period were few. Elsewhere our troops confirmed the presence of elements of 1 Div on the Mandalay-Toungoo axis.

16. Before the general withdrawal of I.N.A. troops from the Popa-Kyaukpadaung-Irrawaddy area more than 300 of II Inf Regt. surrendered at Legyi. A few others, realising that their hope of escape was fading, also surrendered at this juncture. About the same time further East in the Wundwin area I M.T. Coy surrendered.

17. The withdrawal of I.N.A. troops probably began about 6 to 9 April. HQ 2 Div. arrived at Magwe about 17th. IV Guerilla Regiment also withdrew to the Magwe area (some sources say the bulk withdraw to the Meiktila area). II Ing Regimen. moving via the road Popa-Natmauk were eventually disposed with a bn. West of the Irrawaddy, a bn. between the river and Taungdwingyi and a third bn. Between Taungdwingyi and Satthwa. The Regiment, or rather what was left of it, was heading for Prome. Eventually this general retreat brought I Inf Regiment into the front line. This was then located as follows:- HQ. and a bn. at Magwe a bn. at Minbun and a third bn. at Taungdwingyi.

18. The withdrawal, which up to now been uncoordinated due to the speed of the British advance, was hastened into a disorderly "run for life" after events round Magwe during the 19 and 20 April. (The commander of 2 Div on arrival in Magwe said he did not know where any of his troops were and had received no orders. This recalls the remark credited to Bose: "They call me C-in-C of the I.N.A but I don't even know where my troops are"). Commander 2 Div and his staff narrowly missed capture; HQ IV Guerilla Regiment was overrun: HQ and 2 bn. of I Inf Regt. surrendered; the Japanese were attempting to force the I.N.A. to fight againt the Burma Defence Army, while south of Magwe elements of I Inf Regt. were doing the reverse by fighting against the Japanese of the side to the Burma Defence Army; the remnants of IV Guerilla Regiment and II Inf Regt. were completely disorganised but still moving south; and Jifs were being killed by aerial bombing and strafing. Worthless, a considerable portion was able to continue to Prome not all reached Prome, for on 22 Apr. 500 of

II Inf Regt. including their notorious commander, Sahgal, surrendered a few miles north of Allanmyo. The surrender of this anti-British and pro-Bose Indian Army officer was indicative of the exhausted condition of Bose's forces.

19. Elsewhere in Burma the rapid advance of British troops down the Toungoo Road had overtaken the remnants of 2 Div and, on 25 Apr about 8,000 including the commander, surrendered about 26 miles South of Toungoo. The main force of III Guerilla Regiment of this Div is spill alocated.

20. In early May more surrenders took place along the Prome Rangoon exis. There is no reliable news of the where abouts of the remaining. It is possible that they were able to reach Rangoon. If they did they have evacuated it since only 300 INA. were found when our troop's entered the city. It is still believed that many isolated groups involved between the Irrawaddy and the main railway axis.

21. The total number of Jifs who fell into our hands during the campaign exceeds 5,000. Killed and wounded reported by our ground troops exceed 150. In addition, considerable numbers were probably killed by Allied aerial bombing and artillery shelling, and more were incapacitated through sickness. A conservative estimate of total casualties is between 6 and 7,000. This still leaves several thousands to be accounted for and if the expected crop between the Irrawaddy and the main Railway axis is below "several thousands", it means that a considerable portion has escaped eastwards.

22. There are several aspects of this campaign which are worth comment.

Broadcasts

23. Broadcasts on the INA in action achieved an unsurpassed level of exaggeration and complete reversal of the facts. An outstanding example of the latter was the broadcast from Rangoon on 9 Mar referred to the mass surrenderd in mid Feburary of IV Guerilla Regiments, which state that "nearly 500 Indian troops with heavy trench mortars, machine gun and other arms in one of the sectors of the Irrawaddy front receraly voluntarily surrendered to the "Indian National Army". Another tence of these broadcast was the citations of individual commanders. Caused by its absence was the stress on fighting "shoulder to shoulder with the Japanese army, a theme prominently featured during the Manipur operations. No broadcasts of any description were made from Rangoon after about 21 April.

Morale

24. Throughout the camapign there was almost daily repetition of reports indicating that Jifs were in a "Low state of morale considered with othere factors it was difficult to understand why, if Jifs hated the Japanese, and were poorly clad, inadequately equipped, in a muddled frame of mind and of low morale, why they opposed our forces, especially Indian troops.

25. The answer as given by most Jifs themselves was, firstly, fear of Japanese reprisals if escape plans went awry and, secondly, fear of being shot by the Allies if they succeeded. This explanation was not entirely accepted, since many Jifs reported that our "surrender" literature was being seen and was having a good effect; some surrenders occurred only as a result of reading our leaflets.

26. The more important Jifs were unable to give a clearly defined picture of INA morale in view of the conflicting factors involved. They were, however, unanimous on several points:-

    (a) The Bose clique is outnumbered by the remainder.

    (b) The latter cannot negative the actions of the former due to their inability to act concertedly.

    (c) This inability is brought about by the four of betryal if confidence were exchanged.

    (d) This fear is justifiably occasioned by the presence in almost every unit of a "Gestapo" cell which reports on Malaya to Bose.

    (e) The political indoctrination of the forward troops, which attempted inter alia to hide the true war situation.

27. These deterrents to surrender were considered by those responsible for the conduct of Psychologied Warfare, and were to some extent removed by the methods employed. Other self contributory factors to the removal of this operational-cum-security problem which need our troops were, of course, the heavy defeat of the Japanese forces, the disintegration of the I.N.A. command, Allied serial bombing and strafing, artillery shelling, sickness and realisation on the part of the Indian Army element that the chances of returning to Indian if they retreated with the Japanese were becoming more remote. Despite these factors and the number who surrendered to us, it is quite clear that we have not entirely succeeded in our efforts. Future INA

surrenders or captures may well include an increased number of "hardened" Jifs.

Japanese-I.N.A. Relations

28. This requires little comment since the complete lack of confidence in, and the mistrust of, the INA. on the part of the Japanese is now well known. It is also believed that the majority of INA. and it is said, even Bose, are anti-Japanese.

Conclusions

29. This campaign has been a greater debacle for I.N.A than the Manipur campaign. They have suffered many more casualties, their propaganda value has dwindled very considerably, and Japanese opinion of them is very low. One of the most conspicuous features of this campaign has been the complete absence on the part of the Japanese of any concern for, or even any efforts to extricate, their "comrades". It is however believed that Bose still possesses a fair amount of influence. If this is true he may be able to persuade the Japanese to use the INA again. The evacuation of thousands from Burma, though unconfirmed at present, is evidence of future Japanese intentions. Early in 1945 there were about 15,000 troops outside Burma, most of whom were civilians, poorly trained and equipped. If they are met in battle, therefore, they seem likely to be more of a liability to security and administrative staffs than to our fighting troops.

37

Statement of Subhas Chandra Bose Condemning the Treatment of the INA by the British after their Capture[1]

30 May, 1945

Information that has reached us from reliable sources in Burma go to show that vindictive and brutal treatment is being meted out to officers and men of the Azad Hind Fauj (Indian National Army) who have been captured by the Anglo-Americans in Burma. As the whole world knows, the Anglo-Americans and in particular the British have always been in the habit of condemning Germany and Japan for their supposed ill-treatment of Anglo-American prisoners of war. But I would now like to ask what the Anglo-Americans are themselves doing with the members of the Azad Hind Fauj who happened to fall in to their hands in Burma. Though the Allied forces in Burma belong to several nationalities, the responsibility as regards the ill treatment of the officers and men of the Azad Hind Fauj devolves solely on the British Authorities. The British authorities cannot even invent the excuse that we ill-treated their troops who fell into our hands. They were those who voluntarily came and joined the Azad Hind Fauj. And even Delhi Radio admittied some days ago that all those who joined the Azad Hind Fauj received good treatment.

It may be that the British Authorities think that we are not in a position to reliate, and that they can, therefore, do what they like with our officers and men. But I would like to warn the British Authorities that this is not the case. If we are forced to do so we can find ways and means for adopting retaliatory measures in case they continue to ill-treat and persecute the officers and men of the Azad Hind Fauj. But before we are forced to think of retaliatory measures, there is one remedy open to us, which is not only efficacious but also easy. If our countrymen at home take up this matter and carry on a raging and tearing campaign inside India, I am absolutely sure that the British Authorities will be brought to

1. 601/7378/H.S.

their senses and will see the error of their ways. Public opinion in India may not be strong enough to force the British to concede independence to India, but it is certainly strong enough to stop the ill-treatment and persecution of members of the Azad Hind Fauj who have become prisoners of war at the hands of the British. Members of the Azad Hind Fauj are honest patriots and revolutionaries fighting for the freedom of their Motherland. They, no doubt, fought bravely and stubbornbly against the British, but they fought with clean hands and with a clear conscience. They are, therefore, entitled to decent treatment during captivity, in accordance with international usage and convention. Consequently, I appeal to my countrymen at home to take up the cause of their own prisoners of war, who fought for India's liberation and who are now receiving brutal and vindictive treatment at the hands of the British. I appeal to them also to compel the British Authorities to divulge correct information about the fate of these prisoners of war, so that the world may judge how far the British themselves observe the rules and canons of international warfare, to which they pay so much lip homage.

38

Philip Mason, Joint Secretary War Department to Sir Richard Tottenham Regarding the Treatment of I.N.A.[1]

12 June, 1945

My Dear Sir Richard,

When I wrote to you in my D.O. No. 452—JS dated 1st June, I told you that we hoped shortly to let you know more on the subject of the treatment of JIFS. H.E. the Commander-in -Chief has now had an opportunity of forming an opinion as to the policy to be adopted, and would like to discuss this with the Hon'ble Home Member. If the Home Member agrees, the Commander-in-Chief suggests that the joint proposals of the two Departments should then be submitted to H.E. the Viceroy.

2. You know the present procedure which we follow, but for convenience it is set out in the attached memorandum by the DMI. So far there have been comparatively few JIFS whose cases have become ripe for prosecution. Of those who have been prosecuted, some have been convicted and sentenced to death, transportation for life or long terms of imprisonment. A few of these sentences have already been carried out. We are, however, now confronted with the problem of very much larger numbers.

3. The three most obvious courses to take are as follows:

   (a) We could proceed according to the strict letter of the law and bring forward far court martial those against whom there is sufficient evidence to make a conviction possible. This would result in a considerable number of death sentences. (A guess at the numbers is given in the DMI's memorandum). The facts could not remain secret for ever, and in the country as a whole death sentences to this extent would probably do more harm than good. There is already a tendency, as you have observed,

1. F. No. R/3/1/330. Indian Office Library and Records, London. Richerd Tottenham was the Home Member.

to whitewash the I.N.A.; and this course would make martyrs of them as well;

(b) We could limit the number appearing before a court martial, or alternatively could remit the sentences in the great majority of cases. But this course would have the disadvantages of (c) below in that some of those who had acted as traitors would get off virtually without punishment,and there would be the practical difficulty that it would be difficult to set a standard and say who were the worst until the cases of all had been examined; and that would clearly be impracticable.

(c) We might treat all offenders lightly on the grounds that they had merely been mistaken in their ideas of what was patriotic, and that at the worst they had acted under pressure. There is however, a serious military objection to this course since it would almost certainly have an adverse effect on the loyal services of the Army who have fought against these men; and a still worse effect on those loyal soldiers who were taken prisoner of war and in spite of ill-treatment and coercion have refused to betray their friends and fight against their compatriots. And there would no doubt be a civil objection to the immediate release to civil life of a large number of men with such a record.

4. The best course seems to the War Department to be a modification of course (b), by which all Blacks against whom there is sufficient evidence would be brought to trial, and sentenced in accordance with the law imposed by the court. But in only the most extreme cases would the death sentence be carried out, the sentences in the remaining cases being commuted to imprisonment and after a short term of imprisonment suspended on condition of good behaviour. The period of imprisonment which would be undergone should cover the period of demobilisation and of the return of prisoners of war. Those Blacks against whom there was insufficient evidence for trial would be mustered out of the Army after a period of detention which would cover the remaining period of hostilities.

Dark Greys would serve a period in a rehabilitation centre after which their cases would be reviewed and they would then be treated as Blacks or Greys. the number of the latter probably being small.

Greys and Whites. These would be treated as normal recovered prisoners of war. They would be returned to their unit, where their Commanding Officer alone would know their past history and would recommend whether or not they should be retained in the service. If not, they would be mustered out.

5. The advantages of suspension of sentence as opposed to remission of sentence are obvious, but there is legal difficulty. A man sentenced under the Army Act to imprisonment or transportation is automatically discharged from the service, and the Suspension of Sentence Act does not apply to him. If the policy is accepted it would be necessary to examine the possibility of an amendment to the Act to make it possible to suspend a sentence under the Army Act but continue to hold it over a man who has been discharged from the service.

6. As you are in Simla, I am sending a copy of this direct to the Hon'ble Home Member. If convenient to the Home Department, we suggest a meeting at 11.30 a.m. on Friday the 22nd June. If this is not suitable, will you suggest another time?

39

Note by British Military Intelligence on I.N.A. and S.C. Bose[1]

15 June, 1945

1. A captured Jif who was an Indian Army Officer and who recently commended a Guerilla Regiment has made some interesting comments on the effect of Bose's propaganda, and of life in the I.N.A., on those men who have come into our hands.

2. This source is insistent that no compulsion was used against either officers or O. Rs to join the new I.N.A. and that those who joined were sincere converts to the cause of Indian Independence. In support of this, he quotes firstly; the hardships that a great number of 1 Div were willing to endure in the Manipur campaign, especially during the retreat, rather than surrender; and secondly, the determined resistance offered in the areas of Kyaukpadaung, Popa and the oil fields.

3. In this officer's opinion, these men, having no immediate hope, will on return to their depots appear as good and well-disciplined soldiers on parade. Off duty, however, they will probably discuss their past experinces, the Bose movement, Independence, an Indian Army without British officers and more especially the hardships they themselves bore in their effort to achieve these objects. Their stated belief is that they failed solely owing to lack of equipment. The source goes on to state that this will mean a rapid permeation of nationalism through the entire Indian Army. He never expected the Indian Army to revolt except and until the I.N.A. had actually penetrated into the plain of Bengal, when he believed such a revolt would have been universal. Rehabilitation he considers cannot be successful unless it is based on the fostering of a national rather than a communal or provincial spirit.

---

1. F. No. 601/7378/H.S.

4. These views are those of an officer who has held a responsible I.N.A. command in the field and who has fought hard against us. He is one of the fanatical members of the Bose clique, and his views naturally are distorted and exaggerated. They are reproduced here because they reflect the mentality not only of some of the commanders but also of some of the rank and file who have been influenced.

5. The reactions of the I.N.A. to their capture in Rangoon have been varied. Some not only showed remorse and repentance but had already removed their badges before our landings. There were, however, diehards who, while offering no resistance at heart retained their loyalty for the I.N.A. cause. It appears that the "Burma Command" had given orders for the continued flying of the I.N.A. flag, the singing of the "National Anthem" and for prisoners to shout slogans on the march to embarkation.

6. It is reported by a reliable source that a number of the captured members of the I.N.A. have stated that their "march to Delhi" is not over, but will be continued from within India with the ex-I.N.A. as the backbone. They say they will be helped by the British Government's leniency which would leave plenty of men to carry out this mission and that those men would be useful to stage a comeback for S.C. Bose in India.

7. The reaction of Indian troops into whose hands I.N.A. personnel have recently fallen is firstly one of the aloofness until a *genuine* feeling of relief and pleasure on the part of the captive is evinced. One unit in Rangoon reports that I.O.Rs regard the I.N.A. as traitors and would not hesitate to shoot them if so ordered. Among V.C.Os of the same unit there is a feeling that the only course to adopt is to try members of the I.N.A. by court martial and to ensure that none ever return to their homes unless cleared of all guilt.

8. In Rangoon the roundup of Jifs continues. The I.N.A. personnel have all been centred in special camps and civilian members of the I.I.L. and kindred organisations are being arrested. Security authorities are now facing administrative problems as they sort out the suspects into their security categories and arrange interrogations.

9. A short study of Bose by one of his ex-Ministers, a senior officer of the I.N.A., is reproduced.

The following appreciation is in B964's own words:

(a) "S.C. Bose was a leader with a magnetic personality, who was loved and revered by all sections of the people of East Asia. Even the stalwarts of the Japanese nation used to look upon him with highest admiration and respect. He was particularly popular with the Indian students community of Japan who held him in the highest esteem as a national leader. As the Leader of the Movement, Bose would never yield even to the highest Japanese authority whenever the question of his legitimate rights were at stake. No Japanese dared disregard him, and very high ranking officers such as General ISUDA had been seen standing before him with awe and respect.

One of the foibles of his character was that he was a poor judge of men, as a result of which many unscrupulous and dishonest men such as M.Z. Kiani, J.K. Bhonsle, Iyar Sahgal (B 968) Rawat, Swami, Raturi and Shah Niwas got the better of him (by appealing to his weakness for flattery) and formed a olique around Bose which no-one could break. The existence of this reactionary olique disheartened many sincere and student workers for the cause of the Movement, both civil and military. Of such sincere and ardent men was Arabindo Sarkar, MSc, a chemist of Rangoon : N.G. Roy also a chemist: N.K. Banerjee and others, all of whom tried to approach Bose with concrete plans of work, but failed to reach the leader through their inability to break through the olique which surrounded Bose. On the military side the sincere and devoted believers in the Movement were people like Capt. Gulzara Singh, Lt. Col. Loganadan (B 953), Lt. Col. Alagappan, Lt. Col. A.C. Chatterjee, Lt. Col. P.N. Dutt, Major N. S. Bhagat. Nk Capt Amar Singh (Chief Clerk 1 Div.) Lt. Man Singh (B 975) Capt. C. J. Stracey, Capt. Jiwan Singh (B. 983) and a large number of Junior officers. These became disheartened when they realised that owing to the existence of the above mentioned olique, justice and fair play were being ousted and replaced by nepotism and injustice. This dislike of the clique was never outwardly menifested for fear of drastic measures from the all-powerful members of the olique, as well as for fear of bringing about a second crisis in the Movement. Bose had also exhibited weakness in meeting out justice which could only be interpreted as resulting from an apprehension of a likelihood of wounding the feelings or displeasing the members of the olique. The bunch of sincers men although disheartened, went on with their work with ardour and zeal except some of the junior officers and men, expecting that a time would come when they would be able to undo the wrongs and guide S.C. Bose on to the right path. These officers' spirits were elevated when they noticed a breach and rivalry springing up between Bhonale and M.Z. Kiani. With this background, S.C. Bose withdrew from Burma on 24 April 45.

40

In a Broadcast from Burma, Bose Requests the Indian Leaders to Reject the Offer of Lord Wavell as it would not Lead to Full Independence[1]

18 June, 1945

"Sisters and brothers! I listened with great attention to the speech which the Viceroy of India, Lord Wavell broadcast on June 14, from New Delhi conveying the offer of the British Government to India. That was the offer to bring which Lord Wavell made a long pilgrimage to London.

"At such a juncture it would neither be untimely nor out of place to inform my countrymen at home as to how Indians in East Asia have reacted to the British Government's offer. First of all we found out, as the Viceroy has himself confessed, that the only motive of the British Government is to mobilise India's support in the war against Japan. The British people are war-weary and after the termination of the war in Europe they badly need rest, and as such, they want others to fight their battles while they themselves reap the fruits of victory. But the British Indian troops, too, are war-weary, and after the recent successes of the Anglo-Americans in Burma they also desire rest and relaxation. It is, therefore, vital for the British to make the Indian people pour out their money and shed their blood for the preservation of the British Empire. While the fighting was going on inside India and along the Indo-Burma border the British could bluff the British Indian Army with the preaching that it was their duty to fight for the defence of India. The British could also bluff them later on by preaching that the Burma campaign was merely a continuation of the campaign for the defence of India.

"But now that the British want India's blood and money for campaigns beyond Burma and for the compaign in the Pacific, a new scheme must be found in order to obtain India's support for such campaigns. That is why

1. Shah Nawaz Khan. *My Memoris of I.N.A. and Its Netaji* New Delhi, 1946. pp. 247-251. Shah Nawaz has also reproduced the subsequant broadcasts, of Bose on the same theme given from 19th June to 26 June. see pp. 252-276

the British Government has now put forward this new offer which is in reality Sir Stafford Cripps old offer in a slightly altered garb.

"In deciding what reply we Indians should give, we will have to consider what we stand to gain by fighting Britain's war against Japan. It is one thing for Britain to forcibly exploit India for her war of aggression but it is quite a different thing for Indian Nationalists to voluntarily fight Britain's war. To co-operate in Britain's war effort at this stage will mean that we have completely nullified our moral struggle against the British. It will mean political suicide on the part of the Indian National Congress and for us Indians as well.

At an earlier stage of the war British propagandists and their Indian trimpeteers could possibly bluff and bamboozle the Indian people that India's defence was at stake as the Japanese were then knocking at India's gates. But now with the change in the war situation in East Asia, no Indian can have the slightest interest in fighting Britain's war against Japan. It is, therefore crystal clear that any acceptance of Lord Wavell's offer will be tantamount to a voluntary shedding of precious Indian blood and draining our resources in fighting Britain's imperialistic war. But what would India gain is return? Nothing except a few jobs on Viceroy's Executive Council.

"We cannot even argue that by accepting the offer we shall be reaching the 'goal of self-Government', which Lord Wavell and the British Government want us to believe. India does not care any longer for self-government within the British Empire, and India will never be content with anything less than complete independence. But even if any Indian is prepared to accept self-government he would have a much better chance of achieving that objective by continuing the resistance now than by accepting the present offer. The moment we accept the offer it will be inferred by the British Government that we are prepared to compromise by taking something very much less than even self-government. I have no doubt in my mind that the acceptance of this offer will seriously jeopardize all chance of securing even self-government in future, not to speak of complete independence. In short, by accepting the offer we shall gain nothing but we shall lose a lot, and it is Britain that will profit by our lack of strength.

"Under normal circumstances there would not be even a ten to one chance for any Indian nationalist to be enamoured of the present offer, but the British are cunning politicians and they have chosen the proper psychological moment for aiming this offer at India. British politicians are hoping that the Indian people are now overawed by recent Anglo-American victories. The Indian people may, therefore, fell that we stand no chance of achieving independence during the course of the present war and might as well make the best of a bad bargain and take whatever is being offered by the British. This is going to be the attitude of pessimists and moderate politicians like Sri Rajagopalchariar, but this attitude is entirely mistaken and unjustified, and will inevitably result in putting back the clock of freedom by many years.

"I shall refer to the merits of the British proposal. On close and careful analysis it will be found that the present proposal is in essence and in substance identical with that of Sir Stafford Cripps', offered to us in 1942. Three more seats on the Viceroy's Executive Council have been offered to us this time, for example, those of Home, Finance and External Affairs; for these and other portfolios the persons will be appointed by the Viceroy and will be responsible to him and not to the representatives of the people. On the other hand , the most important portfolio, that of the War Member has been reserved for a Britisher namely, the C-in-C. While the present offer is the old offer of Sir Stafford Cripps appearing in a slightly altered form, there are other obnoxious features which render the offer totally unacceptable. In his speech the Viceroy has clearly indicated that he regards the Congress as one among many parties as has been the traditional policy of the British Government. This attitude was indignantly repudiated by Mahatma Gandhi at the Round Table Conference in London in 1931 when, as representative of the Congress, he represented the Indian people. If the Congress accepts the offer now it will repudiate once for all what it has consistently maintained, namely, that it represents the people of India, and it will accept what the British Government has repeatedly held, namely, that the Congress is one among many parties in India. I cannot, for the slightest moment, imagine how any Indian nationalist can think of accepting this offer.

"There is another mischievous feature in Lord Wavell's offer. He has ordered the release of the member of the Working Committee of the Congress, but has maintained that unless his offer is accepted, all those who participated in the rising of 1942 will have to remain in custody. There is, nowewhere, mentioned in his speech that even if his offer is accepted, those who were imprisoned in the year 1939 and 1942 will be set free. It is a well established convention in all democratic centuries that a constitutional change is heralded by an amnesty for all political prisoners. In the case of India, however, this convention has been given the go-by.

"The British Government has been telling us that no constitutional change can be introduced during the course of the war though we have seen that throughout the world far-reaching political changes are being carried out. Here in East Asia we have seen quite a different state of affairs. Right in the midst of the war, several independent governments have been set up and power has been handed over to people. So, you see that this British plea is completely hollow and it is intended to delay and deny the Indian demand. If British really want to set up a responsible government she should lose no time in declaring India a self-governing national and hand over power to the people's representatives.

"Sisters and brothers in India ! You have suffered long and suffered much from the political persecution and economic exploitation of British capitalism. Let us suffer a little longer. We have to resist British imperialism by all the moral and material means at our disposal, and above all, let us keep the flag of independence flying. By continuing our fight against imperialism, and by refusing to compromise over independence we shall be able to keep burning the question of India's freedom before the bar of world opinion. That is the way to freedom. On the other hand, by accepting the offer we will be humiliating ourselves and losing the moral sympathy of the world.

"It may be that some of you are asking what is the best way for achieving the liberation of India. To that my answer is perfectly clear. Firstly, from outside India we shall carry on the armed struggle for our freedom to the last man and to the last round. Secondly there are numerous friends of India abroad who advocate our cause before the bar of world opinion and in all international conference. And, lastly, my countrymen, you too must be prepared to launch a revolution at the opportune moment which will spread like the wild fire of the parties and may even be supported by the British Indian forces.

"Sister and brothers ! In conclusion, I appeal to you not to give up hope. I repeat that the force that are now working inside India and outside are irresistible. There is no earthly power that can stop the Indian people for achieving their goal of freedom. With patience and determination we shall achieve our goal. The viceroy has asked for your goodwill and co-operation. Tell him that your goodwill and co-operation has been reserved for India's struggle for liberty and for none else."

41

Note by the British Intelligence on the Activities of Bose and I.N.A. in Burma[1]

22 June, 1945

I.N.A.

1. At Appendix 'A' are two Special Orders of the Day by Subhas Chandra Bose, dated 23 and 24 April 45. These deal with the establishment of the "Burma Command" and the wholesale promotion of all ranks which took place just before the fall of Rangoon.

Bose Statement

2. After the evacuation of Rangoon, the INA. Radio Station in Singapore broadcast a statement by Bose, dated 26 May, in which he attempted to excuse the failure of the INA. in their march to Delhi. The blame, according to Bose, was to be laid on the Indian Army because, during the Manipur campaign, "it was the British Indian Army more than anybody else who barred the way to Imphal. Calcutta and Delhi" and similarly during this year's campaign, the victories achieved by the Allied forces were mainly those of the Indian Army. He considered being faced in the field by Indian troops, "themselves slaves in their own country", the "most tragic experience" and considered himself thwarted. He derived some consolation in thinking that the meeting of the Indian Army and the INA. would open the former's eyes to the "heroic fight .... of liberation against tremendous odds" and that they would realise that the Provisional Government and the INA. were not puppets of a foreign power, but patriots and revolutionaries. In the course of this broadcast he mentioned that our propaganda had been stressing that the INA. was a puppet force and that "the Azad Hind Fauj has been nicknamed that 'Japanese Indian Fauj' or J.I.F."

1. F. No. 601/7378/H.S.

3. On arrival in Bangkok, Bose announced the safe evacuation of the Provisional Govt. with all its Ministers except. "Lt. Col." Ehsan Qadir, who had been left behind in Burma "on special duty". (As already reported in Appendix 'A' to W.S.I.S. No. 187 this officer is in our hands and under interrogation).

Indians in Rangoon

4. Reports from Rangoon regarding the Indian civilian population contain some interesting aspects of the general security problem facing the local authorities. Following the round-up of most of the I.I.L., interrogation of office-bearers and officials has revealed that this system was based on a form of gangsterism and blackmail. The I.I.L. executives allowed nothing to interfere with their extortion from both rich and poor; donations were given by some people in order to avoid being handed over to the Kempei, to save their women folk being removed, or to avoid being conscripted into the I.N.A. League funds were spent a office-bearers on presents for their wives and mistresses. One source describes the League as the most highly organised and well paid racket of the war.

5. As regards civilians themselves in Rangoon, they are presenting a considerable security problem, imbued as they are with Bose's ideas through continual propaganda from radio and press, and in the form of mass meetings. Bose himself had been in Rangoon for over a year and the INA. and highest officiency. The presence of a government which was more wealthy and more influential than any other of the puppet governments in East Asia had also had a great influence on the population. One result is that INA. deserters (an possibly trained agents also) are being hidden and well looked after by the civilian population who are also reported to be attempting to subvert Indian troops in the city. Before his departure, Bose is believed to have instructed Indian civilains to contact British Indian troops with a view to inculcating a national spirit, telling them about the "movement" and subverting them from their loyalty.

6. In the forefront of these civilian propagandists are the Indian women, especially those who have been members of the Rani of Jhansi Regiment. One of them, whose father was a revolutionary, has been interrogated in considerable detail. She referred to the Japanese as "allies" who, she assured her interrogator, would have allowed the

INA. to take India after the occupation of Imphal. If, however, it had been necessary for the Japanese to penetrate any further into India, Bose would have only had to repay them in cash and they would have left the country. He considered the campaign which has just ended was only an "attempt" and she was certain that further "attempts" would be made. These views appear common to such women of whom there are a considerable number at present in Rangoon in contact with our forces.

7. There is a great deal of talk among the Indian public in Rangoon about the U.S.S.R. and many are confident of a declaration of war on Britain by Russia, to whom Bose would immediately ally himself. There would then be no question of the next "attempt" failing. There has been considerable speculation regarding Russia's future position both by the Japanese and by Bose propagandists, one source going so far as to announce that Bose's Provisional Government had been officially recognised by the Soveit Union.

Azad Hind Fauj
Special Order of the Day
Dated 23rd April, 1945

In view of the developing war situation in Burma. It has become necessary to establish a Special Headquarters in Burma named "Burma Command of the Azad Hind Fauj". It will be in charge of and look after all the Azad Hind Fauj troops in Burma. Maj. Gen. Loganadan will be the officer commanding the Burma command of the Azad Hind Fauj. The Chief of Staff of Burma Command will be Lt. Col. Arshad. Other Staff Officers and personnel of the Burma Command will be appointed by Maj. Gen. Loganadan.

Sd/- Subhas Chandra Bose
Supreme Commander

Azad Hind Fauj
Special Order of the Day
Dated 24th April, 1945

The Supreme Commander of the Azad Hind Fauj is pleased to grant promotion to the next higher rank to all officers and other Ranks (except those officers of General's rank) of the Azad Hind Fauj now stationed in Burma. In accordance with this order when Lance Naiks are promoted

Naiks, the vacancies will be filled up by will be carrried out by the different unit commanders.

The above promotion will be forefeited if anybody happens to leave Burma or if he conducts himself in an unworthy manner.

Sd/- Subhas Chandra Bose
Supreme Commander
Azad Hind Fauj

42

Bose's Faith in the Ultimate Victory of the INA Forces Against the British[1]

26 June, 1945

Subhas Chandra Bose, head of the Provisional Government of Azad Hind has transferred his government to somewhere in Thailand, where he is determined more than ever, to carry on India's struggle for independence. To the British he is a greater menace than a modern army of one millions men. And the astute British Imperialists admit this in their broadcasts. For Netaji has repreatedly told the world that he and his Azad Hind Fauj will battle until India has been liberated from the shackles of British imperlialism.

Condemning Britain's latest offers for India, Bose bluntly declares that "acceptance of Wavell's proposal will mean political suicide for the Indian National Congress and for all Indian Nationalists. It will seriously jeopardise all chances of securing even self-government in the future not to speak of complete independence."

Netaji emphasized that "The British are cunning politicians and they have chosen the proper psychological moment for hurling this offer at India." He outspokely urges his people to refuse such a compromise.

"Outside of India we shall carry on an armed struggle for India's freedom—to the last man and to the last round." He continued "Our friends in the world—of whom we have many will—soon agitate for India's independence before the bar of world opinion and all international conference. And you at home must be prepared for a revolution. There is no earthly power that can stand between the Indian people and freedom. We have only to be firm, unflinching and patient and carry on our struggle under all circumstances."

Launches New Campaign—From somewhere in Thailand, Subhas Chandra Bose has launched another radio campaign directed to his people in India. In his latest broadcast he has pointed out that during the course

1. *Nippion Times*, 28 June, 1945

of the current war, India—whether the British liked it or not—has become "a live issue in world politics—so much so that the British fearfully realise that the Indian issue will be constantly raised in the future."

The fiery Indian nationalist told his listeners "not to forget that the moment there is a compromise between nationalist India and Britain, India will become a domestic issue of the British Empire and it will then be impossible for foreign powers, such as Soviet Russia, to intercede on behalf of Indian independence."

Shrewd, handsome and intelligent, Subhas Chandra Bose towers above them all as a freedom-fighter. He is an Indian, whose heart and soul is in the interest of India. Unlike most Indians who believe in the passive method of battle, Bose has always advocated the active or aggressive method. Call it violence or fanaticism, Netaji firmly believes that it is the only kind of language the British understands.

British educated, he is the personification of physical strength and mental vitality and Britain would move heaven and earth to have him as an ally.

A Menace to Britain—Subhas Chandra Bosc has always been a menace to the British. He has been so from his early twenties. While studying at a university in Calcutta he struck a British Professor after an argument on British polices in India and was expelled from school. The British in an effort to harness this fiery Indian, admitted him into Cambridge University in 1920. While a student there he passed the Indian Civil Service examination. He was only 22 years old then. The following year he obtained his diploma from Cambridge.

He hurried back to India and threw himself in the anti-British movement led by Mahatma Gandhi. His friendships with the revered Mahatma and Jawaharlal Nehru grew. His people elected him to the working committee of the Indian National Congress. Not satisfied with the conservative attitude of the leaders, in 1923 he organised the radical Swaraj faction within the Indian National Congress Party.

When "Forward" the organ of the Swaraj was rounded, Subhas Chandra Bose became its editor-in-chief. So great was the faith of the Indian youth in the leadership of this spirited young man that in 1924 he was made chairman of Calcutta municipal assembly.

The following year he revolted against the Indian National Congress Party and called a meeting of Indian Youths and became leader of the All India Young Men's Congress. This dramatic move by Bose influenced the National Congress Party to be more progressive.

By 1931, Subhas Chandra Bose was mayor of Calcutta. The mayor himself led an anti-British demonstration demanding immediate British withdrawal from India. Such anti-Britsh speeches aroused the anger of the British. He was seriously injured by British officers and thrown into prison. In 1932, he was released, but it wasn't long before he was hustled back in jail. Each time he was set free, he came out with a greater, more passionate hatred for the British.

After being released from prison in 1937 due to illness he was given permission to take a two-month trip to Europe. The British intended to impress him with their "kindly" British attitude toward India, but Bose came back hating the British more than ever before. The British were arrogant, cunning and clung continually to their imperialism.

When his friends and followers saw him, he was firmly convinced that the Indians could except freedom only by fighting for independence.

Bose was the president of the Indian National Congress in 1938 and 1939, but resigned from the position because of factional troubles within the party and organised the "Forward Bloc."

Advocated Open Break. The youth of India allied to the "Forward Bloc" launched one of the most aggressive movements for independence in British colonial history.

With the appoaching world crisis, Bose advocated an open break with Britain. As president of the Congress in 1938 and 1939 he had the prestige and the facilities to extend his influence all over the country and to contact the governments and political parties of the neighbouring states.

In additions to Burma, he extended his anti-British campaign to Thailand, Malaya, Singapore, Indo-China, Iran and Afghanistan.

In the summer of 1939, when the international tension approached the breaking point, Bose urged the Congress to make the bid. He raised the cry for immediate and complete independence. He objected to a compromise plan. He clamoured for an uprising by proclaiming preparation for armed resistance. He preached a holy war on the British. Bose saw in the predicament of the British empire a "unique opportunity to drive the British out of India."

Born to a well-to-do family established near Calcutta in 1897, Subhas Chandra Bose could have lived a comfortable life if he so chose, but his burning patriotism destined him to tread the path of pains and hardships.

Altogether he has lived eight full years in prison. British-prisons, however, could not change a patriot into a traitor.

Worked in Berlin. Late in 1939 Bose disappeared from India. Then he appeared in Germany where Fuhere Adolf Hitler welcomed him. From Berlin he continued to direct his Indian Independence movement.

Meanwhile, the early Axis victories over Britain and Bose's campaign against British army bore fruit in India. Mahatma Gandhi announced the revival of the civil-disobedience movement. But Mahatma and other important Congress leaders were arrested by the British before the movement officoally got under way.

Bose's mysterious trip and unexpected arrival in Tokyo in the spring of 1943, was a happy surprise for the Indians and the Asiatic races. The British and American leaders, however, trembled with misgivings.

43

Bose Future Plan to Free India. Declears Uncompromising Struggle to Continue for Independence[1]

7 July, 1945

Declaring that it has become clear that the Congress Working Committee has already decided to reject Lord Wavell's offer. Subhas Chandra Bose, Head of the Provisional Government of Free India, in a broadcast last night from Shonan to his sisters and brothers inside India suggested a programme for those who carry on an uncompromising struggle in the future for independence, according to a Shonan dispatch to Domel dated July 7.

In the beginning he pointed out that a defeatist mentality was the reason why so many prominent leaders were anxious for a compromise while the war was still going on. He declared that there were two groups, one which thinks nothing is to be gained by continuing civil disobedience insise India and that a compromise will render the possibility of reviving and strengthening Congress and the organisation of the country once again and second, one which thinks if India is to play a role in the camp of the United Nations she must come to some sort of an understanding and represent India at all international conference in the future. Both groups think that through a compromise they will able to work a way toward independence.

Stressing his disagreement with the defeatist mentality. Bose again emphasised that a compromise with the British will the achievement of independence. Regarding the first group's stand, he stated that, no harm will be done if a revival of Congress was postponed for the time.

Regarding the second point, Bose stated that the real question was not who should represent India at future International conference but whom the Indian spokesman will represent—a free India or an India under British rule. As long as Pandit Jawahar lal Nehru and other Indian leaders work under the Viceroy's leadership, declared Bose, his voice at the international conference will not be the voice of free India.

1. *Nippion Times*, 10 July, 1945.

Regarding the future of India, Netaji asserted that the Indians in East Asia are resolved to carry on an armed struggle to the last man and the last round keep the Indian issue alive as an international issue. A parallel movement, he declared should be carried on inside the country with the one aim of seeing to it that as a result of a cooperation with the British government. Congress does not degenerated into a liberal federation.

The *first* thing, Bose pointed out, should be to combine all oppositionists to the Wavell offer into some kind of a central organisation. The *second*, a persistent demand which should be made on behalf of the public and which the Congress Working Committe should place before the country is a programme for a central government and for a provincial government. *Thirdly*, a strong agitation should be carried on for the release of all political prisoner of all categories. *Fourthly*, the public should make a persistent demand of the Congress Working Committee to tell the country to what extent it is going to participate in British Imperialist war in the Far East.

Will India contribute to the UNRRA fund with the approval of Congress? Will Congress demand help for India's recovery or will Congress put out 15 crores of India's money, as a contribution to the UNRRA fund? *Sixthly*, will Congress insist that India's sterling balance be made available to India or will Congress allow itself to be used as a pawn by the British Amercian high finance. *Seventhly*, will Congress take up the question of India's public debt when it accepts the power and responsibility at the centre ?

If agiation and propaganda are kept up on all these points, declared Bose and the Indian insist on each of these points by Congress and the representative give effect to the demand of the Indian public than British power in India will be reduced to the minimum.

44

Special Order by Subhas Chandra Bose on the Surrender of the Japanese[1]

15 August, 1945

Comrades,

In our struggle for the independence of our Motherland, we have now been overwhelmed by an undreamt of crisis. You may perhaps feel that you have failed in your mission to liberate India. But let me tell you that this failure is only of a temporary nature. No set-back and no defeat can undo your positive achievements of the past. Many of you have participated in the fight along the Indo-Burma frontier and also inside India and have gone through hardship and suffering of every sort. Many of your comrades have laid down their lives on the battlefield and have become the immortal heroes of Azad Hind. The glorious sacrifice can never go in vain.

Comrades, in this dark hour I call upon you to conduct yourselves with the discipline, dignity and strength befiting a truly Revolutionary Army. You have already given proofs of your valour and self-sacrifice on the field of battle. It is now your duty to demonstrate your undying optimism and unshakeable will power in the hour of temporary defeat. Knowing you as I do, I have not the sightest doubt that even in this dire adversity you will hold your heads erect and face the future with unending hope and confidence.

Comrades, I feel that in this critical hour thirty-eight crores of our countrymen at home are looking at us, the Members of India's Army of Liberation. Therefore, remain true to India and do not for a moment waver in your faith in India's destiny. The roads to Delhi are many and Delhi still remains our goal. The sacrifices of your immortal comrades and of yourselves will certainly achieve their fulfilment. There is no power on earth that can keep India enslaved. India shall be free and before long.

Jai Hind

Subhas Chandra Bose

1. 601/7378/H.S. This along with the next one were the last orders issued by Bose before his death in the plane crashs.

45

Subhas Chandra Bose's Special Message to His Countrymen in East Asia after the Termination of the War[1]

17 August, 1945

Sisters and Brothers,

A glorious chapter in the History of India's struggle for Freedom has just come to a close and, in that chapter, the sons and daughters of India in East Asia will have an undying place.

You set a shining example of patriotism and self-sacrifice by pouring out men, money and materials into the struggle for India's Independence. I shall never forget the spontaneity and enthusiasm with which you responded to my call for 'Total Mobilisation'. You sent an unending stream of your sons and daughters to the camps to be trained as soldiers of the Azad Hind Fauj and of the Rani of Jhansi Regiment. Money and materials, you poured lavishly into the War Chest of the Provisional Government of Azad Hind. In short, you did your duty as true sons and daughters of India. I regret more than you do, that your sufferings and sacrifices have not borne immediate fruit. But they have not gone in vain, because they have ensured the emancipation of our Motherland and will serve as an undying inspiration to Indians all over the world. Posterity will bless your name, and will talk with pride about your offerings at the alter of India's Freedom and about your positive achievement as well.

In this unprecedented crisis in our history, I have only one word to say. Do not be depressed at our temporary failure. Be of good cheer and keep up your spirits. Above all, never for a moment falter in your faith in India's destiny. There is no power on earth than can keep India enslaved. India shall be free and before long.

Jai Hind

---

1. I.N.A. Trial Papers.

46

Order of the Day by M.Z. Kiani, asking I.N.A. Troops to Stop Fighting[1]

18 August, 1945

To all units and Commands, Malaya and Singapore

(i) In view of the present situation when all nations have decided on peace, the cabinet of the Provisional Government of Azad Hind has decided to cease fighting with effect from Saturday 18 August 1945.

(ii) You are hereby ordered to cease fighting forthwith. Convey this order to all units and troops, under your command at once. Also keep yourself and your troops, arms and ammunication and other military, stores ready to be handed over to the British on demand. Further instructions in due course. Strict discipline will be maintained. Commanders will remain responsible for the welfare and health of the troops under their charge till the British take over or issue other instruations. Normal administration and training will be continued. Troops will be confined to camp area except to move on urgent administration duties in which case they will move in suitable groups under a responsible officer.

1. F. No. 601/7378/H.S.

Interrogation Report of Major Nripendra Singh Bhagat, Who Tried to Wreck the I.N.A.[1]

20 August, 1945

C.S.D.I.C. (India), Red Fort, Delhi

No. 2 Section Report No. 1003 Dated 20 August 1945

Should any of the information contained in this report be reproduced, no mention of the source from which it is received should be made.

The information contained in this report is derived from interrogation. Although every effort is made to ensure accuracy, the original statements on which it is based are difficult to assess, and are often made under the influence of motives not conducive to veracity. A full record of these statements is kept here, and is available for reference if required.

Description of Individual

No. Rank and Name	T/Maj Nripendra Singh Bhagat CSDIC(I) B1020
Unit	R Bombay S & M
Class	Hindu Sikh
Family	S/o S.S. Bhagat (dead); Next of kin: Maj B.S. Bhagat, VC (brother)
Address	"Bhagalkot" PO, PS. Mussoorie Dist: Dehra Dun

1. F. No. 601/7778/H.S. Every soldier who joined the I.N.A. did not do so on account of patriotic records. There were many, who remained loyal to the British Government. Major Bhagat was one of them, who tried to wreak the movement from within. His report is included here to show the other side of the picture of the I.N.A.. Like him there were others who also remained loyal to the British.

Description Age 31 years, height 5 feet 8 inch Slanting linear scar 1.5 inch long below right eye.

Language Speaks English well, also knows Urdu and Punjabi fluently, and a smattering of Japanes.

1. **Introduction.** B1020 was captured, after playing a part in the Malayan Campaign, which earned him a recommendation for decoration, at the fall of Singapore.

As a non-volunteer, he was sent for a period to Borneo, but returned to Singapore in Aug 42, and then joined the I.N.A. as part of a calculated plan to expose Japanese faithlessness. For some time, he commanded the O.T.S., but was then appointed MS by Mohan Singh, in which office his influence was exerted in accordance with his preconceived plan. Partly as a result of the influence, Mohan Singh issued orders for the disbandment of the I.N.A. in the event of his arrest, which took place as expected.

The efforts of B1020 and others to prevent the reorganisation of the I.N.A. were unavailing, and he therefore rejoined with the same intention as before. He was appointed Chief Administrator, Supreme Comd, and then, in spite of his protests, Comd 2 Div, with which formation he remained in Malaya until Apr 44. His activities in the second I.N.A. led in that month to his being brought to Rangoon, and imprisoned.

B1020 escaped from confinement in Zeyawaddy on 19 Apr 45, and reported to our troops a week later.

Many CSDIC (I) 2 Sec Reports have been consulted in compiling this Report. References to them are given in the appropriate paragraphs. This Report should, in addition, be read with 3 FIC No. P/1665, in which B1020 is recommended for WHITE.

2. **Early History.** B1020 was born in 1914 in Alwar State, where his grandfather was in state employment. He was educated at home up to the age of 12 years by his father, who was in the UP PWD. in 1926 B1020 joined the PWRIM College, Dehra Dun, where he contained his education up to the age of 18. He then joined the IMA, and in 1932 was commissioned into the Bengal S & M. A three-year course followed, at the Thomson Engineering College, Roorkee. On conclusion of the course B1020 proceeded on service and took part in the Waziristan operations of 1937.

In 1938 B1020 was transferred to R Bombay S & M, and served in Quetta and Kohat before taking part in the Ahmedzai operation of 1940.

B1020 went to Malaya in Mar 41 as 2, i.e., 17 Fd Coy. In July he was promoted Major, and appointed to command the Coy.

B1020 served throughout the Malaya Campaign, and was recommended for the MC by the CRE 11 Ind Div, and the Div Comd. Maj-Gen Keyes.

3. **B1020's Attitude as a PW.** B1020 was captured, along with about 200 of his Coy, at the fall of Singapore, and attended the Farrer Park meeting two days later.

Note 1 : B1020 has recorded a statement at CSDIC (I) regarding the handing over the Ind PW to the Japanese by Col Hunt of Malaya Command which should finally dispose of any doubts on this subject. The statement is reproduced at Appx A. Although officers should have realised the implications of total surrender, B1020 states that this handing-over left in their minds an impression of having been sold out.

Note 2 : B1020 confirms that Capt Patnaik IMS was wearing a Fujiwara armband at the Farrer Park meeting.

After the meeting, B1020 was sent to Bidadari, and took over an area suitable for the accommodation of his 200 S & M personnel. During his first two days as a PW, B1020 was frequently approached by VCOs and men of his Coy for advice as to the attitude they should adopt towards the new movement. He advised them to ignore propaganda, to treat 'F' volunteers as unpatriotic collaborators, and to cling determinedly to PW status.

B1020's counter-propaganda led, after only two days, to his removal at the behest of Mohan Singh to the latter's bungalow, where he was told to cease his efforts to hinder the formation of the I.N.A. and warned of the consequences of non-compliance. Nevertheless B1020, after his return to Camp, maintained the same attitude, with the result that there were no volunteers from his Coy.

B1020 states that thereafter a proposal to shoot him was made on three occasions, and was only dropped, as he heard, for fear that such action would adversely affect I.N.A. recruitment. This was later confirmed personally by Maj-Gen IWAKURU.

Note 3 : That R Bombay S & M personnel did remain non-volunteers is confirmed by CSDIC (I) 2 Sec Report 850, para 3, column 5, under "Bombay S & M."

4. Deportation. In order to separation B1020 from the men he was influencing, he was sent to Kranji in the first week of April 42, and then subsequently for brief periods to Tengah and Tyersall Park. Ref CSDIC (I) 2 Sec Report 592, para 2. He remained at the latter place for two days only, and was then, together with Coy, abruptly put on board a cargo vessel. At the end of Apr or early in May 42, this ship sailed for Borneo.

Note 1 : For B1020's despatch to Borneo, see CSDIC (I) 2 Sec Report 742, para 6. Name of some men who accompanied him are given in Report 698, para 9. See also 2 Sec Report 586, para 3.

Note 2 : B10200 has been mentioned in CSDIC (I) 2 Sec Report 711 para 6, serial 35 as an anti-British propagandist in Singapore PW camps. If his propaganda had been I.N.A.-inspired, it is unlikely that as an important convert he would have been deported. It is possible that in the early days he had, however, ill-advisedly put about his reactions to the Farrer Park incident, as a "grouse". Between May and Aug. 42, B1020 was not in Singapore.

On arrival at Miri in Borneo, the men were accommodated in three barracks, and put to work as unskilled labour repairing an oil-refinery plant which had been demolished by retiring British forces during the Borneo fighting.

Labour conditions were hard, and rations totally inadequate. B1020's efforts brought some alleviation, when the Japanese allowed 10 cents per day, with which the men were able to obtain some small additional comforts. Fatigues of this nature continued until the end of Aug. 42, when B1020 was put into an aircraft and flown back to Singapore.

Note: He has no knowledge of the reasons which prompted this abrupt removal; but believes that it may have been at the instance of the Hikari Kikan, as no sapper officers had so far volunteered. The removal had no connection with any decision by B1020 to colunteer in Borneo. He did not take this decision until after arrival in Singapore.

On arrival in Singapore B1020 found that with the formation of the Council of Action arising out of the Bangkok Conference, and the renewed Japanese undertakings concerning the future of Indian independence, Mohan Singh's I.N.A. was already well under way as a going concern. B1020 was offered, for himself, the alternatives of joining the movement or of being shut up in a concentration camp.

B1020's appreciation of his situation was then, he states, as follows:

(a) His objects were both to expose the insincerity and emptiness of Japanese promises regarding Indian independence to the leading I.N.A. personalities, who were rapidly becoming dupes, and also to take some active part in causing all possible harm to his former persecutors.

(b) As factors in arriving at a decision, B1020 considered that a continued passive role in a concentration camp, where in any case he would merely be suffering personal inconvenience, would not forward his aims. The I.N.A. had reached a stage of development where it was no longer possible to damage it from outside. The same factor minimised the danger of his example to others; if he volunteered, moreover, his own Coy was away in Borneo. Finally, from his study of Japanese methods in Manchuria and China, and his personal experience of their unscrupulousness, B1020 was convinced that it was essential to match cunning with cunning.

(c) There was no other course open to him but the two alternatives offered by "force majeure".

B1020 therefore decided to join, and in the second week of Sep 42 was offered the choice of commanding a Regt of Grla troops, or of commanding the Neesoon O.T.S., then in process of raising, B1020 chose the O.T.S. as the best means of propagating his ideas amongst the future leaders of the I.N.A. This decision would too, he felt, embroil him least in possibly active participation.

6. **At the O.T.S.** Due to lack of equipment, and other administrative difficulties, the opening of the school was delayed, and B1020 was in nominal command for a short period only.

Note: Ref. CSDIC (I) 2 Sec Reports 553, para 5(a); 596, paras 5 (a) and (b).

These reports confirm B1020's account of the early stages of development of the O.T.S. It is worthy of note that B1020 interviewed all cadets personally, and that there was no propaganda on the only course which took place.

Pending completion of plans for the O.T.S., Mohan Singh in Oct 42 gave B1020 the appointment of MS, and asked him to stay with him.

7. **B1020's Achievements as MS.** Mohan Singh was well known to B1020, as they had been fellow-cadets at the IMA. Before long, B1020 gained considerable influence over Mohan Singh, who referred most matters of importance to B1020 for his advice. B1020 states that in these circumstances he was able to achieve:

(a) The separation of PW from I.N.A. volunteers not yet posted. (Ref CSDIC (1) 2 Sec Report 933, para 42, which may have a bearing on this)

(b) The original officers' segregation camp was abolished and officers were sent to PW camps. (CSDIC (I) 2 Sec Report 957, para 6).

(c) The maltreatment in concentration camps was stopped, and these became purely detention camps for petty offenders.

Note: The substance of this is confirmed by Sub Shingara Singh (B1053), whose Report is in preparation at CSDIC (I).

B1020 worked hard on Mohan Singh, constantly bringing before his notice the Japanese record in other occupied countries, with particular reference to their faithlessness. Mohan Singh became increasingly disillusioned, and agreed with B1020's forecasts on the future of the I.N.A. and Indian independence.

Matters came to a head when, at the time of the despatch of I.N.A. advance-parties to Burma, B1020 suggested to Mohan Singh that in view of the Japanese refusal to make a straightforward declaration on their war aims as far as India was concerned, all further I.N.A. troops movements to Burma should be stooped. To this proposal Mohan Singh agreed.

8. **The results.** Further troops movements were stopped and a meeting of the Council of Action was convoked, which drew up a note for presentation to the Japanese Government containing a demand that the independence clause of the Bangkok conference should be implemented. The Hikari Kikan, however, refused to forward this note, as they said that is constituted an ultimatum.

The crisis became more acute when Gill, on his return in Dec. 42 from Burma, was arrested by the Japanese on charges of attempting to communicate with the British. With the exception of R.B. Bose, the Council of Action resigned in a body. To avert the possibility that the Japanese might replace Mohan Singh by someone more amenable to their methods and aims, Mohan Singh himself sent out a sealed letter to be opened in the event of his arrest, containing instructions for the disbandment of the I.N.A.

Note : A clear account of subsequent events is given in CSDIC (I) 2 Sec Report 953, paras 12-16, which B1020 confirms.

9. **B1020 and the 1st I.N.A. Independent Assessments**. That B1020's own claims have not over-stated his part in breaking up the first I.N.A. is supported by independent evidence available at CSDIC (I). Reference should in particular be made to CSDIC (I) 2 Sec Report 956, para 46(c), which reveals the influence exercised by B1020 over Mohan Singh, and the ends to which that influence was used.

Further confirmation is available in CSDIC (I) 2 Sec Report 897, para 107, in which the four staff officers of 2 Div quoted Bhagat himself on his activities, and also described an interview of the latter with S.C. Bose, who had evidently come to hear the inner story.

Ref should also be made to Report 876, para 8, for a statement by Sub Maj Baboo Ram (B1007) to the same effect.

10. **Post-Crisis Deliberations.** Discussions by the DMB, of which B1020 was a member, continued through early 1943, when the formation of a new I.N.A. was hotly debated. B1020 himself spoke strongly, on more than one occasion, against the proposal.

Note : This is confirmed by CSDIC (I) 2 Sec Report 618, para 4, and connected ref.

At the same time B1020 was approached by R.B. Bose, who offered him command of the new Army if he would consent to join. These efforts were continued until Feb 43, although other persistent non-volunteer officers had already been sent to PW camps. When B1020 himself remained firm, he was sent to Rawang, where he joined parties engaged on bridge-construction and road-improvement work.

There, he continued his anti-recruitment propaganda, and mentions particularly, in connection with individuals whom he so advised, the names of:

1. Sub Walayat Khan R Bombay S & M
2. Sub Painda Khan 5/2 Punjab

He added, however, that increasing pressure was being brought to bear on him, and that if he volunteered, the VCO's were not to follow his example. B1020 remained in Rawang until July 43.

Note: B1020 was not an instructor at the O.T.S. during the Ind I.N.A. regime. CSDIC (I) 2 Sec Report 528, para 3, which shows him as so employed, is considered to be an erroneous reference to his earlier tenure of command there.

11. B1020 Joins the I.N.A. Again. At the beginning of August, soon after S.C.Bose's arrival, B1020 was taken to Singapore, and interviewed by both Bose and the Japanese. He was again offered a choice, this time of volunteering, or of being transferred to a Japanese jail. Basing his decision on the same considerations as before, B1020 again decided to join. Moreover, (with an unfortunate ignorance or misreading of Bose's character), he anticipated that his past experience and knowledge would act on Bose in the same way as on Mohan Singh.

On Volunteering B1020 was unemployed until Oct 43, when he took up the appointment of Chief Administrator, Supreme Command, vice Lt. Col Loganadan (B953), who had proceeded on a tour of East Asia in August, and who, immediately on his return, became a member of the PGI. (Ref: CSDIC(I) 2 Sec Report 953, paras 18 and 20).

B10020 held this appointment until Dec 43, with the rank of "Lt. Col".

12. Other Activities. In Oct 43, B1020 was appointed a representative of the I.N.A. to serve with the PGI. B1020 disclaims any initiative on his own part leading up to this appointment, and any subsequent display of initiative in the affairs of the PGI was rendered impossible by the dictatorial manners and habits of S.C.Bose, who reserved all major decisions to himself. B1020 then found, he states that there could be no question of obtaining an influence over Bose similar to that he had wielded over Mohan Singh, and he was obliged to change his approach, accordingly, to one of more overt propaganda.

In Nov 43 B1020 received orders to broadcast to India. His script was amended by Ayer, the Propaganda Minister. Nevertheless, the contrived to make a broadcast which was ambiguous, as no nations were specifically referred to:

Note: The text of B1020's broadcast is not available at CSDIC (I).

13. A Combatant Command : About the middle of Dec 43, B1020 was posted to command 2 Div, earmarked for operations in Burma. He protested against this posting, on the ground that his experience as an engineer officer disqualified him for the command of combatant troops, His protest, however, was overruled, and he remained in command until April 44. B1020 has added nothing to existing knowledge of 2 Div during the training period.

14. Collaboration with the Japanese from Dec 43 to Apr. 44.

(a) **"Nominal" Independence of the Philippines.** Burma and the Philippines had been granted "independence". Officers returning from Burma, however, reported that the "transfer of power" was on paper only, and the real authority remained vested in the Japanese.

B1020 told all with whom he came in contact that similar treatment was in store for India if, with I.N.A. collaboration, the Japanese invaded the country.

(b) **I.N.A. equipment unsatisfactory**. Equipment issued to 2 Div was inadequate and of poor quality. The interpretation which B1020 put on this was that the Japanese regarded the I.N.A. as a propaganda army only. This expression of B1020's views reached the ears of the Japanese.

(c) **Attitude of S.C. Bose.** In continuation of his earlier efforts with Mohan Singh, B1020 frequently drew S.C. Bose's attention to the Japanese record in Manchuria and China, and attempted to convince him of their real future aims with regard to India. It was evident, however, that Bose was determined to follow his own path, was intolerant of criticism or suggestions from his subordinates, and was fully committed to a policy of collaboration.

On one occasion B1020 referred publicly to S.C. Bose as a civilian. The remark came to Bose's ears, and caused him considerable annoyance.

Note : This is confirmed in CSDIC (I) 2 Sec Report 897, para 107.

(d) **Suggested released of Mohan Singh.** B1020 was one of a small body of officers which was anxious for the release of Mohan Singh, Gill, and six other officers, from Japanese imprisonment.

B1020 pressed these views on both Bose and the Japanese, and later, after the former left Malaya for Burma in Dec 43, on the deputy Bhonsle, the CGS. The discussions and correspondence with Bhonsle were particularly acrimonious.

Note : This is also confirmed in CSDIC (I) 2 Sec Report 897, para 107.

15. **Was B1020 ever appointed CGS in Rangoon?**— CSDIC (I) 2 Sec Report 633, para 22, on L/Nk Risal Singh (B466), gives B1020 as holding the appointed of CGS at Rear HQ in Rangoon in Mar-Apr 44. B1020 states that at that time he was still in Malaya. Moreover, it is plain from CSDIC (I) 2 Sec Report 975 that B1020 only arrived in Burma for the first time early in Apr 44, and was immediately placed under arrest. Furthermore, a letter from S.C. Bose to B1020, dated 5 Apr 44, and referred to in the next paragraph, still addressed B1020 as Comd. 2 Div.

While, therefore, B1020 never actually held the appointment, it is possible, in view of Capt (Col) P.K. Sahgal's (B968's) remarks on the necessity for secrecy at the time of B1020's arrest, that the story of B1020's appointment as CGS may have been deliberately put about among the lower ranks of the I.N.A. as a security-cover. B1020 himself, although he has no first-hand knowledge, gives this as his own explanation of the probable reason for the belief.

16. **Arrest**. On 5 Apr 44, B1020 was informed that S.C. Bose had sent for him to come to Rangoon. He left by air the same day, travelling with:

(a) "Maj" Man Singh

(b) "Maj" S.N. Gupta

(c) "Maj" Lakhshmi Rani of Jhansi Regt.

The party halted for three days at Bangkok, and then left for Rangoon arriving on 8 Apr. B1020 was met at the airfield by two Japanese officers of the Hikari Kikan and "Lt. Col" Sahgal (B968), who handed to B1020 the letter from S.C. Bose which is reproduced as Appx "B" to this Report.

Note : Refer to CSDIC (I) 2 Sec Report 897, para 10

Refer to CSDIC (I) 2 Sec Report 975, para 17

This letter is considered to provide very substantial confirmation of the stand which, in accordance with his intentions from the first, B1020 claims to have taken in the 2nd I.N.A.

B1020 was driven straight to the Kempei Tai Jail in Rangoon, and there imprisoned. He was informed that the charges against him were:

(a) Disloyalty to the I.N.A.

(b) Disloyalty and disrespect to the Supreme Comd.

(c) Participation in anti-Japanese activities.

17. **Imprisonment**. B1020 remained in the Kempei Tai Jail for seven months. One other allied PW imprisoned there was Capt Seagrim who, B1020 believes, was shot for espionage in Aug 44. In Oct/Nov B1020 was removed to I.N.A. custody in Taunggyi, and thence in Feb 45 to Zeyawaddy. There he was told by Hav (Lt) Shiv Singh (B1066) that he was in touch with British officers who were leading Burmese guerrillas; B1020 replied that he would escape at the first opportunity, and join them.

18. **Escape of Capt Brown.** At 0300 hrs on the night 13/14 Apr 45, B1020 was awoken by "Lt. Col" P.N. Dutt, (B1015) commander of the Zeyawaddy area, who told him that a BO had been captured by S.O. Kundan Lal. Dutt asked B1020's advice as to the officer's disposal. B1020 realised that if he gave advice which lead him open to the suspicion of wishing to aid the officer's escape, he would be transferred to Rangoon. He therefore suggested that the officer, a Capt Brown, should be handed over to Inspector Misra of the Civil Police, whom B1020 already knew. Capt Brown did escape as described in the CSDIC(I) 2 Sec Report 997, on P.N. Dutt (B1015), and No. 1010 on Shiv Singh (B1066), and both Misra and Shiv Singh had to go into hiding.

19. **Escape.** Zeyawaddy was heavily bombed by Allied planes on 19 Apr, and was evacuated. In the confusion following the evacuation, B1020 again contacted Shiv Singh, and the two made their escape. B1020 planned to join a guerrilla band, under Maj Carew, but before he could carry out his plan, regular Allied troops arrived in the area. B1020 reported to HQ 5 Ind Div on 26 Apr. 45.

20. **Conclusion**. In addition to the normal interrogation very detailed research has been carried out at CSDIC (I) to establish the exact part which B1020 played during his periods of spasmodic service with the I.N.A. Adequate documentary proof is available to show that B1020 was very largely responsible behind the scenes for the crisis

which culminated in the disbandment of the I.N.A. under Mohan Singh, the process of whose disillusionment was hastened by B1020's cleverly-applied influence. It is, therefore, considered at CSDIC (I) that B1020's membership of the first I.N.A. was the outcome of a well-conceived plan to destroy that organization, and that it was not in any way due to fundamentally seditious intentions.

In deciding, however, to attempt a similar coup under Bose, B1020 committed an error of judgement, in underestimating the new Leader's calibre. Bose would stand no nonsense; it is, moreover, plain from existing records that he had become aware of B1020's earlier activities and probable future intentions, and took step accordingly. The early attempt to win B1020 over by appointment to a nominally high office in the I.N.A. and PGI administration failed; and the clashes of character and temperament between the two men, aggravated by other disagreements with Bhonsle, gradually forced B1020, who intended primarily to work behind the scenes, to show him hand in the open defiance and counter-propaganda which led to his arrest and imprisonment. These consideration, and the circumstantial evidence which supports them, must therefore outweigh B1020's temporary (and allegedly involuntary) command of 2 Div of which a more serious view would have been taken at CSDIC (I) apart from this evidence of creditable motives.

B1020 is deeply reserved in temperament. Nevertheless, his realisation of the position into which Bose has been forced, whether against his will or not, as a puppet of the Japanese, has been made plain both by B1020's actions in the I.N.A., and by his statement at CSDIC (I). He has also revealed a deep aversion to the Japanese, and all their aims and methods.

For these reasons, it is not considered that B1020 represents any danger to security under the present conditions in India.

B1020 achieved some distinction in the Malayan Campaign, and appears to be of the best type of Indian officer, who showed initiative and judgement after capture by the enemy, and also in the manner of his escape in April 45.

It is therefore recommended that he should be categorized WHITE, and that his line of conduct after 1942 should be brought to the notice of the Adjutant-General.

Appendix "A" to CSDIC (I) 2 Sec Report 1003 dated 20 August 1945

Handing over of Indian PW to the Japanese by Col Hunt at Farrer Park Singapore on 17 Feb 1942

The great majority of Indian PW were assembled at Farrer Park in front of a two-storeyed building.

Presumably Col Hunt had been instructed by Malaya Command to hand over officially the Indian PW to the Japanese authorities. He came on the balcony of the first floor and spoke into a microphone as follows, or words to this effect:

"From now on you (Indian soldiers) are handed over into the control of the Japanese authorities, and are under their instructions."

Immediately afterwards the Japanese representative Maj Fujiwara handed over the men in similar words to Capt Mohan Singh.

It is possible that the whole affair was stage-managed by the Japanese to have a desired effect (from the Japanese viewpoint) on the Indian PW. It is my personal opinion that it conveyed a general impression on the rank and file that they were to obey the Japanese, and later on their representatives, wishes on all matters.

Appendix "B" to CSDIC (I) 2 Sec Report 1003 dated 20 August 1945

Arzi Hukumate Azad Hind
(The Provisional Government of Free India)

5th April 1944.

Lieutenant-Colonel N.S. Bhagat,

Commander, No. 2 Division Indian National Army.

Every since you took over command of No. 2 Division, you have adopted a very defiant attitude towards the Headquarters, Supreme command, and in spite of my repeated warnings and advice to you, you have persisted in your attitude and have openly defied the authority of that Headquarters.

Furthermore, you have, by your actions and speeches, exhibited lack of loyalty towards me, as your Supreme Commander, and the Indian Independence Movement.

It is not possible to overlook such breach of discipline and lack of loyalty on the part of an officer holding such a responsible position, and to avoid any trouble in future, I have decided to relieved you of the Command of the Second Division.

Owing the present wartime conditions, I have also decided to place you in protective custody, until such time as your release is considered desirable.

Your future relations with the Indian National Army will be considered and decided later.

Sd/. Subhas Chandra Bose
Supreme Commander,
Azad Hind Fauj.

48

Minutes of the Meeting War Department to Frame Policy with Regard to the INA[1]

21 August, 1945

1. At a meeting held on Saturday afternoon, the 21st July, 1945, in the War Secretary's room, to discuss the policy to be adopted regarding members of the INA, the following were present :

Sir George Spence	Secy. Legislative Department
Mr. G.S. Bozman	Secy. I and B Department
Mr. F. Cracknell	Actg. Jt. Secy Home Department
Mr. G. Smith	D.I.B.
Lt. Gen. Sir John Swayne	C.G.S.
Major-General J.B. Dalison	Actg. A.G.
Major General A.K. Ferguson	D.M.I.
Brigadier D. Young	D.P.R.
Mr. C.M. Trivedi	Secy. War Department
Mr. P. Mason	Jt. Secy War Department

2. The War Secretary began by saying that after some consideration of the problem, the War Department felt that whatever the decision might be regarding publicity or the reverse for the actual individual trials of members of the I.N.A. there should be in the near future an announcement of policy. The policy decided upon was generous and we were entitled to make the most of it. Further, by anticipating questions and making a full statement we should prevent much criticism.

3. All agreed that such a declaration of policy should be made; but there was a difference of opinion as to the form it should take. Home Department felt that the statement should be directed rather to the Indian Army than to the general public. The statement might therefore begin by pointing out the seriousness of the offence of

1. Indian Office Library and Records, F. No. R/3/1/330.

joining the I.N.A. and continue by stating that while the law would be allowed to take its course in the worst cases, the majority were being treated with generosity. I and B Department and DPR on the other hand, felt that the generous treatment was the strong point which it was required to make and that this should open the statement, the seriousness of the offence being given second place. Both points of view were noted and it was decided that they should be borne in mind in drafting a communique.

4. The War Secretary went on to consider the question of whether an attempt should be made to prevent publicity for individual trials by court martial. He pointed out that in some cases the accused would be defended by eminent counsel with political connections, and that therefore they would attract considerable publicity and might arouse much more bitter feelings than the declaration of policy. The fact that they might arouse bitter feelings against Government would be an argument for holding them in camera and suppressing publicity. It was also necessary to save the good name of the Indian Army.

5. Home Department supported this view and were in favour of proceeding by Ordinance to make it possible to hold the trials in camera, and to bind counsel to preserve secrecy. Further, they could rule that counsel must be selected from a panel approved by government.

6. I and B Department on the other hand, (and DIB, with the consent of the Home Member, expressed personal views concurring with those of I and B Department and differing from the official views of Home Department) felt that publicity would inevitably be attracted to the whole subject, whether the proceedings were held in camera or not. This being so, they thought it better not to proceed by ordinance because this would arouse strong criticism in the Press and in the Legislature, and it would be felt that Government were using war time powers for a merely political object at a time when the war situation did not justify it. Further, I and B Department pointed out that such action would be used by Bose and the Japanese in propaganda and would give them a strong handle.

7. Legislative Department did not think that the trials would arouse much interest.

8 D.M.I. Director Military Intelligence said that the trials might reveal information which it was necessary to conceal from the Japanese.

9. Acting A.G. said that from the point of view of the Army,all that was required was to announce the sentences in India Army Orders and the less publicity given to the actual trials the better.

10. C.G.S. Chief of General Staff said that there was no question that the less publicity that was attracted the better,but he was not clear as to whether publicity could best be prevented by an Ordinance or by letting matters take their normal course. It would perhaps be argued that by hushing up trials we were concealing the fact that we were not in fact carrying out the announced policy. He was not,without further examination, prepared to say that it was essential in military interests that powers by Ordinance should be taken to prevent publicity.

11. All except Home Department felt that if an Ordinance was introduced, the provision regarding selection of defence counsel from a panel would prove an irritant and in practice would be difficult to work.

12. I and B Department agreed that if it was felt by the General Staff that it was essential in the interests of security that the proceedings should be secret, there was no further dispute and the wishes of the General Staff must be carried out; but reiterated that from the point of view of the public it would be preferable to avoid such action.

13. Finally,War Secretary thanked the members of the meeting for giving their views and said that it would now be necessary to represent those views to H.E., the Commander-in-Chief and take his orders.

Minutes of the Provincial Conference to Discuss the Policy Towards the INA[1]

24 August, 1945

Present

The Hon'ble Sir Francis Mudie.
The Hon'ble Sir Richard Tottenham.
Mr. F.G. Cracknell, ICS, Deputy Secy., Home Department.
Mr. N.P.A. Smith, D.I.B.
Mr. W. Mck. Wright, Dy. Director, D.I.B.
Mr. M.K. Johnston, Director, D.I.B.
Mr. P. Mason, Jt. Secy., War Department.
Major. Gen. A.K. Ferguson, D.M.I.
Mr. W. Scott Brown, Chief Secy., Madras.
Lt. Col. G.S. Gill. I.G. of Prisons, Madras.
Mr. W.F.A. Hamilton, Supdt. of Police, S.B. C.I.D. Madras.
Lt. Col. Bhandari, IMS, I.G. of Prisons, Bombay.
Mr. W.G. Lang, Asstt. To D.I.G. of Police, Bombay.
Mr. S.B. Bapat, ICS, Jt. Secretary. Home Dept. Bengal.
Lt. Col. M.A. Singh, IMS, I.G. of Prisons, Bengal.
Mr. D. Stephens, Special Supdt. of C.I.D. Bengal.
Lt. Col. A.H. Shaikh, I.G. of Prisons, U.P.
Mr. H.C. Mitchell, Asst. I.G., C.I.D. U.P.
Mr. H.J. Frampton, Chief Secy., U.P.
Mr. AA. MacDonald, Home Secy. Punjab.
Mr. E.W.C. Wace, CIE, I.G. of Police, Punjab.
Lt. Col. N.D. Puri, IMS, I.G. of Prisons, Punjab.
Mr. J. Bowstead, Chief Secy., Bihar.
Mr. B.St.L. TenBrocke, M.C., Dy. I.G. of Police, C.I.D. Bihar.
Mr. T.C.S. Jayaratham, Chief Secy., C.P. & Berar.

1. I.O.L. F. No. R/3/1/330

Mr. D.G. Watson, I.G. of Police, C.P. & Berar.
Lt. Col. N.S. Jatar, I.G. of Prisons, C.P.
Mr. R.A.E. Williams, CIE Chief Secy., Orissa.
Mr. H.J. Vickers, I.G. of Police, N.W.F.P.
Mr. G.W. McElhinny, Chief Secy., Sind.
Mr. G.G. Ray, OBE, I.G. of Police, Sind.
Mr. F.B. Plunkett, OBE, I.G. of Prisons, Sind.

1. The Home Member explained that the policy towards the ex-members of the INA and 950 Regiment was at present confidential and would remain so until a communique on the subject was issued.The main problem was how these people would behave on return to India.There were about 20,000 Blacks and Greys and though at the time this Conference was originally summoned there had seemed to be no immediate prospect of all these coming to hand, developments in the last few days had made it seem likely that the whole number would be caught very soon and the problem had consequently become much more urgent. In dealing with the problem it was essential to have close cooperation between military and civil authorities as well as between the Centre and the Provinces.

2. There were two extreme points of view on the question of policy. One was that the members of the I.N.A. had committed a most serious offence and should all be punished with the penalty that the law provided. The others was that the members of the I.N.A. were not pro-Japanese but that their sole object was to achieve the freedom of India and that, as India is being promised her freedom anyhow in the near future, there was no reason to take a serious view of what these men did.The first of these opinions ignores the circumstances in which many of them joined the I.N.A. and the propaganda to which they were subjected. The second would offend those whose loyalty had never wavered, particularly POW who did not join the Japanese.It would in fact put a premium on disloyalty. The effect of harsh punishment on reasonable public opinion also would be adverse, and would prejudice hopes of a political agreement. The second opinion, on the other hand, would strengthen the hands of those elements in the country who were in favour of achieving their political ends by force and not by negotiation. The policy which had been recommended therefore for the approval of the Secretary of State distinguished between the degrees of culpability. The worst

offenders would be tried and of those convicted, some would be hanged,while the remainder might have their sentences commuted to fairly long terms of imprisonment. These could be described as "Convicted Blacks". Their numbers could be taken as approximately one-tenth of the military "Blacks" shown as belonging to each Province in the statement circulated for the meeting. The question of the numbers to be court-martialled was entirely one for the military, subject to the condition that Provinces had prison accommodation for them. The first point on which Provincial opinions were invited was whether Provinces would have any difficulty in finding accommodation for their own "Convicted Blacks".

3. Provincial Representatives then gave their opinions as follows:

Bengal stated that in view of their special problems the large numbers of terrorists and Bose enthusiasts in the Province they did not want any of these "Convicted Blacks" to be sent to Bengal. They agreed, however, that accommodation was available.

Bombay said that they were of opinion that "Convicted Blacks"should not be kept in civil jails. They also did not want to make alternative arrangements as they did not wish to have "Convicted Blacks"in Bombay Province at all.

Bihar, Central Provinces, Madras, N.W.F.P., Sind and Orissa stated that they would have no difficulty in arranging the necessary accommodation.

United Provinces also said that they would be able to find accommodation in their central Jails without using the Sitapore Jail or the Lucknow Camp Jail.

They said they could also accommodate convicted Blacks from Indian States etc., but this would mean using Sitapore.

4. The Home Member then explained the problem of "Greys". Their activities might be dangerous.

(a) to the loyalty of the Army ; and

(b) to law and order in general ;

and for this reason it seemed desirable to have some scheme for polling intelligence on both points. If a suitable machinery was set up on these lines for civil and military liaison, it might obviate the necessity of imposing restrictions in each case. We gave it as his personal opinion that temporary restriction would be difficult and might raise problems that did not at present exist.In dealing with these men both the civil and military points of view should be considered. The Provincial Governments' Representatives were asked to state their opinions on this proposal.

Bengal said that they wished to be allowed to express on an opinion at the time of the classification, as in the past they had found it necessary to detain persons who had been classified "Grey". They were in favour of the proposal for military-civil liaison in watching the activities of "Greys".

Bombay said that they wished each case to be reffered to their C.I.D. before any military "Grey" was allowed to come back to his village on leave. They were of opinion that no one from Satara District should be released as a "Grey"and they were prepared to make arrangements for detaining all such persons if necessary. They agreed to the proposal for civil-military liaison for watching the activities of "Greys".

The Central Provinces did not consider military-civil liaison necessary; they thought that watching the activities of the "Greys" was entirely a matter for the Police but any information of use to the military authorities could be passed on to them.

Madras were in favour of military-civil liaison and stated that it could be arranged with the Chief Civil Liaison Officer who was in charge of Soldier's Boards.

Punjab stated that they wished to have some information about "Greys" before they were turned loose. They were prepared to accept the classification of military "Greys" but not that of civil "Greys" without further information. They did not think it necessary to have civil-military liaison for watching "Greys" as the Police would be able to obtain all the necessary information by themselves.

The United Provinces were in favour of civil-military liaison that they had the necessary arrangements.

5. At this stage for the benefit of those Provinces who had asked to be allowed a say at the time of classification of "Greys", it was explained by General Fergusson that this would involve their sending representatives simultaneously to widely separated centres such as Multan, Delhi, Singapore, Rangoon and Jhingargacha.

6. Opinions were then invited on the necessity for restricting military "Greys". The Home Member had expressed the opinion that it would not be necessary. He explained that military "Greys" would be given six weeks' leave before discharge, namely in order to give them some money. They would not be in uniform and would not return to their units. The military authorities would be prepared to order them to remain in certain areas around their village during that time if Provincial Governments considered it necessary.

Bengal stated that they would insist on these restrictions being imposed to ensure that the men reached and stayed in his village.They would also impose their own restriction orders in every case on the expiry of the six weeks.

Bombay agreed with Bengal.

The Central Provinces considered that restriction orders would be unnecessary.

Madras were strongly in favour of these restrictions being imposed so as to get "Greys" to their villages. They also wished to be given prior information of their departure for their villages.

N.W.F.P. considered no restrictions necessary so long as prior information of departure was given. They were in favour of warnings being given to "Greys" by *Lumbardars* and also making some local person responsible for the "Greys" behaviour.

The United Provinces and Punjab were both in favour of restrictions being imposed.

It was agreed that "Greys" from Indian States would have to be restricted in their States and the question would be taken up with the Political Department.

7. The question of "Detained Blacks" was taken up. The Home Member explained that there would be about 7,000 ex-soldiers among them and the problems for consideration were how long they could be detained and in what circumstances they could be released. There was also the danger of a political campaign being worked up for wholesale releases. The best policy would appear to be one of gradual releases similar to that which had been successful in the case of Congress. Behaviour of persons released would be a valuable aid in deciding on further releases and for this purpose the cases must be under constant review almost from the outset. For this review

close cooperation between civil and military would be required and a suggested arrangement would be to hold the necessary courts of Enquiry in the various Provinces. By these means it might never be necessary to find accommodation simultaneously for the whole 7,000. A review at the very start might result in a decision not to detain some of them at all, e.g., if persons of a similar type had been released with satisfactory results. If there were difficulties about holding courts of inquiry in Provinces, a solution might be had in having part of the place of detention seperated off as a kind of lock up where Blacks could be kept while the question of their detention was considered by a joint military and civil body.

8. Provincial Government's opinions were then invited on (a) the proposal for constant reviews of these cases and (b) whether they could find accommodation for their "Detained Blacks".

Bengal expressed themselves in favour of the principle of constant reviews but reiterated that they did not want any "Blacks" in their Province. They would not be able to find accommodation for them unless Hijli Jail at present used by American Forces could be made available.

Bombay were in favour of constant reviews but said that they could not find accommodation for their "Blacks".

Central Provinces were of opinion that there should be a sorting out of "Blacks" after about 8 months followed by six monthly reviews. They would be able to find the necessary accommodation.

Madras agreed to the proposal for review after a few months and also said that they would be able to find the necessary accommodation.

Punjab agreed to the proposal that these cases should be reviewed from the start provided that the military officers associated with the review were such as had good knowledge of Punjab conditions. As regards accommodation they said that they would be unable to find accommodation for their "Blacks" unless the Yole Jail was released for their use. They also mentioned the impossibility of obtaining wardens and said that they were already short of them by 600. (The United Provinces mentioned a similar shortage of wardens). It was agreed that the Army might be able to help in this matter.

The United Provinces stated that as they had not been informed of the points for discussion or had sufficient time for fully considering them, any opinions expressed on various points raised in this meeting should not be taken as committing the United Province Government. With this proviso, they agreed with the proposal for constant reviews. As regards accommodation, they said that they could arrange this if the Sitapore Jail were available in the near future. It was agreed that they would address the War Department about the difficulties in obtaining material to complete the construction. They also explained that if the prisoners sent to Sitapore were of Class I or Class II, there would be accommodation for only 750, whereas if they were of Class III,the accommodation would be for 1500. It was ascertained that the great majority of persons to be detained there would probably be of Class III.

It was agreed that the question of the accommodation etc. of Detained Blacks coming from Indian States would have to be taken up with the Political Department.

9. The last point on which Provincial Government's opinions were invited was whether "Blacks" should be kept in one place or distributed as widely as possible or whether, if kept in one place, there would be any difficulty in segregating different classes of prisoners or the dangerous from the rest.

Bengal were in favour of keeping all in one place.

Bombay also were in favour of keeping all in one place but would keep upper and lower class prisoners in separate prisons.

Central Provinces were in favour of splitting them up by classes or according to their behaviour in jail.

Madras said that they could arrange separation by classes but would prefer to keep all in one jail.They could if necessary, remove the more troublesome ones to some other jail.

N.W.F.P. said they would start off by keeping all in one jail and separate them later if necessary.

Punjab said that they would separate them according to their communities.

United Provinces said that they would start off by keeping them in the same jail segregated according to classes and would send the more troublesome ones elsewhere if necessary.

10. N.W.F.P. enquired whether the "Blacks" would be sent to the Province under military escort and were informed that they would. The Home

Member stated that civil "blacks" would also be detained under War Department's orders and would be subject to the same suggested review procedure.

11. It was agreed that Inspector General of Prisons would meet Mr. Mason of the War Department at 3 p.m. and discuss with him the rules for the treatment of "Detained Blacks".

50

Note by R.F. Mudie, Regarding Treatment of the INA[1]

24 August, 1945

1. The decision regarding the number of persons to be court-martialled is for the Commander-in-Chief. The Home Department only comes in if there is any question of sentencing to imprisonment more than could be kept in provincial jails. No difficulty is expected if only 600 men are court-martialled. If it were decided to court-martial 2,000, it would probably be necessary to accommodate some in the new jail at Sitapore, U.P.

2. Home Department agree about the undesirability,both administrative and political of detaining about 7,000 "Blacks" without trial and would like to distinguish between "Blacks" and those to be detained. The classification of "Black" or "Grey" depends on what the individual in question did as a member of Bose's Army. The question of whether or not he should be detained depends on what he will do if released.This again depends on the community or class from which he comes and the state of affairs existing in the part of the country in which he would probably live, if released. Home Department would therefore prefer to look on "Blacks" not as those who should be automatically detained but as those who should be *considered* for detention.

3. The danger that may arise from releasing these men is both military and civil. They may attempt to suborn the Army or spread disaffection in recruiting districts and they may join terrorist groups or other subversive organisations. The difficulty about estimating the extent of either danger is that we have no previous experience to go on. On the one hand these people joined the Japanese or Germans on the assumption that the enemy would win the war. And now that we have won, a great many of them will undoubtedly see the error, or

1. I.O.F. No. R/3/1/330.

the futility, of their ways. On the other hand,their leader Subhas Bose, who has apparently made a deep impression on a great number of them, is a dangerous agitator with influence with the Congress and connections with the terrorists of Bengal and elsewhere. Not only is this the first time that any large number of Indian prisoners of war have joined the enemy, but it is also the first time that an important Congress politician has established his ascendency over any large body of ex-soldiers.

4. In these circumstances Home Department's view is that we must proceed by trial and error. They would like to release "Greys" as rapidly as possible and keep a watch on their doings. This watch should be as unobtrusive as possible and Home Department would prefer if military officers were associated with the police in this matter. As regards "Blacks", Home Department would suggest that as far as possible they be kept for some time out of India till we have some knowledge of the behaviour of the "Greys". When "Blacks" are brought to this country, the question of their detention should be examined by a Joint Committee of military and police officers having knowledge of the state of affairs in the province to which they are to return and the behaviour in it of previously released "Greys" or "Blacks" of various types.This examination should be done in Provinces. The instructions to the Committee would be to be as generous as possible in releases consistent with safety. It would also be their business constantly to examine with a view to release the cases of those that had been detained in the light of further experience gained and of changed conditions. For instance, it would probably be possible to release all detained "Blacks" if we reached a political settlement agreeable to the left wing Congress.

5. If this policy were adopted and if "Greys" and "Blacks" did not create trouble on release, it might be hoped that we would be left with a comparatively small hard cores of those who could not safely be released. These men, it is suggested, should then be court-martialled to obviate the political objects to detention without trial. There must at least be evidence against all that they joined the enemy, which is sufficient.

6. These views are generally in accordance with those of representatives of Provincial Governments with which the whole question was discussed last week.

7. I should like H.E. the War Member to see this note.

51

Note by the India Office on the Role of INA[1]

25 August, 1945

A brief indication of the security problem arising from the return to India of suspect Indian civilians and soldiers from territory liberated from the enemy.

1. The Blacks and Greys, civil and military, whom India will eventually have to re-absorb into her population, have been members while under the enemy's influence of one or more of the following groups:

   (a) The (Jif) Indian National Army in East Asia —as its name implies, this was a military body, organised, trained, equipped and to some extent used as a fighting army. It has existed since the earliest days of the Japanese conquest of Hong Kong, Malaya and Burma. Its development and efficiency have at times been disturbed by internal discord, the luke-warm attitude of individual members, and distrust of the Japanese. Its record in the firing line has in some cases been poor. On the other hand, on occasions the INA has fought well and the Japanese found it useful in Burma: its failure was partly the fault of the Japanese themselves. Membership of this 'army' has made a deep impression on almost all who joined it, whether they were prisoners of war or ordinary civilians. They have been fundamentally affected by the personality of their leader Subhas Bose, who possesses their ungrudging trust, respect, admiration and loyalty, and by his continuous propaganda concerning their mission to liberate India under his command. Some of the INA.'s higher officers have also had great influence on their men. It is abundantly clear that even those INA. members whose low morale has led to voluntary surrender, or who realise that they have backed the wrong horse, and whose

1. India Office Library and Records London, R.F. No. R/3/1/330.

suspicions of Japan have been crystallised by events, in many cases still preserve intact their belief in Bose's integrity and ideals. They consider that he has had a good try, and has by no means altogether failed, for he did at least gain fair treatment and even a measure of respect from the Japanese for the Indian community throughout East Asia. They say, with reason, that. Indians (though a minority) suffered less than any other community from the Japanese and that this was entirely due to Bose. Almost all the INA. are anti-Japanese but they are proud of the INA. itself ("India's first National Army") of Bose's Provisional Government (which "has been recognised by nine great powers. India is at last a State in her own right"), and of their own effort to free India. They expect Bose to try again somehow some day. and would be behind him in the attempt.

(b) **The (Hif) Indian National Army in Europe**— known as the "Indian Legion" or 950 Regiment. This too was a military body, organised, trained, equipped and to some extent used as a fighting force. Unlike the INA. in East Asia, which maintained its independence of the Japanese Army to a great extent (except in actual operations), the 950 Regiment was actually a part of the Reischswehr (and at the last, fleetingly, of the SS). It wore regular German army uniform; a percentage of the officers and N.C.Os. were Germans. Generally speaking, what has been said in para 1(a) above about the effect of propaganda and collaboration in the war against Britain on the Jif INA. is also true of the 950 Regiment. The main differences are *firstly*, that Axis attempts to suborn Indian P.O.W. met with far greater resistance than Japanese attempts in Asia, and the 3000 odd who eventually formed 950 Regiment were therefore on the whole more hardened traitors;

Secondly, that they were never anti-German—on the contrary they have been deeply impressed by German methods, efficiency, equipment and ruthlessness :

Thirdly, that they suffer from the complaint, which is common to many Indian soldiers (not necessarily ex-P.O.W.) who have associated on equal terms with Europeans in the U.K. and Europe, of resenting the restrictions imposed by caste, religion, community and race prejudices, which they find on return to

India. This often finds expression as an "anti-British-in-India" manifestation which, in the case of 950 Regiment personnel, naturally aggravates the effect of the rest of their background. On the whole the men of the Indian Legion are a particularly truculent, ill-disciplined and unregenerate lot of renegades.

(c) **The Jif "Intelligence Corps"**—a convenient term for the many hundreds of Indians, both soldiers and civilians in East Asia who have been trained in various intelligence functions by the Japanese and Subhas Bose's assistants. Generally speaking, the remarks in para. 1(a) above apply to them as to the INA. They are, if any thing, even more affected as a class, by the training they have undergone in sabotage, espionage and propaganda; by the concentrated propaganda to which they themselves were continually subjected; by the feeling that they were volunteers to a corps delite specially selected to help in India's liberation by individual underground tasks, involving great personal danger; and by the more intimate contact they had with Bose's chosen lieutenants, often men with pre-war revolutionary histories. A great many of these intelligence agents are of poor courage, weak moral fibre and low mental calibre. Afair percentage, however, are to be reckoned with as constituting a potential security danger as long as the present regime continues in India. They are the type that might well be readily recruited into the existing revolutionary parties, to whom their determination and acquired knowledge of explosives, etc., might prove useful. It is also possible that a few of them might be prepared to go on working for the Japanese to the best of their ability, however dark the hour for Japan.

(d) **The Indian Independence League**—the "party", on the best Fascist model. This civil organisation served Bose as a medium through which to exercise discipline and control over the hundreds of thousands of Indians in East Asia, to distribute his propaganda, to collect the funds which the Japanese would not provide, and to recruit the men he needed for his army, intelligence corps and other enterprises. Practically all Indian civilians in Japanese controlled territory were ordinary members of the I.I.L. - they had little choice. Most of them are likely to have been infected, thougth in lesser degree, with the same confidence in Bose and pride in his achievements as has been noted on the part of the INA in para 1(a) above. It is, however, only the noticeably enthusiastic among them that seem to deserve particular attention; for the most part these were the usual type of professional agitator-politician, corrupt, unscrupulous, on the make for power and money. They went into the business for what they could get out of it, with "patriotism" as a secondary but still important motive. A few are perhaps the more dangerous for their integrity and sincerity of their misguided patriotism for the rest, the I.I.L., ordinary members and office holders alike, are no more and no less a cause for anxiety than the millions of nationalists already in India. They are generally anti-Japanese as well as anti-British. They are, more specifically, probably pro-Bose and still influenced by what they have witnessed of his work. It turns out that they have backed the wrong horse, but they would probably behave just the same again in similar circumstances.

(e) **The Miscellaneous Collaborators**—a small group who, though prompted by much the same greed for power and money as the I.I.L. politicians, worked directly and voluntarily for the Japanese. They are almost all civilians. They are probably even quicker than the I.I.L. to take Allied victories as a hint that it is time to change their tune. They are unlikely to be pro-Japanese to the extent of continuing to work for a beaten nation. And they are suspect even to the J.I.F.C. on account of their dealings with the Japanese.

Appendix - I

Report on Security Measures taken by the British against the Indian National Army during the War[1]

Chapter-I

Early Security Arrangements on Eastern Frontier–1941-43

Introduction

1. The year 1941 marks the beginning of the Japanese Intelligence offensive against India. With the fall of Singapore and the resultant wholesale surrender of over 36,000 Indian troops, the Japanese began, with the help of Cap. Mohan Singh of 1/14 Punjab Regiment and others, a concentrated attack aimed at suborning the loyalty of POW and of forming the Indian National Army which was to fight collaterally with the Japanese for the freedom of India.

2. Immediate steps by the Japanese were also taken at the same time to organise "Contact Parties" of suborned PW who carried out front-line fifth column propaganda activities. These attempts were continued by the Japanese through-out the British withdrawal from Burma in 1941-42 and with the halting of the enemy on the N.E. frontier of India, a new problem arose, namely, the infiltration into India itself of espionage, sabotage and propaganda agents mainly recruited from Indian P.O.W. Opportunities for the despatch of agents were too simple among the constant stream of refugees, stragglers and escapees from the Burma withdrawal, and the discrimination between genuine refugee and "agent provocateur" became one of the major problems facing security and Intelligence authorities in India. The difficulties of this problem were re-inforced by the allied danger that specially trained agents would also be despatched to India by sea and air as well as by land.

---

1. F. No. 601/ 12539/H.S.

3. The failure of Mohan Singh's efforts and the arrival in June 1943 of Subhas Chandra Bose increased the problem still more. With his arrival in the Far East the activities of the Indian Independence League increased and at the same time the strength of the Indian National Army was augmented by the recruitment of Indian civilians. More and larger espionage schools were opened for the mass production and despatch of agents into India.

4. **Immediate Counter Measure In India**

Immediate measures to prevent the entry of agents into India through the evacuee/refugee stream were planned by military authorities in India (D.M.I.) in conjunction with the civil authorities (DIB) supported by both War and Home Department of the Government of India. Planning visualised the formation of forward refugee camps on the Indo-Burma border with a centralised or Base camp in Bengal. Although these camps were to be mainly relief and medical aid camps for refugees, the extreme urgency of establishing immediately and at the same time an efficient organisation for the examination and interrogation of refugees was emphasised.

5. In consultation with HQ Eastern Army and HQ 4 Corps, the dispositions of relief camps were arranged on the main refugee exit routes on the N.E. border of India. The welfare element of such camps was supplied by the Department of Indians Overseas and was supplemented in all case by an efficient security and interrogation element supplied by and wholly responsible to the military authorities.

6. Refugee camps were immediately (spring of 1942) located as follows—

   (a) Advanced Camps—Ukrul, Kusom Khulan, Palol, Phakekedzumi.

   (b) Collection Centres—Kohima, Imphal, Bishenpur.

   (c) Base Camp—Silchar, Margherita, Dimapur, Chittagong.

7. **Refugee Welfare/Security Scheme 1942**

Forward planning with the object of combining welfare and security responsibilities had the following three stages:-

   (a) Refugees would first be contacted at the military outpost line and it would then be the responsibility of local military authorities to see that they reached the advanced relief camps in the advanced camp line (see para 6(a)).

(b) On arrival at the Advanced Camp, refugees would then be sent to Collection Centres for food, medical relief etc. and would subsequently be despatched to Base Camps. Transport facilities for refugees would be the responsibility of the welfare organisation controlled by the Deptt. of Indians Overseas. Security requirement, namely, the provision of escorts between the advanced and base camps, would be a military responsibility.

(c) On arrival at Base camp the security element would take control of the interrogation and examination of all refugees, and the final segregation of special cases or release of non-suspect refugees.

8. **Formation of Advanced Forward Interrogation Centres, Main Forward Interrogation Centre, and Combined Services Detailed Interrogation Centre, Delhi**

(a) Since the organisation referred to in para 7 above and administered in the main by the Department of Indians Overseas was essentially a welfare organisation, it was logical, in order to maintain a similar efficiency of security, that security camps should be organised to work collaterally with the welfare camps. The main security requirement was the examination and interrogation of all refugees. Security camps or examination centres were, therefore organised at all Base Welfare Camps. The original suggested staff for such camps was:-

One gazetted police officer (preferabley Burma Police),
Three Inspectors or Sub-Inspectors of Police with requisite clerical staff One Military Officer. . .

(b) Examination centres were set up at the following Base Welfare Camps and at the Collection Centre at Imphal :-

Margherita

Dimapur

Silchar

Chittagong

These centres were the forerunners of what were later termed Advanced Forward Interrogation Centres.

(c) In order to avoid congestion at these camps, when suspects were eliminated from the main refugee non-suspects stream, it was essential that there should be one Central Examination Centre to which all suspects requiring further examinati-

should be sent. Action to establish and equip this Centre was taken by the DMI, and the Combined Services Detailed Interrogation Centre was organised in the Red Fort, Delhi. This centre was staffed with selected police and military personnel and with its formation and the advanced interrogation centres already in position, the Security plan for the N.E. frontier of India was completed. The important work of segregating and finally classifying suspect refugees on the basis of interrogation reports was the first step taken to counter-act the influx of Japanesse agents into India. This machinery, installed towards the close of 1942, was working smoothly and efficiently by January, 1943.

9. **Interrogation of Refugees and Escapees**

Formation of HQ Security Corps Functions of Forward Interrogation Centres—1942–43

(a) Towards the end of 1942 arrangements were made by the DMI to attach to HQ Eastern Army an Intelligence officer who was given the task of co-operating the work of the Forward Interrogation centres which had been established in Eastern Army Area, and of co-ordinating also the security arrangements with the officer-in-charge of the organisation set up by the Deptt.of Indians Overseas.

(b) It was also arranged that FIC's would work under the control of HQ Eastern Army, who would be responsible for decdiding their locations dependent on the swing of operations, and for the distribution of information to civil and Military authorities in Eastern Army Area. The staffs of the FIC's were also impressed to maintain close liaison with the local Provincial police. Control of FIC staff, was a GHQ responsibility, as the staffs of these centres would remain on GHQ establishment and would in all cases be regarded as forward detachments of the combined Services Detailed Interrogation Centre, Delhi.

(c) The responsibilities of FIC's were to interrogate all refugees and escapees with a view to :-

(i) Obtaining further information of immediate operational value. This information would be passed without delay to the nearest military HQ for onward despatch to HQ Eastern Army.

(ii) Obtaining information likely to be of value to the civil security authorities.

(iii) Selecting individuals civil and military for detailed interrogation at the Combined Services Detailed Interrogation Centre, Delhi. This would in all cases be done when a man was suspected to be an enemy agent, or where an individual held considerable information likely to be of operational value to GHQ i.e. information about enemy occupied territory whether political, economic or military; or where there were strong suspicions regarding and individual which could not be resolved locally.

(**N.B.** - In all cases, before suspects were despatched to CSDIC from FIC's permission from GHQ(GSI(e)) was first obtained. The object was to control the fluidity of CSDIC holdings as accommodation in Delhi for interrogation purposes was limited.

(iv) Maintaining records of all who pass through the interrogation centre in such detail that individuals, military or civilian, may be traced should subsequent interrogation be considered desirable in view of fresh evidence concerning their activities.

(d) **Formation of HQ Security Corps and Main F.I.C. —**

As the numbers of refugee suspects increased the work of holding them at FIC's prior to sending them to Delhi became more difficult. To meet the problem a Main FIC was established outside Calcutta with its own suspect holding centre. Suspects were sent direct from FIC's to main FIC/Security Corps for holding, prior to being forwarded to CSDIC Delhi. Main FIC was controlled by HQ Eastern Army and ultimately became HQ Security Corps (see para 9(a)).

10. **Principles for preliminary classification by security Corps/FICs further function of FIC's—**

(a) Security corps with its HQ in calcutta was placed under the general control of DMI GHQ and under the control of HQ Eastern Army. Security corps was formed to man up to five FICs only.

(b) In detail the staff of each FIC consisted of :-

1 Gazetted Police Officer

1 Military IO

4 Inspectors or Sub-Inspectors

1 Head Clerk
2 Steno's
1 Record Keeper
2 Typists
5 Orderlies

(c) Escorts for use between check point on the frontier and FIC's, were also provided as follows:-

1 Inspector
2 Head Constables } per F.I.C.
20 Constables

(d) In addition for escort duties between FICs and CSDIC the following were provided :-

16 Head Constables
80 Constables

(e) **Principles of classification by FICs**

(i) **In the check points refugees and escapees were interrogated and sorted into two categories**

Suspect and non-suspect. Non-suspects were directed to the Base Refugee Camps. Suspects were searched and all documents, money, weapons, and personal effects were bundled and listed and sent with the suspect escort to the nearest FIC. Any information of immediate operational importance was immediately passed to the nearest military HQ.

(ii) All refugees and escapees who arrived at FIC were interrogated and classified on the following principles :-

(a) **Whites**—Those whose loyalty was not in question.

(b) **Greys**—Those who were subject to Japanese INA/IIL propaganda and were affected but who were not considered to be fundamentally disloyal.

(c) **Blacks**—Those whose loyalty was definitely in question and who were regarded as a potential danger to security.

(iii) **CSDIC Priorities**— Suspects were sent to GXDIC at Delhi according to the following priorityies :-

(a) All Blacks

(b) All these to whom attached suspicion which could not be resolved locally.

(c) All these (whether White or Grey) who appeared to hold detailed information likely to be of value to GHQ or the Government of India or Burma.

11. **Disposal of military and Civilian personnel classified 'White' and 'Grey' —**

(a) Whites

(i) Military—These were returned to Begtl Centres/Depots

(ii) Civilian—(Other than Burmese)—These were relensed unconditionally

(iii) Burmese civilians mostly were refugees and were disposed of by the Refugee organisation.

(b) Greys

(i) **Military**—Pending the establishment of a reconditioning camp they were returned to Regtl Centros/Depots.

(ii) **Civilian**—These were detained until receipt of orders from the Director, Intelligence Bureau, Home Department, Government of India.

12. **Escorts**

(a) All Blacks and Greys, whether Civil or Military were escorted during transit both in forward areas and when sent to Delhi for interrogation by CSDIC.

(b) Military Greys were placed in open arrest; military Blacks in close arrest.

(c) Civilian Blacks including Burmese were kept in custody. Between Advanced Camps and FICs they were in law subject to an order under rule 129 Defence of India Rules or its State counter–part.

(d) Escorts proceeding to Delhi in charge of suspects brought with them the orders under Defence of India Rule 26 (later superseded by Ordinance IV of 1944) passed by the Officer–in–charge of the FIC covering the prisoners in their charge.

N.B. All Security Corps staff, including escort personnel, were empowered by War Deptt of Government of India to arrest without warrant.

13. **Particulars of refugees and escapees – Interrogation reports—**

(a) Full particulars of all refugees and escapees interrogated by FICs were maintained and recorded. Copies of particulars of civilian Whites and Greys who were allowed to proceed to their homes in India were forwarded together with their interrogation reports to :–

(i) CID of the Province or Resident of the State to which the individual was proceeding.

(ii) DMI GHQ New Delhi.

(iii) HQ Eastern Army.

(b) Particulars of military 'Whites and Greys' who were sent to Reconditioning Camp (or in the interim to their Regtl Centres/ Depots) were forwarded together with their interrogation reports to :–

(i) DMI GHQ

(ii) HQ Eastern Army

(iii) OC Recondition Camp or Regtl Centre/Depot to which the individual proceeded.

(c) FICs were in all cases sent copies of CSDIC reports on individuals forwarded by them for further interrogation.

14. **Suspect Currency** —

(a) The following general principles were observed regarding all Indian currency notes brought into India from Enemy Occupied Territory by individuals passing through FICs and then Check points.

(i) All Indian currency notes were taken out of circulation.

(ii) All currency reasonably suspected of coming from enemy sources was confiscated.

(iii) A man was permitted to retain the equivalent value in fresh currency of any currency notes confiscated under (b) above.

(b) FICs were held responsible for determining whether currency brought in originated from enemy sources or not. Their opinion on this point was recorded in the interrogation report of the man concerned.

(c) The actual Indian currency notes brought in from Enemy Occupied Territory were despatched by the OC FIC to the Manager, Reserve Bank, Calcutta.

(d) The final paragraph of each FIC interrogation report forwarded to GHQ contained full details of the serial and index numbers of all Indian currency notes of Rs 10/– denomination or more, recovered from each individual, as well as the circumstances in which they came into his possession.

(e) The above applied equally to military and civilian personnel passing through FICs.

(f) Japanese currency was in all cases confiscated.

15. **Indian Refugees arriving ex China**

(a) All Indian refugees arriving from China were the responsibility of HQ Security Corps. In all cases the following information was required before the arrival of the Refugee :–

(i) Army Number Not for civilians

(ii) Rank

(iii) Name

(iv) Unit

(v) Father's Name

(vi) Village

(vii) District

(viii) Occupation – Not for military personnel

(ix) Expected date of arrival in Calcutta

(b) In all cases Assistant Military Attache Kunming , telegraphed to Security Control, Calcutta, giving advance information of the individual arrival.

Chapter II

Security Arrangements against INA – 1943 - 1944

1. **Review of events covering the end of 1943 and the year 1944**

(a) By the end of 1943 the Refugee problem, assisted by the welfare and Security machinery organised for its speedy regulation and conclusion, had almost resolved itself. The security machinery, however, with the experience of two years' training, remained to tackle the larger problem which lay ahead, namely the apprehension of fully trained enemy agents recruited from P.W. and Indian civilians. The security not on the N.E. frontier was slightly modified in the light of our operations, but the principle of having advanced FICs as front line check points feeding Main FIC and ultimately CSDIC, Delhi, remained as before, FICs were located as near to Corps HQ as possible and worked in close conjunction with corps 'I' Staffs.

(b) The INA as fighting force did not make its appearance until the

Arakan operations of February 1944, and the Manipur Campaign March – July 1944. In these operations the INA did not engage in independent action but acted mainly in a reconnaissance/intelligence role, or in certain instances as guerilla units in conjunction with the Japanese forces.

(c) Despite the apprehension of a certain number of INA suspects during the end of 1942 and 1943, the main difficulty faced by intelligence and Security staffs both in GHQ and lower formations including CSDIC and Security Corps was the initial lack of detailed information regarding the INA, its strength, composition, methods of training, equipment etc. While considerable information had already been gleaned from captured agents concerning espionage training schools, none of these agents were able to furnish anything more detailed than hearsay reports regarding INA activities generally.

Operations commencing towards the close of 1943 however revealed the location of INA personnel on the N.E. frontier and their subsequent aprehension or surrender gave a considerable amount of new and detailed information which proved excellent foundation for framing a new, or modifying the existing, security/intelligence policy directed at counteracting the INA danger.

2. **1944 – Stabilisation of Security Policy classification and Disposal of INA suspects – military and civilian**

(a) The beginning of the year 1944 produced ample evidence that the Japanese intelligence offensive was being prosecuted with increasing purpose and vigour. More attention was devoted to deep infiltration by agents who had received considerable detailed training at one of the many major 'I' schools sponsored by the Japanese. In addition it was clear from information gained from apprehended agents that plans were already being made for the fifth column employment of INA personnel in the capacity of "stay behind" agents in territory liberated by the Allies in their advance.

(b) At the same time, the beginning of 1944 witnessed the first commitment of the INA as a fighting force in Burma. The first division of the INA accompanied the Japanese both in the Arakan and later in the Manipur Campaign. The end of this campaign, which saw the debacle of the first INA Division, was naturally marked by much important information obtained by means of interrogation of captured or surrendered members of the INA's., and the acquisition of a quantity of INA documents. this information proved invaluable as working foundation for stabilising existing security policy relativing to the INA and for the subsequent classification and disposal of PW who had joined the INA and had either been captured by our forces or surrendered to our forces during the British advance in Burma.

3. **Stabilisation of Security Policy relating to INA Procedure for Final Disposal of Indian, Gurkha and Burmese P.W. recovered from the Eastern Front – 1944**

(a) The apprehension of INA suspects made it increasingly clear that a single comprehensive directive covering all aspects of the problem should be issued to all Armies/Commands (with sufficient copies to Regimental Centres/Depots) for guidance as to the policy for classification and disposal of INA men. Up to the end of 1943, policy on these matters had been dictated by intelligent surmise rather than by experience and it was now essential that the number of letters/directives which had been issued should be co–ordinated into one general policy letter which would meet the demands of all concerned with the problem, which was enhanced by the speed and success of our own operations in Burma.

(b) In April 1944 a comprehensive directive together with draft Indian Army Order (IAO 943/44) was issued to Armies/ Commands and lower formations embodying all previous policy regarding the return to India of P.W. recovered from Japanese hands, and dictating revised instructions based on current experience and information. This directive and IAO co–ordinated also the work of FICs. HQ Security Corps and CSDIC, and centralised the final classification and disposal of INA personnel military and civilian, their responsibilities being vested in GHQ. The attached chart showing the procedure for the disposal of military personnel (and applying generally to civilian suspects) became the last word in this matter until May 1945 when the work of leading with the military INA problem decreased manifestly on the "I" side increasingly becoming an "A" responsibility. In other words, from that time, the security aspects of the problem were overshadowed by the disciplinary factors.

4. **Preventing public statements by recovered P.W.**

The following instructions, which had previously been stressed, were again issued in 1940 by GHQ to all Armies/Commands/ Formations. Local Commanders were instructed to arrange for copies to be displayed conspicuously at all ports, aerodromes and other places where returned P.W. and stragglers might land.

"All ranks who escape from enemy hands are warned that they are forbidden without the express sanction of GHQ to publish in any form whatever, or communicate either directly or indirectly to the Press any account of their escape or experience prior to repatriation, and they will be held responsible for all statements contained in communications to friends which may subsequently be published in the Press or otherwise. This order applies equally to broadcasts, scripts etc., prepared for private circulation, to loose talk, publication in regimental journals etc. In the case of personnel arriving in India, the first military authority to whom they report will bring the above to their notice and obtain a signed statement that they have understood it."

These instructions were published quarterly in unit orders.

5. **Important aspects arising from GHQ Security Policy 1944 relative to the INA**

(a) **Procedure adopted on recovering Allied PWs**

Before any action was taken on the disposal of returned P.W. or stragglers when apprehended by forward patrols or outposts in operational areas, such individuals were, in all cases, thoroughly searched by the officer or NCO in charge of the party, who also listed in duplicate all personal effects, documents, currency and weapons. After signing and dating the lists the officer–in–charge despatched all effects and lists with the individuals under suitable escort to the nearest unit commander giving him at the same time a detailed report of the circumstances under which the individual came into his hands, (i.e. whether he reported himself or was apprehended), together with the number, rank, and name, of the person(s) whofirst confacted the individual(s) (s). The unit commander then checked and endorsed lists and prepared, if this was not already done, a certificate of "apprehension" or "surrender" as specified in IAO 358/44. On completion of this detail the individuals concerned were then despatched to Formation HQ for operational interrogation, and thence to the nearest FIC where normal interrogation was carried out. The certificate of apprehension or surrender was significant as being invaluable when legal action was to be taken by military courts at some subsequent date. The form when completed was in Court of Law and would not necessitate the summoning of witnesses to attend such courts for the purpose of establishing the place, date and the fact of 'apprehension' or surrender.

(b) **Procedure for Quick Release P.W.**

(i) It was natural in the course of operations in Burma that from time to time there were cases when small bodies of our troops or individuals fell into the hands of the enemy and after a brief period in Enemy Occupied Territory managed to rejoin their own units while the later were still in forward areas.

(ii) It was equally natural that certain modifications to the existing procedure should be made with regard to these men (who are adequately described as 'Quick Release P.W.') on grounds of norale and operational expediency, and that they should be allowed as far as possible to rejoin their active units on recovery.

(iii) "Quick Release P.W. were defined typically therefore as follows :–

(a) Men who had been in Japanese hands for a short period (say a month), and who had, under compulsion or otherwise, agreed to undertake an INA mission and had been sent to our lines with this object in view.

(b) Men who had genuinely succeeded in escaping from Japanese hands soon after capture.

(c) Men who during operations had made purposeful hide–out in the jungle; and who after rejoining our forces, had claimed that they had escaped from Enemy Occupied Territory.

(iv) While both GHQ and HQ Fourteenth Army felt that there was an element of danger in accepting any of the three types without careful interrogation, it was agreed that in all cases where unit COs were fully satisfied as to the loyalty of the individual and wished their continued service under their command, they should indicate this when sending men back to FICs at Corps HQ OCs FICs were instructed that in all cases as far as was practicable, "Quick Release P.W." should be given priority of interrogation, and if such interrogation corroborated the unit COs opinion, the men would be returned to forward unit under orders issued by HQ Fourteenth Army and HQ Corps concerned.

(c) **Courts of Inquiry on individuals who escaped from Enemy Occupied Territory**

Although this matter was entirely one for the Adjutant General in India mention of it was made as a general instruction at the same time as the security and disposal directive was issued by the DMI India Command. Instructions laying down principles for the holding of Courts of Enquiry on individuals in or escaping from Japanese hands were published in IAOs (IAO 944/44).

Briefly these principles were as follows :–

(i) An immediate Court of Inquiry could be held without prison reference to GHQ on VCOs IORs who were known deserters, or who believed to have deserterd, or who disgracefully surrendered to the enemy.

(ii) Such Court of Inquiry would be held under the orders of the Bde/equivalent commander provided he was satisfied :–

(a) That useful evidence was available.

(b) That there was a risk of such evidence ceasing to be available if reference was first made to GHQ.

(c) That Security would not be prejudiced by the holding of such a Court.

(iii) Under no circumstances could a Court of Inquiry be held on an officer except under the orders of GHQ.

(d) **Certain factors which subsequently modified principles for holding Court of Inquiry**—It was subsequently considered undesirable that any Court of Inquiry should be held without prior reference to GHQ for the following reasons :–

(i) In order that individuals who had been in Japanese hands should not be brought into contact with other troops more than was absolutely necessary, and in order to avoid possibly dangerous publicity.

(ii) In order that publicity in regard to persons still in Enemy Occupied Territory and who were reported to have behaved treacherously etc might be avoided.

(iii) Because of the fact that once a Court of Inquiry reported adversely upon a VCO/IOR his pay, including all family allotment ceased unless Government orders to the contrary were obtained. It was considered that it might in many cases be useful to keep this liability to cessation of emoluments in a state of suspension by deferring the holding of Court until the appropriate moment.

(iv) Regarding para 5 (c) (i) above, even where the facts of any such incident were apparent to many people in the unit, Bde Comds/equivalent were impressed that it might nevertheless be best in the interests of security to replace a Court of Inquiry by a special investigation by security staff after discussing the matter frankly with the VCOs of the unit concerned.

(e) **Disposal of Recovered P.W. and civilians by classification** :–

(i) **The DMI/DIB Committee**

(a) A Committee of representatives of the DMI and DIB had been constituted as early as April 1943 in order to make final recommendation for the security classification of INA suspects both military and civil. The Committee sat once a week and was presided over by the Deputy Director, Intelligence Bureau, Home Department, Government of India. Included in the Committee were the DDMI (S) GHQ, a representative of CSDIC and representative of the Adjutant General's Branch Legal Section (AG PS 7).

(b) It was at no time possible to interview the INA suspects (JIFs) personally, and the Committee worked from the interrogation Reports furnished by CSDIC and the Forward Interrogation Centres.

(c) Security gradings were as formerly Black, Grey and White according to their actual or potential danger to security.

(ii) **Principles for Disposal of Military and Civilian Suspects –1944**

Classification	Definition		Action
White	All individuals whose loyalty and morale are not, or are no longer, affected.	(i) (ii)	**Military** Direct to Regtl Centres/ Depots or to Regtl Centres/Depots after brief reconditioning at Holiday Rest Camp, Sabathu.
			Civilian Direct to their homes.
Grey	The classification indicated that although an individual's loyalty and/or morale was considered to have been affected, he was not considered to be fundamentally disloyal.		**Military** Sent to Holiday Camp for Course of 3 months recon-ditioning. Thence as White to Centres.
			Civilian Restriction to their homes under Ord III of 1944 under orders of HD G of I.
Black	All individuals whose morale is permanently affected and who are considered to be fundamentally disloyal and danger to security.	(i) (ii)	**Military** Discharge and Detention under Ord IV of 44 under orders of W.D. If sufficient evidence became available trail by SGGM or under the Enemy Agents Ordinance, or the military operational Army (Special Powers) Ordinance 1943 (Ordinance XXXVII of 43), or other Civil legislation.
			Civilian Detained under Ord IV of 44 under orders of War Department, Government of India.

Chapter III

Security Arrangements against INA 1944–45

This chapter describes the further formulation and stabilisation of Disposal Policy in INA regarding the following : –

(a) Policy regarding military 'Blacks' ,

(b) Policy regarding military 'Greys' ,

(c) Policy regarding military 'Whites'

1. **Policy regarding military 'Blacks' Attock Fort**

(a) **Principles**

(i) The guiding security principle relative to military 'Blacks' was to ensure that their return to India from Enemy Occupied Territory was kept SECRET from the Enemy, and in order to effect this it was essential that they should on their arrival in India be denied all communication with outside contacts. It was also considered most undersirable from the security aspect that it should be generally publicised that a person previously posted as "missing" or "P.W." had returned to India, but was not at large.

(ii) Furthermore open dismissal from the Army of military 'Blacks' would automatically involve less of family allotment, and it was considered that such action might have an adverse effect on morale, and consequent repercussions on recruitment.

(b) **Detention Orders** :– Detention order for the holding/ incarcerating of military 'Blacks' were originally issued by Home Department of Government of India under Defence of India Rule 26. Early in 1944 Ordinance IV was promulgated. This superceded DIR 26 and orders for detention under Ord IV of 44 were issued by War Department, Government of India.

(c) **Attock Fort**

(i) It had been decided early in 1943, in order to safeguard security by withholding public knowledge that 'Blacks' had returned to India, that a secret centre should be formed for holding them. It was decided that the Attock Fort was the most suitable Centre for such individuals, and preliminary arrangements were made to alter certain portions of the Fort to house such individuals suspects as would be despatched there.

(ii) **External Precautionary Measures** – Jail Staff for Attock Fort was provided by the Punjab Government. HQ NW Army was made responsible for the provision of military guards. As soon as individuals marked 'Blacks' by CSDIC were confirmed as such by the DMI/DIB Committee, arrangements were made for their transfer from their units to the Intelligence Corps. Arrangements were also made that names and any particulars of 'Blacks' should not be disclosed in Part II orders. They were to be accounted or as "(so many) special prisoner" , and all Controllers and Field controllers of Military Accounts were requested to accept such orders in Audit without calling for the usual particulars. At the same time all relevant Part II orders were to be forwarded under Most Secret cover to the appropriate CMA or FCMA with reference to a specified Most Secret letter from MAE to these Deptts which had previously been received by them.

(iii) **Internal Security Measures**

As soon as Attock Fort was ready to receive 'Blacks' (the first batch went in June/July 43), they were discharged in Delhi and taken over from CSDIC who held them, by military escort provided by HQ Delhi Area. They then went by rail as far as Lawrencepur and were from there to Attock Fort for detention. Once installed in the Fort they were subjected to the following disciplinary and security precautions

(a) Permission to converse with each other only on parades and with cognisance of Supdt Attock Fort.

(b) Permission to sent to relatives Special Field Service Post Cards/letters, directed toSuperitendent Attock Fort, and forwarded examination under Most Secret cover to GHQ(GSI) for onward despatch

(c) For such letters special PO Box 144 was instituted, and this served as the current address for all letters going to and coming from Attock detenus.

(d) Denial of all communication with outside contacts other than by (3) above.

(e) At the same time, the Superintendent Attock Fort was instructed that he had no authoritative powers to communicate with any formation or unit regarding military 'Blacks'. All correspondence to regarding them was sent by him under Most Secret cover to GHQ Delhi (GSI).

(d) **Factor Which Tended To Compromise Attoch Security Policy**

In spite of all secrecy precautions taken between the years 1943–45 certain factors tended to compromise that secrecy or to render it more difficult to impose. Such factors, though never serious, were natural and inevitable and were briefly as follows :–

(i) Relatives of 'Blacks' detained in Attock Fort attempted to visit it or places near it.

(ii) Such relatives even visited Delhi (GSI) offices.

(iii) The companions of 'Blacks' who may have been classified 'Grey' or 'White' communicated with 'Black' and informing them of his return to India.

(iv) When such cases, occurred relatives of 'Blacks' naturally wondar why the men had not been granted leave in India prior to proceeding on "Special Duty".

(v) The policy of Secrecy was compromised when 'Blacks' were required to act as witnesses in trial, or as accused in Courts Martial. (This situation was subsequently eased towards the middle of 1945 by the transfer of 'Blacks' who were required for legal purpose's, to organise Holding and Enquiry Centres under the jurisdiction of the Adjutant General in India, and finally resolved itself and all other secrecy problems with the fall of Japan in August 1945 when 'Blacks' were removed from Attock.

(e) **Number of 'Blacks' held in Attock Fort**

(i) From the time of its inception in 1943 Attock Fort held only the following military 'Blacks' :–

53 who were discharged

66 who were undischarged.

(ii) All these men were subsequently despatched in August 1945 to Holding and Enquiry Centres at Multan or Barasat (Bengal) (Vide Para (d) (v) above.

2. **Policy regarding Disposal of Military Greys**

(a) **The Holiday Rest Camp, Sabathu/Multan – Reconditioning Policy**

(i) **Origin**—With the progress of operations on the Burma Front in 1942 and the recovery of Indian and Gorkha P.W. from Enemy Occupied Territory, it was decided to form a special security centre for these P.W. classified 'Grey' by FICs or CSDIC. The camp was organised in the guise of a Holiday Rest Camp at Sabathu, Simla Hills, and began operating in December 1942, moving to Multan Cantt in October 1944.

(ii) **Purpose.** The classification 'Grey' as opposed to 'White'/ 'Black's was applied to all P.W. who because of their experiences while in enemy hands were physically and mentally of low morale, but who at the same time were not considered to be fundamentally disloyal. The aim of the Rest Camp was, therefore, to bring such individuals back to normal before they were permitted to return to their Regt/Centres/Depots, or to proceed on leave.

(b) **Essentials of reconditioning process**

These were as follows : –

(i) Complete Rest and adequate medical supervision.

(ii) Good food.

(iii) Adequate amenities, radio, cinema, lectures.

(iv) War-time welfare education.

(v) Settlement of domestic problems, pay, allowance etc.

(vi) Facilities for sport.

(vii) Sufficient military parades at discretion of Comd Centre to restore gradually martial spirit and beaming.

(c) **Control and administration.**

The Holiday Rest Camp was joint DMI/AG responsibility. For general administration and control, the comd dealt direct on the following subjects :–

(i) With MI Dte GHQ—On all security matters and intake, length of stay and final disposal of recovered P.W.

(ii) With AG's Branch GHQ—for provision of staff and administration problems.

(iii) With Army/Command through normal channels – for provision of amenities, special funds etc, and matters of local administration.

(iv) With Regtl Centres/Depots/Record Offices – regarding matters of pay, allowances, next of kin, records of individual recovered P.W., etc.

(d) **Progress statements**

(i) After its inception in early 1943, the number of "patients" increased from an average of 40 percent rise in September 1943 to 150 in early 1944, with a definite anticipation for further increase. By June 1944 the number of 'Greys' per course averaged 500, and by the end of 1944 the total number of 'Greys' who passed through the reconditioning course numbered roughly 1500. All these men were returned on the conclusion of their course to their respective Regtl Centres/Depots as 'Whites'. (Adverse Reports on such men were received from Centres/Depots on 2 cases only).

(ii) Originally organised for the treatment of 'Greys' from the Eastern Front (Burma) the Camp also catered for all 'Greys' including those recovered from the European Theatre and South–West Pacific.

(iii) Because of the great numerical increase of 'Greys' the Camp was moved from Sabathu to Multan in October 1944. The original site of the camp at Sabathu remained however with a small staff for the treatment of medically unfit 'Greys' and as a summer resort for the treatment of Gurkhas and 'Greys' from other hill tribes for whom the climate of Multan was not considered suitable.

(e) **Reconditioning Period**

The course for any individual P.W. lasted roughly from 5/8 weeks, at the end of which time the Command submitted a Confidential Report on the individual to MI Ate HQ with the recommendation that he should be sent on leave prior to his return to Regtl Centre/Depot. the confidential Report was in all cases to be closely studied and if no further information had come to light which might change the individual's classification, or prolong his stay in the Rest Camp, the Commands recommendation was accepted and disposal instructions were accordingly issued by GHQ.

(f) **Change in Policy – March/May 1945**

(i) The successful and continued progress of our operations towards the close of 1944, and the wholesale recovery, surrender or apprehension of INA personnel necessitated alterations in the existing treatment of 'Greys'. Because of the large numbers coming through from FICs to HQ Security Corps, the impossibility of holding them by Security Corps and the inability of the Holiday Rest Camp to accept them because of lack of accommodation, it was agreed by DMI/AG that 'Greys' should proceed direct from HQ Security Corps to Regtl Centres/Depots. In this respect 'Greys' would be treated in the same way as 'Whites', and would, on arrival at Regtl Centres/Depots, proceed on leave. In all cases their leave certificates were endorsed "recovered P.W. classified 'Grey' but to be treated as 'White'".

(ii) This change in policy did not immediately affect reconditioning at the Holiday Rest Camp, but out of it there developed a new category of individual namely 'Dark Grey' (A note on this classification is made later)

(g) **General Results of Change in Policy** – May 1945 **Affecting 'Greys'**

The major results from this change of policy were as follows :–

(i) GOC–in–C HQ Eastern Command now had authority to dispose of 'Whites'/ 'Greys'/ 'Dark Greys'. Whites/Greys were despatched to Rettl Centres/Depots, Dark Greys to the Holiday Rest Camp, Multan. In all cases of 'Dark Greys', the classification was first confirmed by GHQ DMI/ DIB Committee before the man concerned moved to Multan.

(ii) Interrogations at HQ Security Corps were undertaken on group basis, as a high proportion of any particular group as resource followed being selected for individual and detailed interrogation. Group reports were issued and contained a list of the persons covered by them, and HQ Security Corps at the same time quoted the reference of the individual reports of any member of the group selected for detailed interrogation. Group reports also showed classification and disposal of the group concerned.

(iii) Categories despatched to CSDIC

(a) Individuals indicated by name by the Central Security authorities.

(b) All individuals who held a commission in the Indian Army other than a VCO commission.

(c) Any individual who held commissioned rank in the INA.

(d) Any 'Blacks'.

(h) **'Greys' of the indigenous races of Burma—**

Men classified 'Greys' and belonging to the indigenous races of Burma did not at any time proceed for reconditioning to the Holiday Rest Camp, Sabathu/Multan. In all cases they were despatched for treatment (similar to that received by Indian Army personnel at Sabathu/Multan) to the Burma Regtl Centre, Hoshiarpur.

(i) **General consideration covering re–posting of 'Greys'**

(i) The general security principle governing the reposting of 'Greys' after they had retuned from leave to Regtl Centres/Depots as 'White' was that as far as possible they would not be posted to any unit which was proceeding to an operational area. (All parachute units were considered as 'proceeding to an operational area' for this purpose. They would at the same time be posted away from their Regtl Centre/Depot as quickly as possible.

3. Policy regarding disposals of Military 'Whites'

(a) As soon as their interrogation was completed and classification 'White' confirmed by DMI/DIB Committee, military 'Whites' were despatched direct from interrogation centres/holding centres to their Regtl centres/Depots, from whence they then proceeded on leave.

(b) The original policy governing their further movements was that they should not be posted to any unit engaged in operations with the Japanese, and that they should on return from leave be posted away from Regtl Centres/Depot as early as possible.

(c) This policy was strictly adhered to until the middle of 1944 when certain factors rendered a change necessary. Reasons for reviewing this policy were as follows :–

(i) The progress of our operations and the existing man–power situation 1944.

(ii) The desirability of re–employing many invaluable and fully trained men (Whites') on the Eastern Front.

(iii) The morale factor – Whites were eager to return and have another crack at the Japanese.

(d) For these major reasons, both DMI and AG at GHQ agreed that military 'Whites' on their return to Regtl Centres/Depots (whether sent direct by HQ Eastern Command, or via Holiday Rest Camp, Sabathu/Multan, or via the Security holding centre, Jhingergacha (Bengal) could be reported to any unit engaged or likely to be engaged in operations against the Japanese subject to the following provisions :–

(i) OSC Holiday Rest Camp/Jhingergacha should in exceptional circumstances endorse the discharge report of military 'Whites' from the Centres, with reasons to the effect that the men concerned should not be reported to any operational unit.

(ii) OSC Regtl Centres/Depots should exclude from posting to any unit with an operational role any individual 'White' of whose morale he was in doubt, or whose reposting would, in the opinion of the OC, have an adverse effect on the unit concerned.

(iii) Main HQ "E Group", SEA and India Commands, and DMI GHQ would from time to time notify Regtl Centres/ Depots of any ex P.W. 'Whites' whose return to any operational unit would be expressly barred.

(iv) No military 'White' who had been examined by CSDIC, Delhi, would be posted to any operational unit without prior reference to any sanction of GHQ (GSI(e)). Permission for such posting would, in all, cases, be given except where the security of CSDIC might be prejudiced if the man was recaptured.

(v) No military 'White' whose personnel safety would be endangered should he again fall into enemy hands, or whose posting would prejudice security generally would be reposted to an operational unit.

4. **Further modifications to Disposal Policy regarding Military 'White' —**

(a) From the inception of disposal policy 1943–44 military 'Whites' (as also 'Greys' and 'Blacks') had been 'Central cases', i.e. to the confirmed by GHQ/DMI/DIB Committee prior to their further move or despatch. Disposal instructions were in all cases issued by GHQ.

(b) The speed of our opeartions 1944 and the mass recoveries/surrenders of PW in the Eastern Front made the existing procedure impossible and for this reason GOC–in–C HQ Eastern Command was empowered to dispose of Whites/Greys locally with the following exceptions no military 'White' could be despatched by HQ Eastern Command direct to Regtl Centre/Depot if :–

(i) He was an officer of Indian nationality

(ii) iIf he was of interest to the Central Security authorities.

(iii) if he appeared to possess operational or security intelligence of nature or degree which would make detailed interrogation worthwhile

(iv) if he appeared to have had his moral so affected, by reason of his having been long time in enemy hands or for any other cause, which would make reconditioning necessary. (N.B. 'Whites' as well as 'Greys' were sent to the Holiday Rest Camp if it was considered necessary).

5. **Military 'Whites' – Leave Procedure**

(a) On returning to Regtl Centres/Depots either direct from Jhingergacha, or via Holiday Rest Camp, Multan, Military

'Whites' were eligible for leave inaaccrodance with AI (I) 265/44. In all cases, before 'Whites' proceeded on leave to their homes, their leave certificates IAFL–1182 were endorsed "recovered PW classified White". All Provincial CIDs concerned were informed :–

(i) that the men had been recovered from Japanese hands

(ii) that they were proceeding on leave.

(b) No detailed supervision by CIDs was asked for in these cases.

(c) On their return from leave 'Whites' general behaviour and morale was discreetly observed for 3 months by Comds Regtl Centres/Depots before further action was taken by Comds to despatch them in accordance with instructions laid down.

6. **Treatment of recovered PW from South – West Pacific Areas**

(a) After the capitulation of Singapore and the downfall of Malaya in 1942 it was known that Indian PW had been despatched as fatigue parties to work for the Japanese in various islands in the South West Pacific. The total number of Indian PW who had been despatched to these islands was not known but it was anticipated that the advance allied operations in the east would gradually regain these PW and security arrangements for their reception and treatment were accordingly made by the despatch of a CSDIC detachment to Australia with its HQ at Brisbane. The object of this CSDIC section was to interrogate recovered PW as and when they returned, as briefly as possible and to arrange for their shipment to India.

(b) In Feb 44, roughly 500 Indian PW were recovered by Allied forces and from them it was estimated that roughly 4,000 more were located in islands in the South West Pacific.

(c) Of this 500, interrogation revealed that none of these men had in fact joined the INA but that they had been through the initial stages of propaganda and, apparently because of obstinacy, had been despatched away from the active INA centre in large fatigue parties to the south West Pacific islands. This knowledge formed the basis upon which guiding principles for the treatment of further South West Pacific recoveries was made.

(d) **Disposal Policy**— The policy governing the disposal of PW recovered from South West Pacific was exactly similar to that governing recovered PW from the Eastern Theatre, and the classification of 'Black', 'Grey' and 'White' applied equally. During the entire course of recovery, no more than 5% of the total number of recovered PW from these areas were 'Grey'. The reminder were despatched on arrival at disembarkation port in India to Regtl Centres/Depots. 'Greys (were despatched to the Holiday Rest Camp, Multan, for the normal period of reconditioning as provided for 'Greys' from the Eastern Theatre.

Chapter IV

The Security Threat From Europe[1]

At the same time as security policy was in process of being considered and made final by the DMI in counter acting the problems created by the Japanese "I" offensive and the INA in the East, similar policy was being framed and directed against the equally dangerous, though smaller threat, which was being developed by the Axis Intelligence machine and employed Indain PW captured in operations in the West. The outline of this development, its origin and charter were as follows—

Introductory

1. Whereas the Japanese "I" offensive was part of an organised and regulated plan which had been carefully prepared in advance, the Italy/German counterpart seemingly originated as a piece of extempore inspiration, if not as an afterthought. The early Axis victories in France in 1940 had gained for them a considerable number of Indian PW whose morale deceased proportionately with each Allied set-back. At the same time in both Italy and Germany there were Indian civilian elements, who, though not at the time pro-Nazi, were certainly anti-British. In spite of this ready material for an immediate "I" offensive in 1940, no serious or concerted attempt was made to forge a fifth column weapon similar to the one operating against the Allies in the East. A hint that Indian PW might to profitably used that revealed itself later in when all the personnel of 22 AT Coy RIASC who had been PW in the battle of France were

1. For details about the formation of India logion in Germany, see T.R. Sareen, *S.C. Bose and Nazi Germany*, New Delhi, 1998.

removed in bulk to German camp for "Special treatment". At the same time it was also noticeable that the Italian Foreign Office commenced to interest itself in Indian civilians in Italy; and in their moribund societies, and from Jun 1940 to the early months of 1941 the period was one of apparent Axis planning and the harnessing of existing peacetime elements and institutions for an "I" offensive.

2. **The arrival of Netaji.**— A fortuitous combination of circumstances augured well for the Axis "I" offensive in Europe. The capture of two large batches of Indian PW in the Western desert at El Mechili in April 1941 together with a further batch during the first Tobruk campaign; the Axis experience which had been gained from studying the reactions to 'special treatments of PW taken earlier, and finally the arrival in Germany of Netaji Subhas Chandra Bose, all combined to promote in Axis minds the need for and the possibilities of a co-ordinated 'I' plan which would use as one of its medium captured Indain PW who had been "treated" and ultimately indoctrinated with Axis aspirations.

These combined circumstances led therefore to the formulation of a plan which had the following initial objects:–

(a) The systematic subversion of all captured Indian troops, by trained Propagandists and recruiters;

(b) The formation of organised Propanganda Centres; which would subsequently form fifth column unit, in the guise of military units;

(c) The exploitation of the propaganda value of such units

3. **The Influence of Subhas Chandra Bose**—

Which the German High Command was more concerned with utilising Indian PW as a trained fifth column unit to operate with Wehrmacht in its plans to advance eastwards through Persia and Afghanistan, Netaji clamoured for pledge from Hitler for recognition by him of the doctrine of independence of India, and for the training of the proposed Indian units as S.S. troops for this purpose. The Italian Foreign Office was extremely sensitive and had its own ideas of how Indian PW captured in Africa should be utilised. The German Foreign Office did not see eye to eye with the German High Command in this particular question, and the presence of the Indian leader had to be kept as a diplomatic secret to avoid contretemps. The Axis 'I' offensive, therefore, gained momentum slowly, and 1941 was a year of trial and error.

4. **The Execution Of The Axis "I" Plan 1941–1944**

Consistent with their policy the Italy/German powers executed a duel 'I' drive.

(a) Through North Africa and Italy

(b) Through Germany and France

It will be convenient chronologically to consider (a) first as this led to the ultimate formation of the IVG (Indian Volunteer Guards) and the CMI (Centre Military India) composed of subverted Indian PW; (b) led to the formation of the 950 Regt.

5. **The Axis "I" drive in North Africa and Italy**

The Italian Foreign Office had already contacted pro–Axis Indian nationals in Italy and Tripoli and had given them their task. This was based on propaganda and subversion of captured Indain PW Selected Indain pro–Axis nationals were to be employed in "walking" Indian PW camps, and would separate any Indian PW who appeared susceptible. Axis sympathisers were flown to camps in Europe, and some specially selected men were trained as propagandists and recruiters. Volunteers were called upon to join a "Free India" movement, for which temptations were offered.

Results, however, were not forthcoming in large measure. A very small party selected Indian PW were despatched Centocelle near Rome and were persuaded to join the organisation referred to earlier as the IVG in March 1942, and in Sep 42 roughly 250 further recruits formed the nucleus of the CMI at Arezzano. Time porved that neither of these units had any quality or calibre to accept a fighting role. They can, however, be described as the "founder members" of the European INA movement of HIFC (Hitler Inspired Fifth Column).

6. **The Free Indian Centre**

During 1941–42 Netaji had travelled extensively in Germany and had convinced the German High Command of his usefulness. He had been successful in his efforts to contact most Indian civilians in Europe who had pro-Axis sympathies. Although he was not given carte–blanche by the German Foreigh Office and the German High

Command, and also realised that he had failed to make himself persona grata with the Italian Foreign Office, he was able to continue with his project of securing India PW reinforcements for his anti–British organisation in Germany. A "Free Indain Centre" was established in Berlin in mid–1942 under the aegis of the German Foreign Office with its own funds and facilities for broadcasting. (A logical extension of this scheme was the opening of a similar "Free India Centre" in Paris in 1943). Pro–Axis Indian civilians coopted by Shri Bose constantly visited Indian PW camps and maintained a forceful stream of anti–British propaganda and, although results were not immediately forthcoming, the ground was being prepared for a large scale campaign.

7. **Annaburg – Bose's Recruiting Speech 1941**

(a) In Dec 1941 Shri BOSE delivered his first recruiting speech at the Indian PW camp at Annaburg. The initial response was not great but special recruiting camps were opened at Messeritz and Frankerberg for what was to become the Free India Legion. Indian PW were sent in batches to these two camps in the hope that they would quickly succumb and join the movement. Those PW who were steadfast in their refusal to join were sôon removed to punishment camps and continued as normal PW.

(b) By July 1942, little progress had been made, there being at time roughly 150 volunteers at Frankergerg. This led to the closing down of that camp and the transfer of personnel to Konigsbruck where accommodation and training facilities were better.

(c) In August 1942 large numbers of Indian PW arrived from North Africa and these were vigorously indoctrinated Propaganda was supplemented by preferential treatment and both succeeded in bringing up the number of "volunteers" sufficiently to form 2 battalions of 10 skeleton companies which were designated 950 Regt (Legion Freies Indian). This was later expanded into three battalions each of 5 companies on the lines of a normal German Infantry Regiment.

(d) In January 1943 an attestation parade was hold Konigsbruk and an oath was taken by all members of the 950 Regt to fight for the freedom of India.

8. The 950 REGIMENT – 1943-44—

Between March – November 1943 the Regiment was transferred to Holland, though not without a certain amount of disturbance, for the news that it was proceeding on active service caused a mutiny to be attempted, which, however, proved abortive. In Holland the 950 Regiment was employed on guard duties at Civil Defence and AA gun sites manned by Germans. In August 1943 it was transferred to SW France where much the same duties were performed in the area between Bordeaux and the Spanish Frontier. During May 1944 a Special Coy (9 Coy) was formed for service in Italy. This was made up by milking other Coys, its strength being 30 Germans and 150 Legionnaires divided into Coy HQ, Mortar Detachment 18 men), and 3 platoons of 36. It was apparent that this Coy was formed mainly to test the reliability and capability of the Legion in action, as also to carry out a certain amount of propaganda work in the front line. Any success, however, which the German High Command might have visualised in promoting the "Special Coy" was negatived by the speed of Allied advance and successes.

9. 950 Regt – Commissioning of Members—

It is noteworthy that no promotions to the rank of Lieut were made up to the time of the formation of 9 Coy (May 1944). At this time a training course of about 3 weeks duration was held in Bordeaux area and was attended by 15 Indians. There had, however, been several promotions to commissioned rank between 42–43 from among original Indian PW converts. These were kept at Regt HQ in "advisory" staff appointments.

10. The Allied Counter Offensive And The Collapse Of The Axis "I" Offensive

(a) With the entry of the Allies into Italy the Axis "I" offensive against Indian PW tottered; with the Allied invasion of France it collapsed. Born out of a continued run of Axis successes, the threat of impending defeat destroyed the foundations of the Axis "I" plan and dismembered the 950 Regt.

(b) No sooner had the Allied invasion of France commenced than the German High Command hastily pulled out the 950 Regt from France. It was then that discipline within the Regt finally broke down not that it had over been very noticeable. Some

Legionnaires were disarmed and there were large scale desertions many being shot out of hand and ultimately open mutiny.

(c) **Conclusion**

When Allied forces entered Germany, the German High Command had in disgust left the 950 Regt to its own resources. Unrelated parties of 950 Regt seeking escape wandered into Switzerland and were interned, or eastwards where they surrendered to the Russians. The Regt was last identified as a body in the neighbourhood of Karlsruhe in the rear position of the Siegfried line.

11. DMI Security Counter Measures 1942–44 CSDIC Detachments At Mena And Cairo

(a) The full story of the Axis 'I' offensive, the HIFIC movement in Europe, and the 050 Regt as told in the preceding paragraph, did not come to light until the end of 1944, and although it was known that a problem similar to that of the INA in the East, was also in existance in the West, its extent, weight and character could not be gauged during the early years of the war. For this reason security measures to counter–act the HIFC problem were conectural and ultimate security machinery grew mainly out of the initial problem which was that of screening and interrogating sick prepatriates prior to their exchange through International Red Cross channels.

(b) The security needs of the exchange of sick repatriates were met by the provision of a small CSDIC Interrogation Detachment which was located at Nona (Egypt) in 1942–43. The objects of this Detachment were limited in scope and were intended primarily to cover the security aspect of repatriates, with operational intelligence as a secondary task. The constant exchange of sick personnel and their arrival at different ports led to an increase in the work of the Detachment, and to the removal of its HQ to Cairo.

(c) Policy now become firmer and the scope of interrogation was extended to PW recovered from the enemy. More time was available for details and for the categorisation of individuals as White/Grey/Black, in accordance with principles mentioned earlier for the classification of recovered PW from the Eastern Theatre. Arrangements were also made for the segregation of dangerous individuals.

12. Formation Of 'X' And 'Z' Sections Of CSDIC (India)

(a) The landing of Allied Troops in Italy demanded the revision of existing security/intelligence arrangements. To this end, an independent section of CSDIC moved in the wake of our forces, and after working in Naples, established its HQ finally at Taranto. During the Allied advance in Italy many Indian PW held in Camps at Avezzano and elsewhere and escaped, and it was the duty of 'X' Sextion CSDIC in conjuction with GHQ CMF and the Field Security Units to bring escapees in for screening and interrogation.

(b) The Allied offensive in France necessitated a similar security arrangement. A self contained section of CSDIC, India, was established in UK with sufficient "I" officers and VCOs to meet the emergency anticipated – this was to be known as 'Z' Section CSDIC India. Co -ordinationing arrangements had been previously made with both sections that as the Allies advanced the southward flow of recovered Indian PW would be covered by 'X' section and the westward flow by 'Z' Section in UK. It so transpired that desertion of about 300 men from the 950 Regt in 1944 before the Belfort Gap closed, and the rounding up of over 1000 Legionnaries in the Hagenan area necessitated a diversion of 1500 recovered Legionnaries and PW from Marseilles to 'X' section in Italy.

13. Procedure Followed by 'X' and 'Z' Sections—

On the arrival of recovered PW at these sections procedure was briefly as follows :-

(a) Their arrival and personal details were signalled to GHQ India.

(b) A preliminary interrogation report was then prepared covering their activities in Enemy Occupied Territory and a security classification made.

(c) This classification was signalled to GHQ India with a copy to HQ Embarkation CMF.

(d) While enroute to India their interrogation reports were sent by FALS to GHQ India, and disposal instructions to HQ

Embarkation Bombay Karachi were made in anticipation of their arrival.

(e) They were then despatched to Regtl Centres/Depots/Holiday Rest Camp, Mutan/CSDIC as dictated by their respective categories.

14. Stabilistaion of the Disposal Policy

With 'X' and 'Z' sections functioning satisfactorily overseas, it was necessary that detailed instructions to all Armies/Commands, and Regimental Centres/Depots should be sent making provision for the treatment and disposal of Indian recovered PW once they were returned to India. The policy governing the treatment of Whites/ Greys/Blacks was the same as that for individuals from the Eastern Theatre but was detailed as below:-

(a) Recovered India and Gurkha PW were sent, on arrival in India to the transit camp of the port of disembarkation pending disposal instructions from GHQ(India).

(b) **White**

(i) Those recovered PW classification 'White' was confirmed by GHQ (India) were despatched from the Transit Camp direct to their Regtl Centres/Depots, unless they were required for further interrogation. The confirmation of 'White' classification (for onward transmission to OC Transit camp) and to Regimental Centres/Depots concerned, as near the time of arrival as was possible.

(ii) **Disposal of 'White' by Regimental Centres/Depots**— On arriving at their Regimental Centres/Depots (whether from the Transit Camp or the port of disebarkation in India or from an interrogating centre in India), 'Whites' were sent on leave in accordance with AI(I) 265/44 and their leave certificates were endorsed "Recovered PW classified white".

(c) **Greys**—

(i) Those PW whose classification 'Grey' was confirmed by GHQ(India) were despatched by OC Transit Camp to the Holiday Rest Camp Multan, for a period of reconditioning. (The reconditioning of recovered PW from the

Western Theatre was identical with that of PW recovered from the Eastern Theatre, described earlier.

(ii) **Reclassification from 'Grey' to 'White'**— After 'Grey' had been reconditioned and their classification from 'Grey' to 'White' was confirmed by GHQ (India), they were sent on leave as soon as possible by the Comd Holiday Rest Camp, and on expiry of leave they rejoined their Regtl Centres/Depots. Their leave certificates were in all cases, endorsed as in para (b)(ii) above.

(d) **Leave notification to Civil authorities**— Ten days before an individual mentioned in para (c) above proceeded on leave, the Comd Holiday Rest Camp, Multan, (or Regimental Centres/ Depot as the case might be), if he considered that the man in question should be observed while on leave would notify the DIG ID of the province concerned giving reasons and suggestion that a discreeting watch should be kept on the man while on leave. It was, however, left to the DIG to decide that action, if any, should be taken.

(e) **Discharge of recovered PW**— If any recovered PW from the Western Theatre was discharged from the service, Comd Regimental Centres/Depots were instructed that in all such cases the DIG CID of the province concerned should be informed of the facts in advance.

(f) **Blacks**— All recovered PW classified 'Black' were sent under escort from port of disembarkation in India to CSDIC for further interrogation. Such 'Blacks' whose initial classification was confirmed by GHQ (India)DMI/DIB Committee were retained at CSDIC, as they were small in number. pending the opening of Holding and Enquiry Centres by the AG in India. (These Centres being opened in anticipation of the mass return of personnel of the 950 Regt.) They were then despatched to these Holding Centres and were not sent to Attock for detention as in the case of 'Blacks' recovered from the Eastern Theatre.

15. **The return to India of personnel of 950 Regt**—

(a) By the end of 1944 sufficient definite in formation about the scope and character of the 950 Regt had been received in India to enable DMI/DIB staffs to consider the problem adequately from the security aspect and to put forward views and recommendations. Upto this time roughly 100 suspects had been repartriated to India, and it was estimated that at least 3,000 personnel of the 950 Regt were still to arrive.

(b) Although DMI/DIB staffs had a fair amount of background history relative to certain members of 950 Regt, it was felt that the work of the DMI/DIB committee in confirmating classification (as for INA personnel), would be impossible because of the lack of interrogation reports on members of 950 Regt individually. The speed of Allied successes and of the capture of 950 Regt personnel and other PW in large numbers and their despatch to India had tended to Swamp the security machine in Europe and Indian PW were being screened in bulk and despatched to India. It was necessary therefore to plan certain agreed action which would meet the situation.

(c) Although the information held by the DMI was insufficient to deal with individual cases categorically, it formed an adequate basis from which the DMI was able to deduce generally principles for guidance in dealing with the problem. The DMI/DIB committee had considered the problem at length, and finally formulated working proposals which, it considered, combined expediency with needs of security and maintenance of discipline. These proposals were then recommended by the DMI to AG in India were accepted by the AG as a working basis for the treatment of all suspect members of 950 Regiment.

(d) **Principles formulated by DMI/DIB Committee**

(i) Officers and VCOs who had joined 950 Regiment, and those other ranks who had promoted to under-officer or officer while with 950 Regt should be recommended for prosecution, or, ir this was not feasible, for summary removal from the service, unless they could show good cause why this action should not be taken.

(ii) IORs recovered before 1 October 1944 (the date by which it was estimated 950 Regiment had withdrawn before the Belfort gap and upto which those who wished to do so had every opportunity of escaping and rejoining our forces), as a general rule should be classified 'Grey' and if they react satisfactorily to reconditioning, be reabsorbed into the Army.

(iii) IORs recovered after 1 Oct. 1944, as a general rule should be classified 'Dark Grey' and recommended for removal from the Army.

(e) It was further recommended by DMI to AG in India that the entire problem was one which should be dealt with more appropriately and efficiently from the disciplinary rather than security angle, by Court of Inquiry set up under AG's Branch to deal with individual cases. It was felt that once personnel of the 950 Regt return to India, they would represent a marked danger to morale if they were retained in their units. It was also pointed out by DMI that the principles set out in (d) above were more severe than those that had hitherto been applied by the DMI/DIB Committee to INA personnel as regards their classification but these principles were considered justifiable, because–

(i) PW in Europe had less justification or excuse for yielding to enemy pressure as, although pressure was admittedly applied, the general treatment of PW and the type of pressure was less drastic generally than that resorted to by the Japanese.

(ii) Much smaller proportion of the total yielded enemy pressure in Europe than in the far East, ie roughly 3,000 in Europe as against roughly 20,000 in the East.

(iii) The 950 Regiment was an integral part of the German Army under direct German Command; its personnel were German uniform and accepted German ranks, whereas the INA remained essentially "and Indian entity" separate from the Japanese Army under Indian and not Japanese officers, with its own uniform, ranks etc. In other words, HIFs joined the enemy ranks—the INA merely collaborated.

16. **Conclusion** The DMI principles referred to above were accepted as a working basis by the AG in India and special Holding and Enquiry Centre for all Western Theatre suspects and members of 950 Regiment was organised at Bahadurgarh near Delhi. These HIFs who were

already in India, either at CSDIC Delhi or the Holiday Rest Camp, Multan, were despatched to the Holding Enquiry Centre Bahadurgarh, were Courts of Inquiry convened by AG's Branch were held on individual cases.

Chapter – V

Transfer of Responsibility from DMI to AG in India

1. **Initial Transfer of Responsibility**

(a) The year 1945 say the initial transfer of policy relative to the disposal of INA personnel and personnel of 950 Regiment– from the DMI to the AG in India. The successful progress of Allied operations in Burma and in Europe, and the resultant mass recovery of disaffected POW, presented a clearer picture of the various aspects and magnitude of the problem which lay ahead, namely the retention/discharge/dismissal of those INA/ HIF military suspects who were in India, and those who would subsequently return.

(b) Numerically the INA/HIF recovery position upto the end of May 1945 was as follows—

(i) Arrival in India by categories

Black	257
Dark Grey	126
Grey	1145
White	1985
Total	**3513**

(ii) This total of 3513 did not include approximately 8,000 ex-INA military suspects who had been taken in Rangoon after its surrender in May 45.

(iii) Estimated Grand total of INA was 20,000

HIFs (950 Regt.)

(iv) Roughly 5000 were already in India with an estimated 2500 still to come. Arrangements were being made by AG in India for the despatch of all HIFs to a Holding and Enquiry Centre to be established at Bahadurgarh near Delhi.

Note : These figure are inclusive of all military intakes from January 1942 to May 1945.

2. **Introduction of a new category viz 'Dark Grey'**

(a) Object of the new Classification

(i) To provide for the discharge from the Army either with or without a period of rehabilitation, of persons whom it was considered undesirable to retain in military duty, but who were not a direct danger to security, e.g., personnel whose conduct while PW showed them to be greatly lacking in soldierly qualities etc.

(ii) To allow for the rehabilitation and ultimate return to units of individuals, who, though initially a danger to security, are likely to respond to reconditioning, but whose treatment would take considerably longer than that of any normal 'Grey' category.

(b) In order to separate the new category 'Dark Grey' it was necessary to amend the existing definition 'Black'. This was redefined as below—

(i) a military subject who it was considered should be brought to trial for a criminal offence.

(ii) any military subject considered to constitute so serious and permanent a threat to security that only detention would meet the requirements of security.

(iii) any civilian considered to constitute a danger to security which could only be averted by his detention.

(N.B. —The definition in (ii) above was intended to allow of the exclusion from the 'Black' category and so to avoid detention of military personnel who could reasonably be expected to react favorably to rehabilitation.

(c) **Definition of 'Dark Grey' Category**— For all FIC/CSDIC calssification purposes, the 'Dark Grey' category was defined as follows:-

(i) A soldier in respect of whom there appeared to be reasonable chance that he might ultimately become fit to a unit, subject to a period of reconditioning considerably longer than that given to a normal 'Grey'.

(ii) A solider in respect of whom it was considered that no amount of rehabilitation would be likely to make him suitable to return to a unit, and who should for this reason be discharged from the Army service with or without a period of reconditioning.

(d) **Action on the 'Dark Grey' Classification by the DMI/DIB Committee.—** The DMI/DIB committee considered the principles to be followed in implementing the new 'Dark Grey' Classifification, having particularly in view the fact that the introduction of this category necessitated a review of many cases. Military or ex-military suspects, originally classificatied 'Black', might on review be 'Dark Grey' according to revised principles. It was agreed by the DMI/DIB Committee, therefore, that a 'Black' must remain 'Black' and could not be 'Dark Grey', if:-

(i) There was reason for accepting the view that his desire to work for the enemy and for Netaji Bose, continued despite his arrest and detention. Bad post- arrest conduct, if it showed determination irreconcilability or strong anti-British feelings, would constitute good ground for taking such a view.

(ii) If he was of sufficiently high calibre to make him dangerous.

(iii) If the place to which he would report on being freed possessed special importance from the point of view of enemy interest and activities.

(iv) If he was considered to be in possession of vital information the disclosure of which would affect the war effort.

(v) If the province concerned was not prepared to accept him when at a future date he graduated from 'Dark Grey' to 'Grey'.

(e) These principles were used by the DMI/DIB committee for the review of all cases of military 'Blacks' and for the confirmation of the 'Dark Grey' classification in other cases where this was merited.

3. **Policy regarding 'Dark Grey'**

(a) It was agreed between DMI and AG that all military personnel confirmed by DMI/DIB committee as 'Dark Grey' should be sent to the Holiday Rest Camp, Multan, for a period of reconditioning, the lentth of the period recommended varying to suit individual cases. The committee's classification would also show into which of the two categories of 'Dark Grey' the man fell viz whether at the time of classification it was the intention to retain him in the service or that he should be discharged/dismissed from the service.

(b) All confirmations of 'Dark Grey' classification made by DMI/ DIB committee would be communicated to AG in India(DPS) as soon as the men concerned were despatched to the Holiday Rest Camp, Multan.

(c) AG in India (DPS) confirmed that no action would be taken by his branch on men categories 'Dark Grey', until their reconditioning period was over, and until the final recommendation of their cases,(i.e. whether he considered they should be discharged/dismissed or retained in the service) was made by Commandant, Holiday Rest Camp.

(d) It was also confirmed by AG that as soon as the Commandant Holiday Rest Camp's recommendation was known a Court of Inquiry convened by AG would be held in each case, and the decision made by the Court would govern the future movement of each 'Dark Grey' concerned.

(e) It was further agreed that forfeiture of pay for the period that a 'Dark Grey' was a PW could only be effected on the recommendation of the Court of Inquiry, the proceedings of which would be approved in all cases by AG's Branch GHQ.

(f) In order to allow for sufficient time at Regtl Centres/Depots to settle all personal and administrative affairs of 'Dark Greys' who after Court of Inquiry would be discharged/dismissed from the service, Courts of Inquiry were in all cases convened one full month before the man's rehabilitation was due to expire, the proceeding being forwarded to AG(DPS), GHQ.

4. **Reconditioning of 'Dark Grey' Treatment**

(a) The essentials for the rehabilitation of 'Dark Greys' were the same as for 'Greys' (vide para 2 page 29)

(b) It was not intended that 'Dark Greys' and 'Greys' should be kept separate, although this had subsequently to happen.

(c) Commandant Holiday Rest Camp was always informed which individuals among those he received were 'Dark Greys' and could inform his staff accordingly.

(d) It was considered undesirable to let a 'Dark Grey' know that his case was in any way different to that of other 'Patients' in the Holiday Rest Camp.

(e) The Commandant Holiday Rest Camp was in all cases informed–

(i) Of the period of reconditioning recommended by the Central classification authorities (DMI/DIB Committee) at the time of classification of 'Dark Grey' was recommended.

(ii) Which of the two classes of 'Dark Grey' any man fell into at the time his classification was made viz. whether it was the intention to retain the man in the service, or whether it was the intention to discharge/dismiss him.

(f) Commandant, Holiday Rest Camp could make recommendations to AG (DPS) modifying (e) (i) and (ii) above, before the final decision as to the 'Dark Greys' disposal was arrived at by AG.

5. **Final Transference of policy from DMI to AG in India—June 1945—**

(a) By May 1945, roughly 4,000 INA military personnel (of the estimated 20,000) were in India finally classified and held or disposed of according to their degree of security classification. At the same time, 7,000 were in Rangoon awaiting security classification and despatch to India, making a combined total of roughly 11,000 in our hands. Planning during the months January -may 1945 by DMI/Ag paved the way for the final transfer of disposal policy from DMI to AG which would govern the future legal, disciplinary and administive treatment of all INA personnel once they were in India.

(b) It was agreed by DMI/AG that once this transfer was finalised, the responsibility of the DMI would be confined solely to the production of security interrogation reports, and to the collection of evidence and material which would be passed on to the Adjutant General in India (DPS) to assist in the finalisation of all cases by Courts of inquiry convened by AG.

(c) It was logical also that a first principle of the transfer would be cancellation of all previous relevant directives/letters issued on the subject of recovered PW by DMI, and the formulation of a new comprehensive directive embodying and co-ordinating all aspects of the problem to be issued by AG, keeping in mind that the basis of the new directive would still be the old DMI security classification black/Dark Grey/Grey/White in individual cases.

(d) The final transfer of responsibility occurred in mid-June 45 after a conference of representatives of DMI/AG and was confirmed by the issue on 30 June 45 of the first AG directive governing the disposal of INA military personnel. This directive No. 98552/PSI(a) AG Branch of 30 June 45, formed the basis for all future "A" policy relative to the problem of disposal and treatment of returned PW and suspected INA recoveries, including also detailed instructions for the disposal and treatment of PW and military suspects recovered from the European Theatre.

6. **Necessity for more detailed policy by AG in India**

(a) The end of the war with Japan, the preparation of plans for the return to India of all recovered PW and the remaining suspect element of the INA, necessitated that more detailed instructions should be issued by AG in India, particularly for the guidances of Comd Regtl/Centres/Depots. These were contained in Ag Branch letter no 98664/PS.1(a) of 11 sep. 45.

Chapter – VI

Evacuation of Indian PW after the War

1. **Planning for evacuation PW from the Eastern Theatres**

(a) Security and administrative planning with the above object in view was given considerable thought and attention during the months April–August 1945 by DMI and AG in India, and a comprehensive scheme termed the "Green Service" was evolved and issued as an anticipatory instruction by mid–August 1945.

(b) Briefly, the "Green Service" may be defined as a plan for the evacuation, hospitalisation and disposal of British, Indian, Dominion, Colonial and Allied PW, including civilian internees, who would be recovered during the course of our operations, or on the termination of hostilities. In all cases individuals would be evacuated through medical channels and the scheme as a whole, although having a major and necessary security aspect, would be administered by the AG in India. AG's Welfare Camps and PW reception Centres would work with security FICs and detachments of CSIDC to be placed where and when they would be required, their location being determined by the swing of operations.

(c) It was decided by DMI and AG that persons known or suspected to have been members of the "INA" would NOT pass through the Green Service Plan. Such persons would in all cases be controlled by security detachments overseas and would be kept out of the genuine RAPWI (Recovered Allied Prisoners of War and Internees) stream.

(d) It was agreed also that civilian internees and Indian merchant seamen would be handled by the "Green Service" within ALFSEA areas only. On their arrival in India they would be taken over by Common–wealth Relations Department and Commerce Department respectively of Government of India.

(e) Green Service reception ports in India would be Madras and Calcutta. The principal Green Service Transit camp in India would be at Bangalore, with a subsidiary camp at Calcutta. Hospitals for recovered PW medical cases would be located at Bangalore, Lucknow and Secunderabad.

(f) It was also agreed that civilian members of the INA and other civilian suspected of collaboration with the enemy would not be evacuted to India unless domiciled in India and required by name by the Government of India. Such persons would not be handled by the "Green Service" in India, but would be despatched in Main FIC/HQ Security Corps, Jhingegacha (Bengal) for interrogation and disposal in accordance with existing 'I' instructions.

(g) The responsibilities of DMI were as follows–MI Directorate, India, was responsible for the security classification and any necessary interrogation of all recovered prisoners of war and civilian internees (RAPWI) who may be evacuated to India. Security classification was dependent on past records and interrogation reports where these were deemed necessary.

Interrogation could be divided into–

(i) Interrogation for tactical intelligence.

(ii) Interrogation for strategical intelligence

(iii) Interrogational respect of circumstances of capture and conduct in enemy hands.

(vi) Interrogation in respect of atrocities witnessed.

(v) Security supervision of non-Indians, where desirable.

The organisations available or required to deal with these commitments were :-

(i) FIUs (within ALFSEA area only)

(ii) S Sec CDIC(I) (detailed interrogation in cases which were of immediate operational interest to ALFSEA only.

(iii) Main FIC

(iv) CSDIC (I)

(v) 'E' Group

(vi) FS Personnel

A detachment drawn from CSDIC(I) and main FIC was made available to work wit the Green Service in India. All elements of this detachment came under command of the appropriate Green Service units for administration so as to avoid duplication of accommodation, messing, relationing etc. arrangements. The composition of this detachment was on an ad hoc basis, as required to deal with the situation from time to time.

The work of the above organisation was subject to the following factors :-

(a) Normally interrogation was carried out as follows:-

(i) Before departure from ALFSEA— Tactical Security (as necessary).

(ii) After arrival in India— conduct etc. atrocities, strategical and security.

(b) Persons known or found to be dangerous to security including all members of INA were removed from the Green Service as early as their medical condition permitted. Thereafter their evacuation was by usual channels for the disposal of suspect personnel, the Green Service having no further responsibilities in respect of them.

Responsibility For Interrogation is Sub-Divided as Under

Responsibilities	Classes of RAPWI						
	Indian Mil personnel (Apparently genuine recovered PW ex-Camps Jails etc)	**Indian Civilian internees**	**British Dominion and colonial mil personnel**	**British Dominion and colonial civilians**	**Allied military personnel**	**Allied civilians**	**British, Indian and Allied merchant seamen**
(a) Interrogation for tactical intelligence (to be carried out in ALFSEA Area)	FIU	FIU	FIU	FIU	FIU	FIU	FIU
(b) Interrogation for strategical intelligence	Det CSDIC/ Main FIC	Few, if any, exp-ected. They will be taken over on arrival in India by C.R. Depot who will supply nominal roll to DIB who will arrange interrogation if required	E Gp assisted by Detc CSDIC/-Main FIC	Will be taken over C.R. Dept on arrival in INDIA. No interrogation except in special cases when arrangements will be made.	Det CSDIC Main FIC	Will be taken over by CR Dept on arrival in India. CR Dept will supply nominal roll to DIB No interrogation except in special cases when arrangements will be made.	Will be taken over by Commerce Dept on arrival in India Commerce Dept will supply nominal roll to DIB. No interro-gation except in special cases, when arrangements will be made.
(b) Interrogation	Det CSDIC/ Main FIC		E Gp		Nil. any adverse information will be passed to Govt. concerned.		
(d) In respect of atrocities witnessed	Det CSDIC/ Main FIC		E Gp		Det CSDIC/ Main FIC		

(c) All interrogation was subject to Medical agreement that RAPWI were fit to undergo it.

2. Procedure within ALFSEA

The following procedure was followed while RAPWI were in ALFSEA.

(a) ALFSEA decided that existing interrogation organisations, i.e. FIUs were adequate to deal with interrogation. A small CSDIC(I) section ('S' Section) was also made available to ALFSEA. This section however, was intended to carry out detailed interrogation for operational intelligence and generally could give little or no assistance as regards the Green Service.

(b) FIUs and 'S' CSDIC(I) were provided with a black list by GHQ, (combined section). Persons on this list, all members of INA and other RAPWI military or civilian, who were considered to be suspect, were removed from the Green Service and dealt with under the existing arrangements for disposal of JIF personnel.

(c) All other personnel were evacuated under normal Green Service procedure to Green base in ALFSEA; ALFSEA responsibility ceased on their departure from Green Base.

3. Arrival in India—

On arrival in India personnel remaining in Green Service were disposed of as under:–

(a) All service personnel through Green channels to Green transit camps and hospitals.

(b) Civilians (except Merchant Seamen) were taken over by Commonwealth Relations Dept on arrival in India. They did not normally go to Green Reception Units. Commonwealth Relations Dept supplied a nominal roll to DIB.

It was anticipated that interrogations were only necessary in exceptional cases, when arrangements were made to bring such persons to CSDIC (I) Delhi as guests. Civilian (except Merchant Seamen) were taken over by Commonwealth Relations Department on arrival in India. They did not normally go to Green Reception Units. Commonwealth Relations Department supplied a nominal roll to DIB. It was anticipated that interrogations were only necessary in exceptional cases, when agreements were made to bring such persons to CSDIC (I) Delhi as guests.

(c) Merchant Seamen (British Indian Dominion and Allied), were taken over by Commerce Department on arrival in India. They were not normally sent to Green Units. Commerce Department supplied a nominal roll to DIB. Interrogation was seldom necessary. Where required, 'ad hoc' arrangements were made.

4. Procedure At Green Reception Centre In India

The following was the procedure at the Green Reception Centre in India:–

(a) It was the responsibility of CSDIC/Main Fic detachment to ensure that all recovered PW completed, as soon as possible after arrival, a questionnaire designed to show whether the individual possessed any intelligence of strategical or security interest, or was a witness of atrocities. The detachment was responsible for reproducing these completed questionnaires for distribution to GHQ India, to E Gp representatives at the Green Transit Camps, and in appropriate cases to the FSP who might be made available to the camps. GHQ India then sub-distributed to the appropriate security authorities where thought necessary to the interested British, Dominion, or Allied authorities.

(b) CSDIC/Main FIC detachment then proceeded to interrogate in such detail as appeared necessary, all persons whose cases justified the course. In the case of British Dominion and Colonial personnel, E Gp carried out the interrogation, but CSDIC/Main FIC detachment could be required to assist.

(c) CSDIC/Main FIC detachment classified all Indian military personnel. It would be emphasised that this was not expected to entail the individual interrogation of every man. All those classified 'White' were despatched by Green Service Regtl Centres as soon as their interrogation was complete or CSDIC/ Main FIC detachment certified that no interrogation was necessary. Suspects were despatched to CSDIC (I) Delhi or to Main FIC, Jhingergacha as directed by DMI.

(d) DPW was to arrange office accommodation and interrogation room at or adjoining Green Transit Camps. DPW also arranged facilities for holding any suspects who were picked out at the camps until they could be evacuated to CSDIC (I) or elsewhere as ordered by DMI.

(e) CSDIC/Main FIC detachment referred to DMI the case of any non-Indian whose previous activities or present attitude indicated that he might be a danger to the security of India. The detachment would also request FSP to keep such persons under unobtrusive observation. It was not thought probable that it would be necessary to place such persons under actual restraint, but if this was considered necessary, British, Dominion and Colonial military personnel were handed over to Provost and all others were segregated in the camp under local arrangements. This course was only adopted in extreme cases. Suspects who were medically unit were segregated in the Green Hospital or Green Convalescent Camp under guard.

5. **Documentation—**

(a) Green Service had to supply to GHQ (GSI (e). Six copies of lists of all persons taken into the service. As far as MI was concerned, the only information required was :–

(i) Green Service Serial Number

(ii) Name, rank, Number (Home address in case of civilians)

(iii) Unit and nationality

(iv) Place and date of recovery

(v) How recovered e.g. PW camp, work gang small party, straggler, in enemy ranks etc.

(b) Green Service also supplied to GHQ (GSI (e)) six copies of nominal roll of all parties embarked for India showing–

(i) Green Service Serial Number

(ii) Name and rank (Home address for civilians)

(iii)) Date of embarkation/emplaning.

---

1. Note (i) Asiatic civilians not domiciled in India were Not brought to India.
Note (ii) French and Netherlands subjects wre Not brought to India.
Note(iii) Civilian members of INA and other civilian collaborators with the enemy were not brought to India unless they were domiciled in India, and also demanded by name by the Government of India.

6. **Modification of the plan after 15 August 1945**

(a) The "Green Service" Plan for the evacuation of recovered PW was in operation as soon as hostilities with Japan terminated in August 1945. The speed of evacuation however was so great that DMI security resources, both overseas and in India were not able adequately to cope with the flow. There was, therefore, the inevitable danger that RAPWI and possibly INA suspects in the guise of RAPWI would arrive in India, and subsequently at their Regtl Centres/Depots, without any record of their having been interrogated overseas.

(b) In order to counteract this problem a small CSDIC detachment was despatched for location at disembarkation point Madras, with the object of screening as speedily as possible all RAPWI and detaching suspects from the RAPWI stream.

(c) As an additional precautionary measure the DMI issued instructions to Commandants, Regtl Centres/Depots to guide them in the events of men arriving at Centres/Depots without any records of previous interrogation. Briefly these instructions were as follows–

Commandants Regimental Centres/Depots should in all cases where men arrived uninterrogated

(i) Complete a nominal roll and despatch it immediately to GHQ, GSI (e). This roll was then checked individually against the suspect INA 'Blacks' List at GHQ, and instructions to Regimental Centre/Depot concerned were issued as soon as "Suspect check" was completed. Any INA suspects were then routed either to CSDIC or Jhingergacha (Bengal) for further interrogation.

(ii) Commandants Regimental Centres/ Depots were also instructed to interrogate all RAPWI briefly, with the object of finding out whether they held any information on the subject of enemy atrocities and war criminals. Where RAPWI hold such information, Form 'Q' (copy attached) was completed in duplicate and signed by the deponent. His signature was withnessed by the interrogating officer. The completed Forms 'Q' were then sent to GHQ (GSI(e).

(iii) Commands were instructed that both (i)) & (ii) above should, as far as possible, be complete prior to the despatch of RAPWI on leave.

7. **Concluding note on Security Interrogation Plan — INDIA**

(a) It had been originally estimated (and this estimation served for the future as the basis of a working figure) that of the 45,000 military personnel who were taken prisoners of war in Malaya in 1942, roughly 20,000 had susequently joined the Indian National Army. Up to September 1945 roughly 12,000 of this number had been apprehended, or had surrendered, and were in India leaving a balance of 8,000 overseas.

(b) The first principle of the Security Interrogation Plan, India, had been the elimination of INA suspects overseas form the normal RAPWI stream and the routing of INA suspects through Security and not welfare channels, to India. The responsibility that INA suspects might merge with RAPWI evacuation had not been overlooked (vide para 2 above), and arrangements to counteract this danger had been made.

(c) Evacuation of RAPWI worked consistently from September 1945 – January 1946 and by Feb 46 the problem had almost resolved itself to a matter of routine.

(d) Inevitable though it was that some INA suspects might evade all security screening both overseas and at port in India, it was gratifying to realise that of the 8,000 INA military suspects awaiting despatch from overseas to India between September 1945 – January 1946, only 263 evaded security scrutiny overseas and arrived in India as RAPWI, either at disembarkation point – Madras, where they were speedily removed from the RAPWI stream and despatched to Jhingergacha, or at Regimental Centres/Depots, from where they were despatched to CSDIC/Jhingergacha for interrogation.

8. **Conclusion**

Final treatment of all ex-PW cases by AG in INDIA in conjunction with DMI — January 1945 to date

(a) By the end of November 1945, 14,000 of the estimated 20,000 INA personnel had arrived in India and in addition to this figure 4,000 HIFs were also sent over to India. The return of these personnel and the arrangements for the subsequent return of the residue marked the last stage in the treatment and settlement of all INA and HIF cases by the Adjutant General in

India. Courts of Enquiry were set up in the AG Holding and Enquiry Centres where such personnel were sent at Barsat in Bengal, Multan and Bahadurgarh. These Courts of Inquiry dealth only with the cases of IoRs and VCDs. ICOs who had joined the INA were despatched via CSDIC to Bairagarh pending finalisation of their cases by AE and C-in-C India. A certain number of officers were also held under AG's authroty in an Holding and Enquiry Centre for officers at HQ Jumna Area Delhi Cantonment.

(b) The part played by Military Intelligence in concluding all cases was to satisfy AG that classification of individual cases was from security point of view correct before AG Courts of Inquiry were held, and also to satisfy Commands Regimental Centres/ Depots when queries or enquiries from these sources were made. Thus the collective policy of handing suspects that necessarily marked the years 1944-45, now was changed into individual policy governing individual cases, and by June 1946 the Military Intelligence responsibility for initiating action on individual cases on INA and HIFs was transferred completely to AG in India. By May 1946 all investigators held in enquiry centres had completed their work and June 1946 onwards saw merely the winding up of individual cases, with Commandant Regimental Centres and Depots.

Appendix-II

Memoirs of Lt. General Kawabe Explain Japanese Policy towards I.N.A. and S.C. Bose (Extract)[1]

Bose Starts Negotiations with Japan in Berlin

Towards the end of October 1941 a strange visitor came to the Japanese embassy in Berlin. Besides the ambassador Oshima, he was received by the military attache col. Yamamoto, who was later on became the head of Hikari Kikan. This was the first time that the two Japanese diplomats met Subhas Chandra Bose. This meeting was sought by the ambassador, who had put in the request to the German Foreign office. Col. Yamamoto had also received orders from the staff headquarter to meet Bose at the first opportunity. Bose did not show any sign of sneakines normally found in political exiles, nor did he show any puffed up attitude. His behaviour during this meeting was just like a normal human being. But one could readily feel the patriot in him. The hosts readily came to know the scholar in him, and felt that it was nothing strange that the Germans would be so much engrossed in him. For Bose also this meeting had a great significance. Taking advantage of this meeting, Bose became a regular visitor to the embassy, meeting the embassador twice or thrice a month, to whom he expressed his views and desires without any reserve. Bose also met Col. Yamamoto frequently which continued till the colonel returned to Japan just before Bose went to Japan in December the following year.

As intimacy grew between ambassador Oshima and Bose, the latter expressed his discontent over the way the Germans were handling the affairs. He revealed that he could rely only on Hitler, and even regretted his hasty step in coming to Germany. Although he had European education yet he embraced grave enimosity towards England. His grievance against

1. General Kawabe compiled the above memoirs in Japanese incorporating the account which he had already given to the foreign office publication. "S.C. Bose and Japan". The english transation of the relevant portion is included here.

Germany originated not only from the attitude of the German authorities who tried to utilize him as a tool; but perhaps from the differences in skin as well. As against this, he expressed great admiration for Japan

Bose's activities in Germany were followed with keen interest by the Japanese government and military authorities. To what extent these assessments influenced the Japanese course of action will be described in detail in later chapters.

As for Japan, 8th December 1941 was a fateful day for Bose as well. Japan's declaration of war against England, USA and Australia gave him the opportunity of realizing his long cherished goal of opening up a joint war front against England.

On 26th December, Bose suddenly rang up embassador Oshima seeking an immediate interview. Bose came to the embassy a little before midday and a meeting was held where Col. Yamamoto was also present besides the ambassador. That day Bose appeared very tense, and it was clear that he wanted to discuss something serious. It was during this meeting that Bose put forward his desire to go to Japan. He said.

"...Had Japan started war with England when I left India I would have gone to Japan at any cost. Before long Japan will occupy Malaya, and after capturing Burma its forces will reach up to the Indian border. Is there any Indian who does not want to join hands with Japan for fighting the Britishers? As the second best alternative, I have come to Germany to carry on my struggle. Now Japan has given me the chance to open my front in the East. It is of no use to remain in Germany when this unique opportunity has come. I want to fight with England even in the capacity of an ordinary soldier. I want you to convey this sincere desire of mine to the Japanese Government."

He spoke these words in German, which was not as fluent as his English; but he could put forward his point forcefully showing his firm resolution at the same time.

Till then neither the ambassador nor the colonel had at any stage suggested to Bose about going to Japan. After the outbreak of war in the East, no instruction came to the embassy on the Indian question. Again, the Germans were not at all inclined to let Bose go, whom they knew to be a great stake. Both the Japanese officials expressed their sympathy, and nothing materialized beyond prayer for success of Bose's scheme.

However, this sincere appeal of Bose moved the embassador greatly who promised to communicate this desire of Bose to Japan.

It was immediately communicated to Japan, but no reply came indeed a reply came but it was too cold and brief "the matter is under consideration at present."

After destruction of British flee* in the battle off Malaya, the Japanese forces advanced south in Malaya without meeting any resistance worth mentioning. Towards the middle of January, the Japanese forces crossed into Burma. Singapore fell by 15th February.

The military alliance concluded on 18th January among Japan Germany and Italy hardened his conviction of the success of the axis powers. Slowly news came about the formation of Indian Independence League in the Japanese held territories, as well as the raising of an army from among the surrendered Indian soldiers to fight for India's freedom. As the attitude of Japan towards these became clear, Bose resolved to take up this second front as his sphere of activity.

After the fall of Singapore, Bose vigorously pressed the Japanese ambassador to take up the case for arranging his travel to Japan.

Japan's attitude towards this was rather lukewarm. Moreover, a number of hurdles stood in the way of his going to Japan, to cross which was not sos easy. Position of the ambassador was very dedicate as Bose had placed all his reliance on him. As the German authorities were keen to utilize Bose for propaganda purpose, they were reluctant to allow him to slip out of their hands. Thereupon, the ambassador accepted the suggestion of the German foreign office and placed Bose's desire directly before Hitler. Luckily Hitler agreed adding that it was but natural for Bose to start working from South East Asia now that the region has been over run by the Japanese forces. The second difficulty was whether Japan would acceed to the demand of Bose and provide him with a base as desired by him. Letters were exchanged between Berlin and Tokyo for the next few months, and ultimately clearance for Bose's travel to Japan was obtained on principle in August. This unconcerned attitude of the Japanese officialdom not only impeded the working of the Kikane but it also hurt the feeling of Bose. The third difficulty was the problem of travel to Japan. At that time communication between Japan and German was noexistent, excepting for a few blocked breachers. Of course that was one air route still open. It was acroses soviet sky from Ukrine, the journey to carried out during night, by Lufthansa plane. Premier Tojo refused to agree with this cause saying that it would mean breech of trust against Soviet Union. A little after this the war situation in Russia worsened eliminating any possibility of air travel. Hearing that an Italian pilot had succeeded in flying to Peking. Bose went to Rome along with Col. Yamamoto and met Mussolini through the good offices of the Mussolini agreed to reserve a seat for Bose in case à second plane were to be sent to Far East. However, the Italian authorities gave up the idea, and Bose had to return to Berlin. Thus the last alternative left was a secret voyage on board a submarine. The prospect of submarine voyage was studied in the very beginning, but as neither Japan nor Germany had any surplus submarine for such a voyage, it was put into cold storage. But as air travel proved to be impossible, the interest in this was revived, and the German agreed to carry Bose in one of their submarines going to Indian Ocean side, proposing the Japanese side to send a submarine to carry Bose acroses the Indian Ocean. The Japanese side agreed somewhat, reluctantly to this proposal, and that also after some delay. When the Japanese approval was conveyed to Bose, he was besides himself with joy, and this was somewhat strange for Bose to react in such a fashion, as he could suppress his feelings easily.

As the travel was very dangerous, the Japanese authorities went as far as even ordering col. Yamamoto to accompany Bose in the journey. Bose was, however, least worried about the dangers involved. and he was busy making preparations for his journey.

It was decided that the submarine carrying Bose would leave in Feb. 1943. Just before his departure, he was accorded farewell by ambassador Oshima, where a telegram just received from the staff headquarters of Japan was delivered to him. It ran as follows, which only amused Bose:

"Please inform Bose that his coming to Japan is unconditional, and that he may have to work under other Indians depending upon after hearing this quietly Bose laughed and replied.

"I am interested only in the independence of India. For achieving my goal I am prepared to work under anybody."

The ambassador was aware of the position of Rash Behari Bose in Japan, and hinted about it to Bose. The ambassador was very much impressed by the reply Bose gave.

"I do not have any special demand from Japan. The only thing I want is to work to the extent I can.

One day in the middle of Feb. Just before the day Bose left Berlin for the submarine base in northern France, Bose gave a lunchaon party where he invited a few of his closest associates, Mufti Hussain of Syria, Gailani Afgani the exiled premier of Iraq, and Lt. Col. Higuachi who had come as military attache after the departure of Col. Yamamoto and who was assisting Bose for his voyage to Japan. Of about twelve person assembled there, the secret of his voyage was known only to Nambier, his most trusted associate, and Lt. Col. Higuachi, besides Bose himself. The Party went on as usual, and during the course of talks, Bose said that he would go to Vienna area on the following day for discovries with the infuential Indian living in the region, and that he would be away from Berlin for about a month. The talks naturally record round trip. After the party broke up. Bose invited Higuchi to his study and discussed about his future course for about one hour. Finally he said :–

"...I want to take my comrades, the Indian unit of Europe consisting of about three command men, along with me. But as transport is a problem, I want to go along for the being as a taken of that cannot real. As there are a large number of patriots in the Far East headed by Rash Behari Bose, they will be in a position to achieve them even if we do not go there. In case some accident happens on the way, please inform Rash Behari Bose that I prayed for independence till the end. The movement in Europe will be looked after by Numbiar after my departure. In case of necessity he will work maintain intimate liaison with Rash Behari Bose. In that case I shall request you to arrange all possible help for establishing close contacts."

On the following night Bose left Berlin secretly. The last man to call on him was the Japanese ambassador Oshima, and to him Bose introduced his only companion and secretary and said:

"It was a difficult task to select the man to accompany me as volunteers were many. The future of India depends upon Hindu-Muslim unity. So I have deliberately selected this Moslem young man as my companion."

This Moslem young man Abid Hassan not only accompanied Bose in this voyage, but remained one of his most trusted followers closest to him till the end of war.

At last journey to Japan which Bose had been advocating for more a year earnestly was realized. Once he had confided to the ambassador that he was worried whether Japan would admit him as a welcome guest suppose he successed in reaching Japan secretly? But the position now has changed completely. A Japanese submarine was coming to receive him. He never once thought the danger and hardships of the journey. Indeed he showed the spirit that can normally be expected of great freedom fighter.

It will be appropriate here to mention the opinion Bose had of the Germans, which he expressed off and on.

He was a great admirer of Hitler, which has been mentioned above already. Although the dictator was already acting in irrational manner in conducting the war. Yet his dictatorial system appeared to be superficially sound without any sign of cracking. Bose quite often admired the efficient manner in which political maneuvers were carried out. He also admired the swift decision taking, Bose studied the words and actions of Hitler with great interest as he felt that twenty years dictatorship was a political necessity for India after independence.

Towards the end he was disgusted with the German Foreign Office officials. He also felt that the German army top brasses were too rigid and formality bound. However, he did not expresses any aversion towards German Defence Ministry. Of course it must be mentioned here that even Japan approved Bose's journey to Far East in August the year before, Bose lost all interest about Germany and German affairs.

Indian National Army

Japan declared war on England and USA on 8th December 1941. The F-Kikan got orders over wireless, and launched the Malaya operation in right earnest. On the following 10th the IIL declared its existence openly by at Hat Yai, a small town near Malayan border, and began the struggle for liberating motherland India.

The members of the F-Kikan accompanied the advancing Japanese soldiers making propaganda among the local Indian and Malays. They protected the local people and the Rajahs from violence of the Japanese soldiers, thereby restoring confidence among the people. Some of the Kikan members penetrated deep behind the enemy lines commanding the Harimau band. In the meeting of Indians sponsored by the IIL, the Head of the Kiken took great interest to explain the fraternal ties binding peoples of Asia, necessity of restoring peace, and Japan's support to the liberation movement of the Indian people.

On the 14th December, a British Indian battalion surrendered unconditionally along with the British battalion commander and other Indian officers in the vicinity of Alor Star. The credit for this goes to the daring correct assessment of situation by the head of the F-Kikan. This was the first group surrender since the opening of hostilities, and one of the four company commanders was Capt, Mohan Singh, the founder of the Indian National Army.

On returning to Alor Star along with the surrendered soldiers, the Head of the F-Kikan found that looting had broken out in the town taking advantage of the vacuum created by the breaking down of police administration. Maj. Fujiwara the head of the F-Kikan, boldly decided to deploy the just-surrendered Indian troops to restore order in the town. The order was conveyed to Capt. Mohan Singh who allotted the task to Capt. Akram. Capt. Akram restored order in the town in no time along with about seventy to eighty soldiers. This news hightened the prestige of the F-Kikan among the Japanese officers and men, and also created goodwill towards the Indian soldiers.

Following this Indian soldiers started surrendering in hundred and placed themselves under the command of Capt. Mohan Singh.

Although Capt. Mohan Singh was an officer of the British Indian Army, yet he passionately desired freedom of India. His attitude toward the Japanese army was mixed. Although he was impressed by the attitude of local Japanese forces, yet he was highly critical of the policy of the Japanese government and the activities of the Japanese armed forces elsewhere. His firm conviction was that any struggle for freedom of should get the blessings of the Indian National Congress. However, he admitted that the Great East Asian War was the golden chance for the colonial nations to attain independence. For this, he felt that a great revolutionary like Subhas Chandra Bose should be invited to Far East, which reflected the aspiration of the Indians in general living in the Far East and South Asia.

Subhas Chandra Bose was the undisputed leader of the Indians in East and South Asia. However, the clearance of the German Government was necessary for bringing Bose to Far East. As this was bound to take time Mohan Singh thought that proper liaison should be established with Bose in Berlin and the movement for Indian independence should be developed on global scale. These views of Mohan Singh were communicated without any delay to the Imperial Headquarters.

For five days following surrender, both Maj. Fujiwara and Pritam Singh tried to persuade Capt. Mohan Singh to raise a revolutionary army to fight a revolutionary war, but without any avail. He stuck to his gun: the intention of the Japanese should be evaluated carefully, support of the compatriots - especially of the Indian National Congress need be obtained, and firm backing of the Indian officers and men must be secured. Round about this time Pritam Sigh and Mohan Singh had an interview with Lt. Gen. Yamashita, the commanding officer of the region. Both of them were very much moved when the General expressed frankly the support of the Japanese army to the Indian independence movement.

In the mean time the IIL movement developed steadily, branches were opened at Penang and Taiping, and many influential local Indians joined the movement. Seeing the great response to the movement, Pritam Singh started thinking in raising a volunteer army for launching an armed a struggle in India.

Finally on 31st December 1941, Capt. Mohan Singh visited that F-Kikan headquarters and expressed his willingness to organise Indian National Army for liberating India provided the following conditions were accepted by the Japanese army.

1. Capt. Mohan Singh will organize the Indian National Army.
2. The Japanese army will render all assistance to this army.
3. For the time being, the INA and the IIL will be brotherly organizations assisting each other.
4. The Japanese army will entrust the command of the Indian prisoners of war to Capt. Mohan Singh.
5. The Japanese army will accord friendly treatment to the Indian prisoners of war, and release those willing to join the INA.
6. The INA will be treated as an ally by the Japanese army.

Pritam Singh had advocated the name Volunteer Army for Indian Independence, but Mohan Singh opted for the name Indian National Army, because he believed that such an army could succeed only if it received unqualified support from the nation. In the discussions that followed it was pointed out that it was technically difficult to accord the state of allied army to the INA right at the moment, and it was decided to postpone the issue to a later date. It was decided that Mohan Singh would raise the army mainly from among the Indian prisoners of war with actgive essistance from the IEL. This proposal was approved by Gen. Yamashita. Thus the INA was born in taiping within about a month of the start of the Great East Asia War.

This news was immediately circulated to all the branches of the IIL. The IIL propaganda squads went behind the enemy lines to urge the troops of the British Indian Army to desert and join the INA.

In the meantime the INA was busy raising its own propaganda set out of hand picked soldiers. Capt. Mohan Singh himself took up the job training and educating them about freedom movement. These people were formed into small bond, and provided with necessary dresses to disguise as stragglers, ordinary people and army regulars. They were also given the symbol 'F', the sign of F-Kikan, a certificate from the F-Kikan and handbills urging the Indian soldiers to join the INA.

The Indian soldiers who surrendered after reading these handbill were literally received with open arms by the INA officers and men. Capt. Mohan Singh also addressed them personally to allay their apprehensions.

Thus the propaganda squads of the IIL and the INA advanced into the enemy territory along with the Japanese army, despite such difficulties like lack of understanding, misunderstanding, and obstructionist tactic of the British forces. However, the Japanese forces soon realized the effect of the presence of the propaganda squads, and messages started pouring in to the headquarters about large scale surrender of the Indian soldiers. Seeing this the front line Japanese soldiers started cooperating more and more with the propaganda squads, and the squads themselves in them gained more and more confidence in their ability.

This smooth sailing of Indo-Japanese cooperation in Malay front was quickly communicated to the Imperial Headquarters; and the people on the spot also conveyed their view on the future course of Indo-Japanese cooperation whenever occasion arose. These mainly ran in the following line.

The ideal of setting up a new order in East Asia can succeed only if it receives the support of 35 crore Indians. For this it is necessary to bring about capitulation of England. As the war situation stands at present, the war is going to be long drawn, which Japan cannot afford. Perhaps the Japanese army will have to stop after capturing Burma. The advance of Japanese forces into India will be resisted not only by the British forces, but also by the Indian, as can be judged from the attitude of the masses towards Japan. Hence a policy should now be drawn up to allow the Indians fight for their own liberation. Japan should abandon all designs on India and should the movement of the Indian people without reserve.

It was necessary to invite Subhas Chandra Bose as early as possible in order to give a concrete shape to the above line of thinking. However, the immediate problem was to intensify the IIL activity in order to mobilize millions of Indians living in East Asia. On the military side it was necessary to raise the strength of the INA by recruiting the Indian prisoners of war and Indian volunteers. Moreover concerted efforts had to be made to let the people in India know the existence of these two organizations so that they would be roused to carry out violent anti-British movement.

Contrary to the general feeling of the officers in the field, the Japanese government and the Imperial Headquarters did not show any enthusiasm on adopting a grand scale policy on India. Rather it may be more correct to say that execution of such a policy was beyond Japan's capacity. Moreover, capture of Singapore was the burning issue of the day. However, the activities of the IIL and the INA deeply impressed the leaders of Japan considerably, and it cannot be denied that they started giving a serious thought over the question of inviting Bose.

To come back to the activities of the IIL and the INA, the British forces got wind of the affair and started replacing the front line Indian soldiers with white troops. The Indian soldiers were withdrawn to Singapore. Despite these difficulties, the operation of the IIL and the INA went on smoothly, and by the time Kuala Lumpur fell the number of Indian troops surrendered exceeded two thousand five hundred.

Capt. Mohan Singh firmly believed that the patriotism had induced the Indian prisoners of war to join the INA, and put forward the following requests to the Japanese side; to give arms training to a section of the soldiers, to organize a strong propaganda contingent in order to foil any British attempt of retreat, and to use Saigon Radio for making effective propaganda broadcast to India. The Japanese Army immediately accepted all these demands and immediately sent light arms sufficient to arm two companies. This was the first step in arming the INA, and armed sentries started guarding the camp gates.

Moreover, the INA volunteered to repair the army air field of Kuala Lumpur, and completed the work in a very brief period mobilizing about one thousand soldiers for the task.

Towards the end of January, the Imperial Headquarters sent a high level mission to Malaya to make on the spot assessment of the work of F-Kikan, ILL and INA, in order the draw up plan for dealing with Indians. This mission thoroughly appreciated the activities of the above three bodies, and also realized the sincere aspiration of the Indians to have Subhas Chandra Bose in their midst. In early February the F-Kikan received order to send some of its members to Burma to assist the operations of the Japanese army there. A section of the IIL and the INA was to accompany, and this was precisely what Pritam Singh and Capt. Mohan Singh had been demanding. Although attack on Singapore was imminent, yet the IIL and the INA accorded higher priority to Burma as about two million Indians lived there and moreover it had common border with India. One unit consisting of a squad of propagandists and a group of liaison officers was immediately organized and sent to the 15th Army which was then poised to strike acrose the Salween river. There already the Thakin Party under the leadership of Aung san and its armed wing the Burma Independence

Army trained by the Japanese Army were active in inciting Burmese people to rise against to British rule. It was feared that the INA and IIL activities were destined for a rough sailing in Burma because of latent anti-Indian feeling among the local people. The Indians were aware of this, but they were not disheartened because their sole aim was liberation of mother land.

On February 8th, the Yamashita Army launched overall attack on Singapore. The INA threw all the available propaganda squads into the operation. The main objective was to secure the surrender of as many Indian soldiers as possible in case the British decided to retreat to Sumtra and Java, or to mobilize the Indian soldiers and the Indian civilians through propaganda for destruction of the British forces in case the British thought of last ditch stand. After sending about sixty trained propagandists to Burma on the eve of this operation Capt. Mohan Singh had no other alternative but to raise new propaganda squads as quickly as possible. The INA propaganda squads made a very commendable job in this operation. Disregarding heavy firing from both the sides they made appeals to the front line Indian troops at the risk of their own life. The effect was electric, and more than one thousand soldiers surrendered by the 13th evening. The British forces finally surrendered on the 15th and the F-Kikan along with INA and the IIL started making preparations for accepting surrender of the Indian soldiers.

The formal ceremony of handing over of the Indian soldiers to the Japanese forces by the British was held on the 17th. The head of the F-Kikan explained to them Japan's sincere desire to assist the Indian for gaining independence, a speech received with tumultuous applause. He also indicated that those willing to join the INA would cease to be prisoners of war, rather the Japanese Army would help them with everything so that they could fight for the independence of their motherland. The speeches of the next two speakers, Pritam Singh and Capt. Mohan Singh, were also equally applauded, and it appeared that all were keen to join the INA.

In Singapore, two very influential local Indians, Goho and Menon, join the IIL.

Just at this time Premier Tojo delivered his historic speech before the Imperial Diet promising liberation of the nations of East Asia, independence of Philippines, and overall support to the Indian Independence movement.

After the fall of Singapore the centre of activity of the IIL and INA shifted to Singapore, and Capt. Mohan Singh devoted all his energy in consolidating and strengthening the INA.

Tokyo Conference of IIL

In March 1942, Rash Behari Bose sponsored a meeting of the Indians of East Asia to deliberate on the question of liberation of India.

While planning for war, the Imperial Headquarters gave a serious thought over the Indian question only at a very late stage as it was realized that the large number of Indians living in the region have their own peculiar problems. Following this the Imperial Headquarters succeeded in establishing contact with the IIL movement, and Subhas Chandra Bose in Berlin through the Japanese ambassador resident there.

Although the IIL was trying its best to mobilize the Indians, yet the Japanese leaders were skeptic about its capacity. They admitted that only a leader of Subhas Chandra Bose's stature could lead such a struggle for Indian independence from outside India which would receive proper response from the Indians of India at the same time. But it was felt that there was no chance of having Bose in East Asia in near future as the clearance of German government was needed for the purpose. Again even if the German Government agreed, the difficulty was transportation.

Thus the Imperial Headquarters was left with the alternative of locating an Indian leader in East Asia who would have the confidence of the Indians and at the same time who would be willing to act in collaboration with Japan. The only person who could satisfy these conditions was Rash Behari Bose.

This exiled leader was already a naturalized citizen of Japan, and expressed his wholehearted cooperation with Japan on the day Japan declared war believing that this was the golden opportunity to drive the British out of India.

In no time liaison was established between the Imperial Headquarter and Rash Behari Bose. He was Pro-Japanese with a good understanding of Japanese situation and naturally both the parties understood each other. At that time the Imperial Headquarters confined their objective to obtain support of the Indians in the operational areas, rather than thinking in terms of eliminating British from the Indian scene. Even then Rash Behari Bose indicated his intention of cooperation without any grudge. The manifestation of the understanding between the two sides was convening of the Tokyo Conference. Invitation went to the leading Indians of East Asia under the name of Rash Behari Bose, and the Imperial Headquarters rendered all possible assistance. The array was as follows.

IIL representatives	:	Pritam Singh, Goho, Menon, Raghavan, Swami, Aiyer
INA representatives	:	Capt. Mohan Singh. Lt. Col. Gill. Capt. Akram
Shanghai delegation	:	Osman (Baba Hari Singh)
Hongkong delegation	:	Khan (D.M.)

Swami was the director of the Culture Centre of Bangkok, and there existed serious differences between him and the IIL. But they sank their differences for the noble cause of freedom of motherland.

However, on the way, Swami, Pritam Singh, Aiyer and Akram died in plane crush, and especially the loss of Pritam Singh was irreparable. He was the central figure of IIL, and Japan had placed much hope on him.

In the conference Rash Behari Bose took the chair. There were delegates from Philippines and Japan as well. The plane accident cast a shadow of gloom over the conference. Beside famous Indian revolutionaries like Sahai and Mahendra Pratap living in Japan did not participate. Somehow the conference failed to give an impression of success. In the resolutions adopted, Japan's assistance to Indian freedom struggle was appreciated, chance provided to the Indians to fight their war of independence due to Japan's military success were rightly evaluated unqualified support was expressed to the ILL and INA activities in South Asia, the principle of evolving policy after thorough and democratic discussions among the leaders of East Asia and political mobilization of the Indian masses was adopted, and finally recognition was accorded to the IIL as the sole representative organization of the Indians in East Asia. The conference leaders also had a meeting with Premier Tojo to ascertain his views directly. The conference dispersed after agreeing to meet again at Bangkok in the middle of June.

This being the first conference of its kind it left serious doubts about the outcome. Moreover, serious ideological differences came to the fore between the leaders from South East Asia and those of Japan. The leaders from south thought that Rash Behari Bose had lost much of his Indian-base, whereas the Indians of Japan thought that the representative of IIL were not seasoned revolutionaries like them. Only till the other day they had been loyal subjects of British. Thus the Tokyo Conference ended with a mixed note.

In the Tokyo Conference, the Japanese side was represented by Maj. Fujiwara, the head of F-Kikan and Col. Iwaguro, the head of a new Kikan (Lit. organization) the Japanese government had proposed to set up to replace the F-Kikan in view of the importance of India. During this period animated discussions were going on between the Imperial Headquarters and the Japanese officers who were associated with the Indian in South East Asia. These officers demanded open occupation policy declaration and unqualified support to the struggle for independence by the Indian people. The Iwaguro Kikan which was to replace the F-kikan should be an embassy type body, which was one step ahead of the thinking of the Imperial Headquarters. The Imperial Headquarters had drawn up what can be termed as Indian stratagem and not Indian policy. It was after a long and heated debate that the Imperial Headquarters could finally be persuade to change their mind; and the establishment of Iwaguro Kikan can be taken as the turning point in the Imperial Headquarters policy towards India.

While this drama was being enacted, on the war front the Japanese forces over ran Lower Burma, Java, Sumatra and Andamans.

Although the IIL and the INA were not very happy with the outcome of the Tokyo Conference, yet they did not get disheartened. After returning to Singapore Capt. Mohan Singh devoted himself wholeheartedly in organizing and strengthening the INA with renewed vigour. However, the activities of the IIL got a great shock due to the death of Pritam Singh, and the timing of replacing Major Fujiwara right at that very time created much apprehension among the ranks. After all the major had nurtured the organization. This major and the devoted band under his command had done much in establishing the bond of friendship between the Japanese front line troops and the Indians in general.

Birth of Iwaguro Kikan- Bangkok Conference-Vicissitudes of India Policy

Subhas Chandra Bose was regularly in touch with the development of the IIL and INA movements, and continued with his persuations with the Japanese government for coming to East. He also came to know that a section of the Japanese leaders were keen to invite him to East Asia.

At that time India was not on the priority list; but even then he was a very well known figure in Japan, and the general consensus of the people dealing with India was that Bose should be invited to East Asia without any delay and handed over the leadership of the movement of the India people. The Iwaguro Kikan was established in place of F-Kikan under obvious premise that Bose would be invited to Far East without much delay, and all the plans were prepared to cater to this.

Although the above was the line of thinking in the Imperial Headquarters and the General Staff office, yet Premier Tojo and the top leaders of the war Ministry did not show any positive interest, and it became clear that an immediate invitation to Bose will not be forthcoming.

Part of the responsibility for this can be placed on Rash Behari Bose. As an Indian revolutionary living in exile in Japan for long he had a good understanding of the Japanese conditions, and the Japanese leaders also had a good understanding of him. Hence they were reluctant to invite Subhas Chandra Bose, whose attitude towards Japan was not clearly known. Thus they were inclined to back Rash Behari Bose, although his political standing was much lower.

The final outcome of such a situation was that although all efforts were made to establish Rash Behari Bose as the Leader of Indian freedom movement, yet negotiations were also carried out simultaneously to comply with the desire of Subhas Chandra Bose and call him to East Asia. In their turn both the leaders showed selfless patriotism, each propagating the other's cause; personal ambition never raising head before the noble cause of the country.

However, both the central leaders and the persons on the spot agreed on one point that Indian should get greater attention, and that a more powerful Kikan should be established for the purpose. As the head of this the choice was Col. Iwaguro, a brilliant army officer, who was recuperating from wounds received during Malaya campaign. In view of his future assignment he was also ordered to take part in the Tokyo Conference.

On taking up the new assignment, the first thing that Col. Iwaguro resolved was to secure Subhas Chandra Bose's arrival, and at the same time accord open political support to the freedom movement of the people of Indian origin led by Subhas Chandra Bose. Stratagem should have no place in the activities of the Kikan. However, he also realized before long that the leadership in the centre had a different thing in mind the topmost person who could take a decision on this matter was premier Tojo himself, and he was yet to be convinced. This aspect came to the forefront during the Bangkok Conference. Before dealing with this it will be appropriate here to describe the set up of the Iwaguro Kikan.

(a) *Political Section*—This was the most important section in the Kikan and a Diet member with expert knowledge on India was appointed as its head. A number of experts on Indian affairs were placed under his disposal. The main tasks were to strengthen the IIL, looking after the political affairs and maintaining proper liaison with the IIL etc.

(b) *Intelligence Section*—Beside collecting information about the Indians both in India and abroad, it established a training centre called "Swaraj School" in Penang appointing a leading lawyer of the place Raghavan as its head. Here also a Diet member was appointed as the special duty officer who was assisted by appropriate military and civilian personnel. The objective was to train youngmen for sending them to India by submarine and by para-dropping, as well as to foster young IIL workers.

(c) *Military Affairs Section*—The main tasks were to organize one field division three guerilla regiments, one intelligence unit to collect information from the border regions, one secret service unit to carry out sabotage behind the enemy lines, etc. from among the surrendered Indian soldiers. The founder commanding officer of the INA was appointed the overall commanding officer of this whole military set up. Although higher ranking officers like Lt. Cols. Bhonlse, Gill and others were there, yet Capt. Mohan Singh's contribution to the founding of INA was thus acknowledged.

(d) *Propaganda Section*—the main tasks were to drop leaflets from aeroplanes, and making broadcasts from Singapore, Saigon and Rangoon radio stations.

The new Kikan gave priority to the political affairs, especially strengthening of IIL, and launched a crash progarmme for achieving this from July 1942, which lasted for about two months. Following this priority was shifted to the military affairs, planning to complete all arrangements by Nov. 1942.

In the meantime Bangkok Conference was convened in the middle of June according to the decisions of Tokyo Conference, and efforts were made to make it as representative in character as possible. More than hundred delegates gathered at Bangkok from all over East and South East Asia, and resident ambassadors of Japan, Germany and Italy attended the inaugural session along with about two thousand Indians. Rash Behari Bose took the chair and Sahai attended as the representative of Indian in Japan. The inaugural session was brought to a close after reading the following message of Subhas Chandra Bose.

"-------------My experience of the last eighteen months since I have left India has shown that Japan, Germany and Italy have made a common cause with us in fighting British Imperialism. But the Independence of India must be won by the Indians. The last phase of Indian Independence movement is armed struggle. Independence of India will signify the collapse of British imperialism, and this is also the objective of the invincible Japanese Army. I pray for the success of this conference, and I firmly believe that it will pave the way to success."

The conference elected an executive committee of five members, Rash Behari Bose, the Chairman, Capt. Mohan Singh and Lt. Col. Gilani to represent the INA, and Raghavan and Menon to represent the civilians. The conference also set up various constituent bodies of the IIL . Working committee delegates council, local committee and local branch. The delegates council consisted of eighty members, forty civilians representing all the regions, and forty INA representatives. It was decided to locate the headquarters of IIL at Bangkok for the time being and that of INA at Singapore.

Finally a resolution of about sixty clauses was adopted after closed door deliberations lasting three days in various sub-committees. It was next forwarded to the Japanese government for a clause by clause official reply. The resolution sought funds from Japanese government for setting up a government of the Indians repayable after gaining independence, and demanded that after independence India should be treated as an ally. The keynote was the relationship of equality between the Indian side and the Japanese side.

This demand for a clause by clause reply embarrassed both the Kikan members and the General staff office, and gave a pretext to premier Tojo and other top leaders who been lukewarm towards India from the very beginning to accuse the Japanese officers concerned of irresponsible action, and giving over indulgence to the Indians. Reflect this hardened attitude of top Japanese leaders, the reply was very curt. "Japan fully appreciates the patriotism of the Indian people, and will do everything possible to assist the Indian independence struggle." This was immediately interpreted as insincerity on the part of Japan, and the Indo-Japanese reliance built up with great effort since the outbreak of war appeared to stand on the brink of a precipice.

Thus although the thinking of the Indian side had taken a concret shape, yet the Japanese side lacked any concrete proposal and this difference in approach created a lot of problems and misunderstanding during subsequent negotiations. This continued even after Subhas Chandra Bose assumed the leadership of the Provisional Government of India and the Indian National Army. As no serious attempt was made to bridge the gap between the thinking of the two sides, the future Indo-Japanese relations were destined to be plagues by it.

Following Bangkok Conference, the Indian Independence League convened a meeting of about twenty five thousand Indians in Singapore on 12th August pledging for independence. Similar meeting was also held in Rangoon on 10th April.

The cold reception of the Bangkok Conference resolution created distrust in the minds of the Indians, and the anti-Rash Behari Bose factious became all the more doubtful about his role. To make the matters worse, just at this time, towards the end of Nov, an incident of sabotage occurred concerning Capt. Mohan Singh and the INA.

In fact Capt. Mohan Singh was the founder of the INA. Moreover he had a great contribution in laying the foundation of collaboration with the Japanese Army, as well as strengthening the INA. In recognition of his merit, he was appointed the commander of the INA by the Japanese army command. However, he also started expressing his doubts about the Japanese intentions, got entangle with factional fights of the IIL, and grew more and more presumptious. As his action went beyond tolerance, the Japanese Army decided to put a stop to it and arrested and interned him at St. John Island. His staff officer Lt. Col. Gill was also similarly arrested in Singapore on charge of abettment of the crime, and the INA was ordered to disband. Simultaneously, Goho and Menon of Singapore who supported Mohan Singh and challenged Rash Behari Bose and his supporter Raghavan for the leadership of IIL were removed from their posts.

Immediately after this the task of reorganizing the INA was taken up. As a precondition it was also decided to purge and purify the IIL. Two real patriots Narayan Swami were located in Singapore, and under their leadership the IIL was organized as the party of real Indian patriots. The INA was also organized simultaneously as a collaborating body to this new setup. Lt. Col., Bhonsle was appointed its commander; and he remained the leader of the Indian National Army till the end of the war. This can be termed as the third stage in the growth of the INA, its moulting, its rebirth.

Special mention must be made here to the contributions of Mizun a member of the Iwaguro Kikan in clearing up the whole mess and success in reorganizing the INA and the IIL. He was an extreme left leader, and his experience in leading the leftist movements had helped him in his task. It is also commendable that Rash Behari Bose never doubted the intentions of Japan, although he found himself in a very tight corner.

It will be appropriate here to make a thorough dissection of the causes that led to the INA incident. The attitude of the Indian side towards Japan was very much biased due to the propaganda of the allied powers—which constantly alleged that the IIL and the INA were puppet organizations of the Japanese militarists. Whenever an incident occurred, the Indian side tried to evaluate it with this as the scale. As a colonial people with long history of oppression they have developed some sort of prejudice, and whenever liberation has been proposed they have tried to assert equality with other nations which was beyond their power. Moreover the outlook of the exiled revolutionary leaders was much different from that of the just surrendered prisoners of war. On the other hand Japan also cannot claim a clean slate. Basically they lacked a clear understanding of the Indian people. Moreover, they failed to evolve a concrete policy regarding Indian, and nor did they show any inclination to draw up a policy that would satisfy the Indians. Under such a situation, the activities of the Japanese officers associated with the IIL and the INA gave an understanding of total Japanese support out of their idealistic approach and good will. When the contradiction became apparent, the Indian side was left with no other alternative but to act contrary to the Japanese expectations.

Under the above situation it was natural that the attention of every body will be focussed on Subhas Chandra Bose.

The resolute action of the Japanese Army against the IIL and the INA at last eliminated the undesirable elements, but it had its repercussions on Japan also. It was at this point that the Japanese side both at governmental and national levels, started giving a serious thought over evolving a concrete policy towards India. This incident also helped in bringing the people of India and Japan closer to each other. The IIL also slowly reestablished itself under the able leadership of Rash Behari Bose and Raghvan. The INA also went on strengthening itself under the able leadership of the new commander Bhonsle.

During this period the Kikan carried out broadcasts beamed towards India from Singapore, Siagon and Rangoon, and from this time sent special work groups into India by para-dropping, submarine landing and over the Indo-Burma border. Although the Iwaguro Kikan started with about ten members, yet it became a grand organization of about two hundred and fifty members; and it worked in perfect harmony with the Supreme Command of the Southern Forces as Maj. Fujiwara, the ex-head of the F-Kikan was the liaison staff officer with the Supreme Command. After the house was put into order, Col. Iwaguro was transferred in May 1943, and a new set up under the name Hikari Kikan was established with Col. Yamamoto as the head to cooperate directly with Subhas Chandra Bose's activities in East Asia.

After the Bangkok Conference the standing of Rash Behari Bose also the leader of IIL became shaky, and in every meeting between the India and the Japanese sides, the Indian side pressed for inviting Subhas Chandra Bose to East Asia. For Japan it involved two risks. One was the possibility of the submarine venture of Subhas Chandra Bose ending in a disaster. The other was the possibility of clash of personality of the two leaders. In spring 1943, Maj. Gen. Arisue, of General Staff office was sent to Singapore to make on the spot study of among other thing the question of inviting Subhas Chandra Bose. In view of shaky position of Rash Behari Bose, the Iwaguro Kikan frankly recommended Subhas Chandra Bose. When the general sought the opinion of Rash Behari Bose, he said: "....for the independence of India Subhas Chandra Bose must be called to the East. The situation has now gone beyond my control. I will by very glad to work under him as his lieutenant......"

In this way the matter was settled.

Hikari Kikan

When it became clear that Subhas Chandra Bose would come to East, the Japanese government felt the necessary of reorganizing the Iwaguro Kikan of ensuring closer cooperation and better coordination. As the head of this new Kikan Col. Yamamoto was selected as he was personally known to Subhas Chandra Bose in Berlin and was associated with the negotiations for inviting Subhas from the very beginning. After a through evaluation of the situation in Tokyo, the colonel went to the field for reorganizing the set up. The first thing he did was to abolish the Political Division as it was decided to entrust this work to the provisional government of India. Again, accommodating the wishes of the Indian side, especially of Subhas, the Propaganda cell was also abolished. Here the Japanese obligation was to supply funds and provide facilities. With this reorganization, the new Hikari Kikan—this was the name of the reorganization set up—lost its political nature and become more of a military body.

This change in the character of the Kikan can be interpreted to reflect the basic tone of Japan's policy towards India. Japan recognized the aspiration of the Indians that the world war provided with a golden opportunity to fight for their own freedom, and Japan's friendly role in assisting such a struggle. The role of the Hikari Kikan was to spearhead such a policy of Japan and render material help to the Indians. This left the nominal and actual leadership of Indian freedom struggle to the Indians, relegating the Kikan to secondary background role. Col. Yamamoto could give a concrete shape to the above line of thinking of Japan because he had a first hand knowledge of the personally Subhas as well as Subhas's outlook on politics and independence movement.

With the change in character of the Kikan, most of the Kikan member were replaced by military personnel, excepting for a few experts on India like Mr. Senda.

The Japanese Government had made it clear that it had no design on post independence India. Subhas also disliked very much to act in any manner that may compromise his position/and brand him as a puppet of Japan, many Japanese civilian experts on India had a tendency to think in terms of future Japanese interests in India. So Col. Yamamoto took great care to restrict the number of so called experts on India in the Kikan to absolute minimum.

Subhas Chandra Bose in Tokyo

Subhas reached Tokyo on 16th May 1943. At last the chance came to fulfil his long cherished dream. He wanted to meet the leaders of Japan as quickly as possible and lay bare his mind. He did not have any time to think of the fatigue of his submarine and plane journeys. The only thing that occupied his mind was liberation of motherland.

However, somehow or other his meeting with premier Tojo did not materialize. For a week following his arrival he met only the low ranking officials of army, navy and foreign office. The talks did not touch upon the points Bose had in mind, and some of the officials went even as far as testing his personality. Ultimately he could meet the Chief of General Staff Sugiyama, Navy Minister, the chief of the Board of Command, and foreign Minister Shigemitsu. These talks were not at all satisfactory, and often ended in exchange of greetings.

When Bose met the chief of general staff Sugiyama, the first words he uttered were : "It seems that Japan has already won the war." At that time Japan was having trouble in Guadalcanal area; and this bold conclusion can be attributed only to the 1st hand impression Bose got about superior human resources of Japan. In a very casual manner he also said during this meeting that Japan's sending of forces into India was of minor significance so far as India's independence was concerned. The essential precondition was that the Indians should go into India and start armed struggle. To this goal Bose was committed. However, the chief's reply was far from satisfactory to Bose. Even then Bose took great interest in explaining the necessity of advance into India, and as a concrete proposal put forward Chittagong as the immediate goal. Just at that time a section of the staff headquarters officers was thinking of launching operation against India in order to recover the war initiative. Bose's arrival and proposal for starting operation in India directly or indirectly encouraged this line of thinking. This doyen of the Japanese army had great interest about India since his younger days, and hence this meeting was conducted in an atmosphere of great cordiality and understanding. But Bose left this meeting with a heavy heart feeling that he could make little progress with his project.

In the mean time he spent about ten days visiting schools, factories, hospitals and military installations etc. in order to get an idea of the real strength of Japan.

In this way June came, but even then premier Tojo postponed the meeting under the pretext of being too busy. This exasperated Col. Yamamoto the head of the Hikari Kikan to such an extent that he requested the general staff office to relieve him of the post.

What was the reason behind this attitude to Tojo. One of the reasons was that a section of the war ministry officials was cold to the idea of Indian operation, raising all possible objections. The main cause was that the premier had developed biased views about India following Bangkok Conference and Mohan Singh incident. The Chief of general staff and the foreign minister tried to soften the attitude of Tojo, but failed. Finally Tojo agreed to meet Bose around 10th June.

The first meeting cleared all the misunderstanding of Tojo. The attitude of Tojo as the leader of the East Asia was indeed dignified during this meeting. Again, Bose deeply impressed Tojo by his arguments and sincerity, and the leader started admiring each other. At the end Tojo himself proposed a second meeting after a few days. Tojo also impressed Bose deeply, and the latter realized that he could count upon the Japanese premier as a sincere friend.

The second meeting was held on the 14th June, when the two leaders exchanged frank views on politics, reconstruction of East Asia, independent of India and other topins. There was complete identity of views. Foreign Minister Shigemitsu and other Japanese leaders were also present during this meeting.

On the 16th June Bose visited the 82nd Extraordinary Session of the Diet, where the Japanese premier delivered his historic policy statement on Grant East Asia Declaration. After explaining Japan's firm policy towards each country of this region, looking at Bose, who was listening the speech intently, said.

"......India is still under cruel oppression of England. I express my profound sympathy to the Indians struggling for independence. The Empire will render all possible help to the Indians for achieving independence. I firmly believe that India will become free before long, and it will attain great prosperity. The liberation of East Asia will come through the successful conclusion of the Great East Asian war, and welfare of the East Asian nations can be realized only through the establishment of the independent nations of East Asia. ..."

He concluded his speech by saying that India should grab this unique chance of new dawn in East Asia, and solve its long due problems of independence.

In may the year before, Tojo had declared in the Diet that the golden chance had come for India to become free. Later on in January he had reported to the Diet that a section of the Indian was cooperating with the Empire and fighting for Indian's independence. Finally before Bose he declared that the Empire assured all possible hope so that the devine mission could be fulfilled. This time he showed more positive attitude because the premier come to know Bose personally, and was to a certain extent inspired by his enthusiasm. Thus a new bond tying down the destiny of Indian Independence with Japan was established.

After this Bose made his first public appearance. On 19th June he held his first press conference, attended by about sixty Japanese and foreign journalists. Here Bose emphasized the following points.

(a) During the last world war the Indian leaders were deceived by the British politicians. This failure should not be allowed to repeat this time again.

(b) I believe in the ultimate victory of Japan, Germany and Italy. The Indian masses know it very well that this victory means independence of India. Moreover, they know that those three countries will render positive assistance, and not simple lip service.

(c) Under the prevailing international situation the independence movement was bound to develop into armed struggle, and there is a very good prospect of its success.

(d) Premier Tojo have promised all possible support to the Indian struggle for independence on the Diet floor. This will serve as a great stimulus to the movement of the Indian people.

The above assessment of Bose is very significant as the first of statement after coming to the Far East. His statement in the press conference will be quoted below as it would give deep insight in the view of Bose.

On 21st June night Bose made his first broadcast to India from Tokyo. Here he explained his belief that the English power in India should be swept away by the armed struggle of the Indian masses which had a great appeal to the thirty five crore Indians. The masses, especially the youth, were very much impressed by his speech broadcast from Tokyo, the heart of the Great East Asian war. He pointed out that Japan would win in the long run, and that the Japanese leaders had personally assured him all possible help without any string attached. It must have made a great appeal to the common people. The gist of the speech will be given below. The gist has been given here.[2]

Bose made his second broadcast from Tokyo on the 24th, in which he informed the people of India of the declaration made by premier Tojo in the Diet. In this broadcast also he expressed his firm belief in the ultimate victory of the axis powers.

Following these broadcast, Bose made broadcasts to the German and the Italian people in German and Italian respectively, where he stated about his conviction of final victory of the axis powers after seeing the conditions in Japan. He also said that the spirit of immortal Marshal Yamamoto was alive among the Japanese people. Again, the Indian people would fight hand in hand with the axis powers till ultimate victory was won. He also urged the Indian living in Europe to devote wholeheartedly to the struggle for liberating India.

Another important event was the meeting with Rash Behari Bose, the president of the Indian Independence League sometimes early June. Although this was their first meeting, yet they had exchanged messages regarding the Indian Independence League, and had helped each other as much as possible. Both of them were working for the noble goal of Indian

2. Not Printed here.

Independence, and hence were committed to help Subhas in great esteem, as the greatest leader of the Indian people, and Subhas also reciprocated by respecting him as a veteran revolutionary. They laid to rest all the fears the Japanese leaders had about any possible friction between the two personalities. Subhas appreciated highly the contribution of Rash Behari in organizing the IIL and proposed to place himself under the leadership of Rash Behari. As against this Rash Behari said that the IIL had already decided to have Subhas as the leader, and hence no delay should be made in assuming the leadership. Thus Subhas became the undisputed leader of the IIL.

Both the Boses next visited the grand old man Toyama. After greeting him Subhas said: "You must come once to India after India becomes free." Next Subhas also added that he expected that Toyama would lend all possible help to the Indian freedom struggle. Hearing this, the grand old man said: "You both have the same surname. But I think that you both have by now one soul. Hence you both should fight for the freedom of India."

During this stay Subhas did not have any desire to meet any person not connected with the government. He visited Toyama because the latter had helped the Indian patriots in Japan in all possible way. Rash Behari respected him like his Guru; and of course this meeting impressed Subhas greatly.

During this stay, the state funeral of Marshal Yamamoto took place. As the presence of Bose was not officially announced at that time, he did not attend the funeral officially, but he paid respect to the dead here by standing on the route of the funeral procession.

Although Bose was very busy, yet he made it a point to visit the headquarters of the Yokusan Siejikai Party on the afternoon of 23rd June. The purpose was to explain the actual position of India to this most powerful party, and to enlist its support and cooperation. Here he met the chairman Abe and other leader of the party, and made a speech of about two hours titled "My India" to about four hundred party members. It started with the subjugation of India by Britain through intrigue and deception, the great Indian Mutiny of last century, image of Japan in recent times, anti-Japanese feeling following the Sino-Japanese. Incident, and ended with revival of Pro-Japanese feeling following the outbreak of great East Asia War. He also mentioned that the Indian masses sincerely prayed for the victory of the axis powers. His refined but forceful rhetoric held the audience spellbound, and helped promoting better understanding about India among the leading politicians.

For the first ten days since his arrival in Tokyo, Subhas passed his days without much to do, but later on he became very busy, and utilised his time very effectively. Presently the time came when he was to leave Tokyo for his new scene of activity in South Asia.

A few days before Subhas left Tokyo, he presented the proposal for setting up a Provisional Government of Free India to the Japanese authorities. As the matter was of grave importance, it was not possible for the Japanese side to give an immediate reply. Being aware of this Bose also did not press for a decision, and was happy to keep it at the probe level. His last act before leaving Tokyo was a broadcast to the Japanese people. He stayed about forty days in all in Tokyo, and the impression he got of Japan was quite encouraging. He became all the more firm in his resolution, with an insuppressable passion for making India great. The above broadcast was titled 'My Greetings to the Japanese people it was recorded and broadcast on 28th June after Bose's departure. It ran in the following line.

Before leaving Tokyo Bose received a telegram from the Burmese premier Ba Maw dated 23rd June, in which he expressed his happiness over Bose's arrival in the East, and promised all possible help to Bose and the Indians in their struggle against England.

Subhas Chandra Bose in Singapore

Subhas arrived in Singapore on 27th June, received by the leaders of the IIL and the INA, and the local Indians, besides the important officials of the Hikari Kikan. On 4th July a convention of the IIL was held in Singapore where the Chairman Rash Behari Bose introduced Subhas as the new president of the IIL. As president, Bose delivered his first speech in this meeting where he declared his intention to establish the provisional government of free India.

After the speech, telegrams of felicitation received form premier Tojo and others were read and resolutions expressing gratitude to the Japanese Prime Minister, and appointing Rash Behari as the top most advisor were adopted. Thus Subhas became the undisputed leader of the Indians in East Asia, and launching his long cherished armed struggle was now a matter of time. On the day the convention was over, Subhas visited Gen. Terauchi, the head of the Southern Command, along with Rash Behari. The general was very pleased to meet both the leaders, and told Subhas the reliance he had placed on the future activities of Subhas. The meeting was held in a very cordial atmosphere without any air of official formality, and Bose readily realized the sincerity of the old general. Bose was deeply moved and expressed his resolution to fight English with every possible means.

On 5th July, a military parade of the INA officers and men was held in honour of Subhas in the municipal plaza of Singapore, where he was appointed the supreme commander of the Indian National Army. After the parade Subhas made a speech propounding his policy as the supreme commander, and the principles the INA should follow.

Around this time premier Tojo paid a visit to Thailand and Malaya and the two leaders got another chance to exchange frankly their views. He held a parade of the INA in the honour of the premier, and pleaded for assistance for strengthening the INA.

Next a conference of the Indians living in Singapore was held on 9th July. In his speech Subhas described his experience of freedom movement for the past twenty years, his going to jail for eleven times on suspicion of involvement in violent and non-violent movements, and other experiences. He also asserted that external help was an essential precondition for Indian independences' and that there were two aspects in this external assistance. On the spiritual plane the Indian people should be made to believe in ultimate victory, and on material plane military assistance should be obtained from external sources. It was the duty of the overseas Indians to grab the chance provided by the world war and the willingness of the axis powers, especially Japan, to provide military assistance in launching armed struggle to free India. He said that he was building up an army with sufficient force to be capable of attacking the British regime in India, and intended to announce this noble step to the world. He also declared his intention to establish provisional government of free India and urged all the Indians living in East Asia to stand solidly behind it mobilizing all resources. He concluded his speech by saying.

"I must say that time has come for the three million Indians living in East Asia to mobilize all there resources, both money and men. We should abandon vacillation. I want total mobilization. As the enemy is saying always, this is going to be the decisive war......

Out of this total mobilization I expect to raise three lakh soldiers and three lakh dollars. I hope that the Indian women will come forward and form a regiment not afraid of death, and will stand up with sword in hand as done by the Rani of Jhansi during our first war of Independence.

For some times past we have been told about the second front in Europe. It is a second front of imagination. In fact it is our brothers in India who are earnestly desiring a second front being unable to bear British tyranny. I promise you the second front, it is the second front of Indian independence."

It is needless to say that this speech had its desired effects. Thus within a few days since his arrival in Singapore, he captured not only the IIL and the INA, but the Indian masses as well. The people, in turn, placed almost religious faith in him.

Responding to his call, the famous Rani of Jhansi Regiment was formed with Miss Lakshmi as the head. The idea of Subhas was not to have a regular fighting women's unit. Rather he wanted to exploit the impact such a regiment would have on the youth in India, and also aimed at the propaganda value such a regiment would have with the ordinary INA soldiers, as was amply evident from the role of British auxiliary women's corps.

In Singapore Subhas devoted himself in making preparations for establishing the provisional government, meeting the Indian people, maintaining liaison with the Japanese military authorities, and keeping closest touch possible with the top military leaders of the INA. In his speech to the INA officers lasting for a few hours, he explained his political past including a number of trips to Europe in order to obtain first hand knowledge of the international situation, and the course leading to his present stand of armed struggle with external help. Luckily the axis power were willing to help, and although fifty thousand was a formidable strength, yet he wanted to raise the strength to three lakhs.

A careful study of his actions will show that his means were clearly dictatorial. However, this was unavoidable under the prevailing situation. As seen above, the first step in his modus operandi was to convince and to proceed after convincing completely. He also utilized propaganda machinery effectively for this purpose. So people at that time tended to interpret him as an agitating politician, but this was a rash and superficial assessment.

Concept of Political Organization and Fighting Force

Establishment of the Provisional Government and consolidation and strengthening of the INA were the two goals Bose had in his mind when he came to the East. When Bose met the Japanese premier, he discreetly sounded the proposal of establishing Provisional Government which received ready approval. So he put forward the proposal in concret form just before he left Tokyo to the Japanese authorities concerned. To this the reply of the Japanese government was:

"On principal there is no objection. A concrete reply will be given by the premier directly to Bose during his trip to South Asia.

Thereupon, after reaching Singapore Bose openly declared his plan to establish the Provisional Government to the Indian both in India and abroad, and proclaimed its essential nature. Establishing the Provisional Government was his personal decision, as he felt that the existing IIL would under no circumstances be able to mobilize all the Indians in East Asia behind it, and moreover it would not be in a position to make its weight felt in India. In reality also, this decision had a great propaganda value. It had not only a great impact on India, but also succeeded in rallying all, the Indians in East Asia behind it.

After the declaration, came the two problems of actual constitution of the government and official recognition by the Japanese government. To mobilize suitable talents for constituting the government indeed was a great problem. Originally he thought to have a very modest start setting propaganda as the principal objective. So he did not ask for participation in administration of various areas, and nor did he seek exchange of diplomatic personnel. Even then he had to make intensive tours to hunt out suitable persons and maintaining personal contact with the comrades of the various areas. Bose thought the questions of recognition by the Japanese government to be an absolute condition, and as agreed upon in Tokyo, premier Tojo conveyed the approval of the Japanese government in establishment of the Provisional government during his Singapore tour. After this only official procedure were left and excepting for minor disputes, the entire procedure went on quickly. The Provisional government was officially proclaimed in Oct, which was recognized immediately by the Japanese government. Profound understanding and active help of the Japanese authorities were important contributory factors here; but the credit for this goes to Bose who could impress both the Japanese officialdom and the masses and convince them of his cause during his stay in Japan.

Although Bose had started with the idea of having a very simple set up of the Provisional government, yet a study of the subsequent development will reveal to what extent he deviated from his original idea. One reason was the necessity to put the whole system in proper order. But the main reason for this was the practical necessity to maintain factional balance, and different religious group, province and castes had to be provided for appropriately. The creation of the ministers without portfolio was another manifestation of this. Again, Bose had to reorganize the administrative set up a number of times involving increase in the number of minister and other official. These reorganizations had to be carried out in order to satisfy his followers rather than from practical business consideration.

Again, that the Provisional government did not have any administrative right was a source of great discontent of the local Indianst. This was because they thought of utilizing the Provisional government for improving their economic position and to secure privileged status compared to the Malays and the Chinese. Again, the Indians of Bangkok expressed dissatisfaction over lack of diplomatic representation to look after their interest. The repeated demand for donation created a feeling of distrust among the populace, especially the business community. A section of the businessmen utilized this pretext of donation to cover up their black market activity. This brought sharp protests from the Japanese authorities, which put the Provisional government and the Hikari Kikan into difficult position.

Again, controversy for sometime continued over Andaman and Nicobar the only administrative territory of the Provisional government, but this fortunately went to the background and never raised its head again.

Thereupon it became urgently necessary to advance into India, the idea which Bose had from the very beginning in order to cover up the above shortcomings. Hence this became the cardinal point in all his plannings. Initially Bose had thought of locating the Provisional Government in Burma, which was to constitute his jumping pad; but as the Burma government disapproval of this idea, he had to opt for the second alternative place, Singapore. Singapore was selected out of consideration of its strategic location for effective propaganda, advantage of maintaining liaison with the Southern Command, and transportation facilities etc. Next when the Japanese army planned Imphal operation he forced on his will to cooperation overcoming all difficulties, and taking advantage of this situation he shifted the government to Rangoon after giving an understanding that it would not interfere with the internal administration of Burma. The direct motive behind this shifting to have a greater impact on Indian people and rouse the fighting spirit of the Indian National Army.

The immediate purpose of the establishment of the Provisional government was to advance into India. As soon as the failure of Imphal operation became known, various kinds of dissatisfactions and accusation against the Provisional government started to be voiced. By Autumn 1944, even Bose started showing worries over the working of the government. The details will be discussed at appropriate places.

Next an outline of the Indian National Army will be given here.

The Indian National Army was more or less an organized army even before Bose took over as the supreme commander. In organizing the army the emphasis was on quantity, so the principal of strict selection was sacrificed. Hence a large number of inefficient officers above the rank of field officers were recruited indisceminately. This detrimentally affected the quality of the whole army. Of course some of the top officers were very brilliant. And the low ranking officers and men were brave and volunteered out of patriotism. However, majority of the officers were of doubtful loyalty, joining out of sheer opportunism. Especially the field officers and above usually lacked military skill, and as Bose selected unassigned officers from among them, a mistaken notion was created that carrying favour with Bose was the only way to success. This naturally brought about a further deterioration in the fighting quality of the army.

The army was thirteen thousand strong, lightly armed for guerilla warfare which was the principal objective. After coming to Singapore, Bose made a demand for increasing the strength as it was too small. As stated earlier, he earnestly tried to raise the strength with fifty thousand as the target. But the Japanese army was in a position to supply arms for about thirty thousand men including the already organized troops. Again such a sudden expansion had the danger of rendering the army into a multitude with few fighters. Even then Subhas decided to increase the strength of the INA to thirty thousand organized into three divisions, and a volunteer force of about twenty thousand. He thought of raising the force from among the prisoners of war and the Indians of East Asia. The assessment of Hikari Kikan was that thirty thousand was the maximum limit of the regular forces considering from the number of officers and the quantity of arms the Southern forces could spare. The volunteers would be just a multitude without officers to command and also with any arm. Tojo was well aware of the attitude of Subhas, and hence when requested arms after the parade by the INA Tojo agreed to help as much as possible cautioning at the same time about the danger of the army being reduced to the status of a disorganized mob in quality. However, because of bad interpretation this caution was not conveyed properly to Subhas. As a result, Subhas was unhappy over the role of Hikari Kikan, thinking that it stood in between Tojo and himself and interfered with strengthening the INA.

In 1944, the volunteer force was amalgamated with the regulars, and he decided to raise twenty thousand volunteers after. As the passion of the Indians had already started coolong off, it became clear that the target will never be reached.

Although he organized the INA into three division, yet guerrilla warfare remained the main objective, and the divisions never got the strength to fight as strategic division. His objective was more of propaganda than of actual fighting. For example, he once said:

"The Britishers are in a habit of inflating their strength ten times. The Indians believe this and are cowed down. Following the example of the British we also should make propaganda that we also possess thirty divisions. We should raise units and name then as division with the establishment of the Provisional government, Subhas became the supreme commander of the Indian National Army in his capacity as the head of the Provisional Government of Free India.

The question of the command of the INA had to be sorted out. As in the case of world war I when the French and British forces were placed under unified command. Bose agreed to place the INA under the command of the Japanese forces, and conveyed his verbal approval of this to Col. Yamamoto, the Kikan chief. But when the actual implementations of the formula came, the idea met with considerable opposition from the Indians, and following certain incidents in Malaya during autumn of 1944 over the relation between the two armies arising out of the question of Defence of Malaya. Bose went as far as even denying his verbal commitment to the head of the Kikan. The Japanese side was both unhappy and disappointed over this stand of Bose.

Similar problems arose during the Imphal operation as well. It was the earnest desire of Bose to let INA have the charge of one front in the operations. It was just to keep up his face and utilize this for the propaganda purpose. The top officers of the INA did not press for this fas strongly as Bosc did as they knew the real strength of the INA. But at the same time these officers were afraid that their role may be reduced to that of errand boy of the Japanese army. The details will be discussed later, but it clearly gives a picture of the thinking of Bose.

Busy Bose

After coming to Singapore, Bose was very busy working hard to put all his plans into practice. After capturing the IIL, initiating the move for establishing the Provisional government, and drawing up plan for enlarging the INA, Bose made extensive tour of South East Asia, establishing contacts with the government in the region, and meeting the Indians settled in the region. Burma was scheduled to become independent on the 1st of August, and this gave Bose pretext to visit Burma which he was to use as the jumping pad.

Bose came to Rangoon on 29th July, received in the airport by the chairmen of the local branch of the IIL, and , a large number of Indians, and the Japanese and Burmese army personnel and officials. Unlike Singapore he could feel the atmosphere of war here.

On 30th he addressed a rally of Indian Youths, unfurling the national flag himself deeply moving all those present. He attached great importance to the youth. Next he addressed the meeting of the chairman of the local branches of the IIL. Following this he addressed a mammoth rally of the local Indians.

Bose attracted a lot of attention in the ceremony of founding of new independent Burma on 1st August and the ceremonial dinner that night. He was indeed very much moved to see Burma, which had been under British subjugation for long, free with his own eyes.

Bose did not let go the chance provided by the occasion in making a call to the local Indians, indicating how deeply he was involved with Burma.

Bose visited Bangkok on 4th August. for the second time, and succeeded in meeting the Thai premier Phibun who was away on tour during his first visit. The meeting was very cordial. Here Bose also established contact with the various organizations of the axis powers. He also addressed a largely attended meeting of the local Indians in the University auditorium commemorating the first anniversary of British repressions against independece movement of 9th August. On 9th, he went to Saigon, meeting the local Japanese military authorities and the Japanese ambassador. He also addressed a meeting of local Indians.

After returning to Singapore Bose addressed a meeting on the 14th August, the first anniversary of Gandhi's arrest. On 3rd September, Bose addressed a meeting at Kuala Lumpur lasting two house where he gave a call for donation exceeding two million dollars.

In this way Bose went round various regions of East Asia for uniting the Indians for establishing the Provisional government. As the day of establishing the Provisional government approached he felt that he should warn and encourage the Indians once more. Another reason for this was capitulation of Italy in the beginning of September to the Anglo-Canadian forces. This had its impact on the Indians as well. The feelings of the Indians in general at that time can be seen reflecting in the above address of Bose. Deep insight of Bose can also be discerned easily when one goes through the speech a bit carefully.

The above speech too fiery even in the standard of Bose. Especially the later part of the speech where he requested funds from the moneyed class clearly shows that the general feeling among the Indians at that time appeared to him somewhat not very encouraging. One can see here the worries that harassed Bose just before the time he was about to establish the Provisional government and start his work right in earnest to realize his long cherished dream. We cannot allow ourselves to be swept away by the enthusiasm of the cheering masses surrounding Bose whenever he addressed them.

Birth of Provisional Government of Free India

Establishment, composition etc. of the Provisional government have been described here. Speeches, Declaration of the Azad Hind Government, order of the day to the INA of 24th Oct. after the parade before the municipal office plaza etc. have been given here.[3]

Thus the establishment of the Provisional government was one of the most important steps of the freedom movement of Bose. It was his brain child and outcome of his sole personal efforts. At no stage did Japan drop any hint about it, and it was not at all the puppet the Japanese government. However, the government thus established, to what extent did it satisfy the dream of Bose; Although Japan hurriedly recognized this government, yet it was more of spiritual support not backed by official steps of diplomatic nature. Even such vital question like exchange of diplomatic missions postponed under the pretext of war, to which Bose had to agree. Again although the southern Comma declared that it would render all possible assistance, yet in practice it gave lip encouragement to the INA urging it to advance into India. The Southern command carefully avoided any statement regarding opening a common war front with the

3. See the documents in Volume III

INA. Not only this, the setup of the Provisional government itself contained many contradictory aspects as already discussed in the preceding chapter. A careful study will reveal that Bose's objective was not fulfilled in many ways. It will be unreasonable to think that versatile Bose was blind to the reality. In spite of all the practical difficulties Bose hurried with the establishment of the Provisional government only to take advantage of the propaganda value. Even though the government was on foreign soil, yet it could carve out its own territory through victory. He firmly believed in the hope the government of two million Indians and three lakh soldiers headed by him would inspire among the Indians in India, as well as the threat it would pose to the Anglo-Americans. That this self-confidence of Bose was neither baseless nor preposterous can be vouched even now from people who know his virtues and strength. This self -confidence was based on the strength of Japan and the Japanese army, which constituted the unique ally of the Provisional government and the INA. It was also indirectly based on the strength of the axis powers in Europe. How did Bose interpret the debacle of Guadalcanal which exposed the limitations of the Japanese army, and the crack in the axis camp created by the surrender of Italy? Did he rash through his plan recklessly overlooking these vital development? No. It was these development which, on the contrary, forced Bose to hurry with his plan. He placed all his reliance on the sincerity and resolution of Japan, and thought of materializing his plan of penetrating into India as quickly as possible mobilizing all the available strength before the development of any situation which night force the Southern Command to review its assessment of strategic inviability. This notice of Bose can be seen in all the subsequent developments.

Great East Asia Conference

Bose paid a second visit to Japan towards the end of Oct. 1943, just after the establishment of the Provisional Government. The main objective was to thank the Japanese government for reorganizing the Provisional Government and extending all possible cooperation. The other objective was to attend the great South East Asia Conference which was scheduled for early Nov. This was the first visit of Bose as the head of the Provisional government. He was received as state guest, and the residence of Vicount Shibusawa at Shiba was allotted as his residence.

After finishing the official formalities in the palace on the following day, Bose paid a visit to premier Tojo in his official residence and expressed his gratitude for the goodwill of the Japanese government. Bose confided to Tojo his ambitious plan of independence movement and sought earnestly Japan's cooperation.

On 2nd Nov. afternoon the German ambassador in Japan visited Bose and handed over an official telegram from the German Government indicating the official recognition of the two axis power excepting Italy which had already surrendered.

On the afternoon of 3rd November, a get together of the participants of the great East Asia conference was held in the official residence of the Japanese premier Tojo. Excepting for premier Ba Maw of Burma, all were new faces to Bose. Premier Chang of Manchukuo, chairman Wang of China, President Laurel of Philippines, Prince Wenwai of Thailand all gave different impression to Bose. Bose, however, mixed with all these leaders with great amity. His interesting impressions of this occasion will be described below.

The conference was inaugurated on 5th Nov. and as agreed beforehand. Bose took observer's seat. He took the observer's seat because in his view that the Great East Asia co-prosperity sphere did not include India agreed with the Japanese interpretation. Bose's party included his Finance Minister Chatterjee, chief of staff Bhonsle and four other Indians, besides his political advisor Senda.

Premier Tojo took the chair, and the conference started with the speeches of the representatives of the different countries. The famous Great East Asia Declaration was adopted on the second day. There was no direct reference to India in this declaration.

After the adoption of the above declaration, Ba Maw the premier of Burma moved a new resolution after delivering a forceful speech that the liberation of Asia cannot be achieved without the liberation of India. The resolutions. "We pledge to offer all possible sympathy and support to the struggle for Indian independence" was adopted unanimously. With the adoption of this resolution, the conference became all the more significant. Here for the first time the provisional government got integrated in the community of East Asian nations. Bose was very much impressed by the goodwill of the Burmese premier and all the leaders of the East Asian nations for initiation and immediate adoption of the resolution. Bose stood up amidst thunderous clappings and expressed his thanks for the sympathy and promise of assistance of the above nations. He also expressed his happiness of being able to attend the conference in observer's capacity.

Premier Tojo took the floor after Bose's speech was over, and pledged firm support of Japan to the Indian independence struggle. He made the following important declarations.

".......I have repeated/stated Japan's earnest desire to assist India to achieve its cherished goal. Now that the provisional government has been established and that the Indians have rallied around this government with patriotic spirit, I declare here that preparations are under way at present to hand over Andaman and Nicobar Islands to the provisional government as early as possible, which will signify the first step in establishment of independent India."

Thus ended the Great East Asia conference. Through this conference Bose succeeded in making his weight felt all over Asia. For Bose also, this very day was the most glorious moment of his two year's step in East Asia. It is not known how the later historians will evaluate the Great East Asia conference, but they will surely not fail to appreciate the heroic stand of Bose in this conference as the leader of Indian people, bearing the burden of India's future.

Taking advantage of the good chance provided by this conference Bose made a radio broadcast to the Indian living within and outside India where he argued that six conditions essential for gaining independence were already ripe.

"....The six conditions essential for capturing independence are already present. They are:

(a) a study of the real war situation will show who are at the tight spot.

(b) all the forces outside India opposed to British imperialism are our allies,

(c) proper understanding has already been established between the India patriots living outside and inside India.

(d) the struggle for liberation of India is closely linked with the struggle for establishing new order in the world.

(e) the provisional government of free India has already been established.

(f) the question of military aid from foreign countries is being worked out to our satisfaction.

Thus the national liberation movement of India has entered the final stage. I am very happy to report my compatriots in India that all the above conditions excepting the last condition are established facts, our only problem is how to drive England out of India.

Some of the leaders of the Indian independence Movement are of the view that independence will come to us automatically as a ripe fruit I always had the belief that if we desirc independence, we should rise grabbing the chance provide by the war. This belief became more and more firm in me when I was in jail in November 1940. We the Indians living overseas will before long cross the Indian border and hoist the national flag of liberation on the Indian said. The day is not far when the INA will advance upto New Delhi and unfurl the national flag over viceroy's lodge."

On 8th Nov Bose addressed a public meeting at the Hibiya Park, where he tried to enlighten the audience about India. He admitted the mistaken notion about India which has been transplanted in minds of the friends and sympathisers of India, and stated that it was a result of enemy propaganda. It will be important here to recollect the main points he tried to emphasis as we are trying to make a serious attempt to understand India now.

The first point he tried to emphasize was that the Indians did not know unity in the past, and factional feuds were very common. Hence a very strong force was needed to control and maintain law and order in India.........Britain subjugated India about hundred years ago. In the century preceding, India had fought with the British. The history of India says that about two thousand three hundred years ago India was unified, and it included the present day Afganistan and a part of Persia. From the glorious age of Buddhist monarchs upto the Imperial Moghal age India had seen a number of cultural, political and economic golden age. It was indeed a very regrettable fact that India did not try to resist England unitedly during the century of resistance struggle. Another reason was that India lacked good leader.

However, the Indians have learnt a lesson from the above experience. The state that the Indians had dreamt of and where they had placed much confidence has not died. So long the Indian tradition lives no power will be able to destroy the spirit of the Indian.

The second point he tried to bring out concerned religion. The enemy has tried to create an impression that India has been divided into Moslem India and Hindu India ever since the days of Moslem domination. However, this was entirely baseless. The history says that India was unified again under the Moghuls. The religious problem was a British creation in 1906, prior to which date the question was unknown. To break up the resistance of the Indians, Britain disarmed the Indians. Next they created a set of native rulers and divided India into British India and native states, retaining all the powers. Next when freedom movement gained momentum, they tried to bring about division between the Hindus and the Moslems.

The third point he tried to clarify was the overnight discovery of special class by Britain recently, which also has failed miserably like the religion-division policy.

The fourth point he said was the British attempt to perpetuate British rule by dividing India into four or five provinces.

Thus Bose claimed that such problems generally acknowledged as the cancer of India were just creation of Britain for propaganda purpose and tried to refute them whenever he got chance. An example of this was his closest associate Hassan, who was a Moslem. He also tried his best to break the food habits based on religion, and took a lead in the matter to set example to his followers. His firm belief was that before the great enterprise of independence, difference of religion or race was of minor significance. However, the problems were not that easy to solve, and the division of the country into India and Pakistan at the time of independence will gave little consolation to the departed soul.

During this stay, Bose visited sick Rash Behari Bose, the Indian students and local Indians. He also met the officials of the Japanese foreign office and the Japanese army and the navy. He laid special emphasis on the negotiations concerning strengthening the INA, and sought aeroplanes and naval vessels for building up air unit and naval unit. He went as far as persuading Japan to train up Indians for the purpose.

During a press conference a reporter asked Bose about famine in India, and the policy of the provisional government over the issue. Regarding the policy of supplying food to India, Bose said :

"The policy can be put into practise in two ways. Either to carry the food in our possession by boat to India, or to call the Britishers to take food from out ports. I have adopted the latter policy. Although I have said that I would give food without any string attached yet they have not yet come. Not only they are not taking food from us, they have even rejected all our offers and are callously watching the death of the Indians...."

Bose had indeed negotiated the above steps with the Burma Area Army through Hikari Kikan, and had broadcasted the offer to India quit a number of times.

Next, it will be interesting to know the impression Bose got of the Great East Asia Conference, where he was present as an observer. The following are from the notes he made and views he expressed on occasion with minor modifications.

Atmosphere of the conference in general :Interpreting that the speech of the Burmese premier Ba Maw touched upon the main objective of the conference, he quotes the following expression of Ba Maw: "The representatives of the various nations of East Asia are perhaps using different languages and different expressions, but at the background exists the same philosophy, objective and resolution."

The Burmese premier has expressed the feeling of the different delegates with wonderful precision. The passionate feeling 'Asia is one' pervaded the whole conference.

Premier Tojo : Faced the conference with firmness befitting a military statesman. His expressions were sharp and clear, reflecting idealism. His theoretical approach was quite appropriated.

Manchukuo Premier Chang: Had the air of old and vateran politician, and created the impression of an old sea captain steering a boat safely to the port through rough weather.

Chinese chairman Wang: A versatile genious with a good understanding of own standpoint. Possessed strict but mute resolution, and hence did not feel the necessity of convincing others.

Philippines President Raurel: An eloquent vateran parliamentarian spitting fire. Could move the listeners to tears with sincere earnest feeling.

Thai Representative Prince Wanwai: Courteous and refined aristocrat conscious of the proud tradition of Thailand. The prince would dazzle any social gathering anywhere in the world.

Burmese Representative Dr. Ba Maw: to borrow his words, he was a soldier right from the front, well aware of the danger of the motherland, and firmly committed to deliver a decisive blow to the enemy. Hence he devoted all his energy to create a united and free Asia.

Conference Proceedings: It is necessary to write a word about the chairman of the conference who carried out the affair quite efficiently. When we go through the records of similar conference we come across one or a few personalities who control the whole show. In Vienna conference we have a Metternich, end in Versalle Conference we have Clemenceau and Lloyd George. It is unavailable that the international Conferences are conducted in such arbitrary fashion. The stronger nations possess the weapon to reject the demands of the weaker nations. Harassing them by adopting various means of deception like flattery, seduction of intrigue. However, this conference was not monopolized by the strongest power. Moreover, there was no trace of flattery, seduction, concealment of scheming.

Bose's Visit to Nanking, Manila and Java

On way back home from the Great East Asia Conference, the Chinese chairman Wang stopped overnight at Fukuoka. Here he expressed his wish to invite Bose to Nanking to his two advisors Shibayama and Toraoka, after making the following remark about Bose.

".........This time I met Bose, the Head of the provisional government of free India. He kept silent during the conference, and only at the end he made a speech about his belief. Befitting to his good physique and looks, he was full of energy and spirit. His speech was solid, and acted like a revolutionary in the real sense of the term. He has been tempered through eleven imprisonments and seven hunger strikes. Again he has been educated in England and Germany, and apparently a man of firm resolution...."

Wang's assessment of Bose is quite interesting when it is viewed in the light of Bose's assessment of Wang.

Wang got a very good impression of Bose in the first meeting and hence went as far as inviting him to Nanking. He wanted to invite Bose to China after getting the concurrence of the Japanese authorities. He sent his propaganda chief Lin Pei Shang home ahead of him in order to have all the preparations for receiving the state guest.

Visit to China had been a long cherished desire of Bose. He left Tokyo on 11th November along with Bhonsle, two other Indians, his political advisor Senda, Col. Yamamoto, and foreign secretary Ota, and flew straight to Nanking.

The Nanking government received him as the head of a friendly nation, sponsored a public meeting, and showed him round military academy etc. Bose paid courtesy call not only on the Chinese chairman, but also on Hata, the supreme commander of the Chinese expeditionary forces, and the ambassadors of Japan, Germany and Manchukuo.

However, the real purpose of Bose's visit to Nanking was something else. He wanted to get a chance to express his conviction to the Chungking government and the Chinese masses.

On 26th night he made a forty minute long speech addressed to the Chungking government, expressing his views on the prevailing political atmosphere in China, and the necessity of maintaining peace in East Asia. It was also the call from an Indian who had risen above to prejudices normally found among the Indians over the Sino-Japanese question.

It will be appropriate here to add one more line. Bose delivered this speech selecting the contents out of his free will. Neither the Wang government, nor the Japanese government had hinted anything about the contents of the speech. He never compromised\his position as the head of the provisional government.

Bose made a second broadcast to Chungking on the 23rd (recorded speech broadcasted after his departure) titled 'Second Appeal to Chungking whereas his first speech was full of sympathy over the division of the Chinese people into two warring camp, this was a protest against the activities of the Chinese forces on the Indo-Burmese border. Here he attacked the attitude of the Chungking government which had cast its lot with the Anglo-Americans. This speech is very significant it contains much of his political conviction.

From Nanking Bose went to Shanghai on the 21st and addressed a meeting of the local Indians. On 22nd he went to Manila as the state guest of the newly independent Republic of Philippines.

During this visit he had talks with President Raurel, the Japanese ambassador and the Japanese army and navy commanders. On 23rd he addressed a meeting of the local Indians. Here the people were not very enthusiastic about joining the INA as they were in Shanghai, hence main emphasis was laid on fund collection.

Bose returned to Singapore on the 25th Nov. On 10th December Bose flew to Jakarta, and after meeting the Japanese army and navy chiefs, addressed a meeting of the local Indians on the 11th. He also visited Jakarta, Surabaya, Borneo and Sumatra before returning to Singapore on the 14th.

Thus Bose visited the Indian communities all over East Asia, and the two millions Indians come forward joining the INA and donating the properties and wealth to the cause of the country. Although Bose was in a very high spirit at this time. Yet all these imposed heavy burden on his shoulder.

The existence of the provisional government led by Bose was advertised rapidly and effectively through the Great East Asia Conference and his subsequent activities. And the main mission of the government, viz. invasion of India, became the decisive issue. Bose devoted all his energy in giving a material shape to this objective.

The objective of invasion of India entailed the fulfilling of a number of basic conditions. The first condition was the stage upto which the organization and equipping within India. To what extent the people and the Indian soldiers inside would respond to the initial thrust of the INA. And the last important condition was whether the Japanese forces would agree to the plan of joint war of the .provisional government, integrating it with its strategy.

As already stated, numerical the strength of the INA increased steadily as more and more men joined it, but it was very ill trained and equipped. There were very few good officers at the top, and hence the so-called divisions lacked the capacity to fight as strategic unit. Some of the units composed of ex-army men were well trained as guerilla units, and hence were already deployed along the Indo-Burmese border. Hence it was just impossible to give a green signal to the INA to launch attack on India single handed. Again the proposition of cooperation with the Japanese forces had to be evaluated in the light of above handicap.

Even before Bose came to East, steps were taken to carry out propaganda to the people within India and gather information. Again, trained people were sent into India. After assumption of leadership, points were emphasized very much. Of his few ministers, one was allotted the portfolio of propaganda, and he personally supervised this, thus raising the efficiency. Besides utilizing the broadcasting facilities of Tokyo and South East Asia, he dropped leaflets in India utilizing the Japanese air units. However, as the Japanese army lacked planes suitable for such a campaign, very limited success was achieved, although he had information from India that dropping leaflets was much more effective than dropping bombs.

Every two or three months Bose got information on domestic situation from his associates in India, via Afganistan, Berlin and Tokyo. Again, once or twice secret messengers came from Bengal across the Burma border. In April 1943 two groups equipped with wireless transmitters were para-dropped, who kept sending information till early following year. The persons sent to Tinsukia were captured by the enemy, and those sent to Calcutta could do very little useful work because of insufficient training. In May 1944, a number of spies were landed on the east coast of India and Ceylon by submarine. Some of them started sending information since July, but these were found to be of little importance.

Bose took great care in selecting persons for these jobs, and the training took five months, two months' preliminary course, and three months' proper course. No Indian could be found to head the training programme, and the results were not very encouraging. Again, there were cases of planned defection on reaching India. In 1944, a group of twelve persons were thus betrayed to the enemy. Bose's zeal for communal integration got a severe blow as the defector in this case was Moslem.

At any rate, the provisional government took all the care to make as thorough preparations as possible with in its means' but excepting for propaganda value, very little concrete things were achieved.

Thirdly, the relation with the Japanese army constituted the life and death question of the plans of the provisional government. As well known, it was not very smooth, and can be said to have ended in a pitiable tragedy. This point will be discussed in its proper perspective.

Provisional Government of Free India Shifts to Burma

The provisional government of Bose shifted to Burma on 7th January 1944. With this he came one stop nearer to his goal of penetrating India.

Before shifting to Burma, Bose paid a visit to Andaman and Nicobar island on 29th December 1943. He appointed Lt. Col. Loganadan as the administrative head, and raised the tricolor flag of freedom on this soil of free India.

Bose came to Rangoon via Bangkok, where he renewed his contacts with the Thai leaders. In Rangoon he was received by Dr. Ba Maw and other Burmese leaders, the INA officers and men, IIL leaders, and the Japanese ambassador to Burma Sawada, Bose claimed this advance to Rangoon as the last step in liberation war, and thanked the Burmese Government and the Japanese army for rendering all possible assistance.

From the very beginning Bose wanted to locate his government in Rangoon, but could not do so for various reasons already discussed. After that the situation changed a lot. But even then the Japanese forces took a bold decision to attack India.

The Japanese forces occupied almost all of Burma by April 1944, restored law and order in the country, and helped in the establishment of independence Burma.

After subjugation of Burma, the 15th Army, which undertook the operation, studied possibility of attacking India. The possibility was also discussed in the Supreme Command of the Southern Forces in Singapore. The views were communicated to the Imperial Headquarters in due course. In fact, the Imperial Headquarters was also very much interested in Indian operation so that the Japanese and German forces, which were advancing towards Suez, could join hands in the Indian Ocean.

During this period the Iwaguro Kikan was busy organizing and training the INA for playing a military role in case of such operation. A branch of the Kikan was established in Rangoon helping the Indians, but reaction to the activities of Indians in Burma was not very encouraging and the military leaders also did not show much interest in the project.

In autumn of 1942, the front line forces reinvestigated the idea of Indian operation, but lack of soldiers and inadequate logistic facilities were found to be greatest impediments. Again, the Indians in general were not very well disposed towards Japan at that time. So Iwaguro Kikan advocated against the operation. So it went to cold storage. The military decision at that time was that the operation was not feasible for the time being irrespective of the progress of the work of the Iwaguro Kikan.

The conception of the Indian operation was based on the momentum of military victory achieved till that time, and the situation in India was totally overlooked. Again, there was no move for combining the political strategy with the military strategy.

After retreating from Burma, the British forces started regrouping, and slowly gained strength with the help of the Americans. Next they went one step further and launched attack on the Japanese forces in Akyab and Assam fronts. Under the above situation it was decided to reorganize and reinforce the Burma Area Army in to three armies and ten divisions, and Lt. Gen. Kawabe was appointed as the new commander. As some action had to be taken, it was proposed to attack the enemy, occupy a certain territory, drew the main strength of the enemy there & deliver a crushing blow. For this Imphal was proposed as the prospect target. The final clearance of the Imphal operation came from the Imperial Headquarters during January 1944. Before Lt. Gen. Kawabe left Tokyo to take up his new assignment, Premier Tojo had indicated to him that the objective of the Burma operation had been to pave the basis for India's independence.

After reaching Rangoon, the general met the head of the local branch of Iwaguro Kikan, the commander of the INA and the commander of local units of the INA. When it became clear that Bose would come to the East, preparations were made to coordinate the political offensive with the military offensive. It was also decided to shift the provisional government and the INA at an appropriate moment, and persuade the Burmese government to approve of it. At that time it became an important topic as to how to coordinate the plans of the provisional government with the strategy of the Japanese army. Although the feeling in India was anti-British, it was not necessarily pro-Japanese. As it was assessed any attack on India would be interpreted as aggressive act and would harm the independence movement, the possibility of harmonizing Bose's movement with this operation was studied carefully. As the basic policy of Japan was for

Indian independence, it was decided that the territories occupied during the operation would be handed over to the Indians immediately. The military fight between Japan and Britian would thus turn into politics fight between India and England, and Bose would be the focal point of the military and political struggle. Again, as declared, all efforts would be concentrated for Burmese independence, and at the same time cooperation would be sought of the independent government of Burma to allow its territory to be used by Bose for launching the Indian Operation. Again, a common anti-British front would be created among the Burmese and the Indians, again, the INA would be given a front where it would be possible to achieve success. A section of the INA force would be deployed with in Burma to work as intelligence unit, special duty unit etc. The Burma Area Army conceived of the whole operation on the above lines.

However, the whole conception ran into difficulty in the very beginning. The commanding officer and below were too much engrossed with the strategic aspect of the operation, and had no time to think of the India policy. Again to associate the INA with the operation was interpret as political muddling which was strongly opposed. Leaving apart the propaganda aspect, the association of the INA would create more problem for the whole operation.

At this stage there was a visit from Bose to Rangoon in the end of July. The commander of the Burma Area Army was won over by Bose in the first meeting itself. As the commander had got hint from premier Tojo about the political objective involved in the operation, he was very encouraged by the attitude of Bose and felt that political aspect also could be fitted into the strategic planning. He met Bose along with his staff officer Katakura a number of times, and ascertained the intent of the provisional government after explaining the policy of the Burma Area Army regarding the India operation. Bose also grabbed this chance to express his intention without any hindrance from the Hikari Kikan.

Bose explained his experience of long political struggle, and stated that he grabbed the chance provided by the world war to launch armed struggle against England, and had resolved to join hands with any country that considered England as its enemy. He also said that this was the reason why he parted company with Gandhi. Finally he asserted:

(a) The INA should be given charge of one section of the front. This would signify advance of resolution.

(b) The war was going to be a protracted affair. Hence a fighting cadre should be built up through the war.

(c) The war was going against the axis powers. Immediate action was needed as any delay would encourage collaboratory attitude among the people.

(d) To check this, INA should penetrate into the Indian soil, set up provisional government administration, and attract the Indian revolutionaries there. Once Japan's support became known, more and more people would come and join the ranks of the INA.

As the plan for attacking India was still shrouded in great secrecy, time was not yet ripe for indicating the views of the Japanese army over the above contentions of Bose, and hence the first negotiatious ended in oral support by the Japanese side. However, it was at this time that the Japanese military leaders in Burma were won over by Bose, and they seriously started thinking of assisting Bose as much as possible.

The question of selecting an appropriate front for penetrating into India preoccupied Bose very much, eversince he reached Berlin. After the fall of Singapore, Bose visited the Japanese ambassador Oshima in Berlin and conveyed his expectation that the Japanese forces would occupy Chittagong after occupying Burma, which was the next objective of the Japanese forces. He wanted the Imperial Headquarters be informed that a great confusion would start in Indian in case Chittagong was occupied by the Japanese army. Bengal was the cradle of revolution in India, and chittagong was its vital spot. He had this firm conviction all through his stay in the East.

However, the Japanese army held that any large scale army manoeuver in the coastal area was impossible as this would immediately come under enemy naval and air attack. Moreover, the supply line was also not very encouraging. Hence the idea of Bose could not be accommodated out of strategic considerations.

As the Burma Area Army came to know Bose, his personality, ideas and political and military outlook, intimately, it started thinking seriously how to incorporate Bose's ideas in the Imphal operations, after the operation got clearance from the Supreme command of the Southern Forces. It was decided to entrust the extreme left wing of the 15th Army to the INA. The motive behind this was that it would be easier for Bose to advance on the Chittagong from here. Again the INA forces would be present all along the front as special units for dealing with the surrendering enemy forces and collecting arms. These were communicated secretly to the Indian side.

The question of shifting of the Indian leaders and the provisional government to Burma became important as the above plan was drawn up. As there were many impediments on the way, Burma came forward to assist Bose in eliminating all the hindrances. It was only in the end of Sep. that the Burmese government finally cleared the idea of allowing the provisional government to work from Rangoon after protracted negotiations by the Burma Area Army and the ambassador Sawada.

This shifting, however, raised a number of new problems. One was the establishment of the National Indian Bank. Bose had thought of establishing the National Indian Bank in Rangoon and issue paper currency. This idea met with Burmese opposition and had to be abandoned. The question of the persons arrested for violating military regulation also came up. Many persons were released at this time. As the INA came to Burma, a number of tricky problems involving relation with the Japanese forces cropped up. The biggest problem that cropped up involved exchange of salute. The Indian soldiers had the tradition of shedding blood over the question of exchanging salute with the whites. Bose demanded equality in exchange of salute as an allied army. After some negotiations, the Japanese authorities accepted Bose's demand. The credit for persuading the Japanese side goes to monk Maruyama of the Nichiren Sect.

Even more tricky problem involved the question of commanding the troops during the joint operation. Here also Bose demanded equality in resolute terms. As this involved directly with the operation, the Japan side adopted hard line, and the negotiations had a very hard sailing. After protracted negotiations, the India side yielded the command right upto the army corps level. As the Indian side was reluctant to surrender command of the lower formations. It was agreed that appropriate action should be taken in the field to avoid confusion in the command. Regarding criminal code it was decided to hand over the Indian soldiers violating the Japanese military regulations to the Japanese authorities. The Indian side was permitted to have its own military criminal code.

The question of the authority of the Japanese military policy (Kempei) over the Indian soldiers also came up. Bose had a sentimental aversion for the Kempei. Again, the Kempei was dreaded both by the Indian military personnel and civilians. Hence Bose firmly opposed the idea of the Kempei having jurisdiction over the military and civilian personnel of Indian origin. After negotiations, the right of action of the high ranking kempei officers was recognized under special circumstances when the security questions came up. The lower ranking officers were forbidden to interfere with the Indians.

Propaganda was the strongest weapon of Bose. Hence he sought independence with regard to broadcasting, which was indeed very logical. The Burma Army took a sympathetic view, and allowed Bose to use the Rangoon Radio without any interference.

There were also many problems still left to be solved. In short, Bose carried through his idea of armed struggle maintaining its independent character, by the sheer weight of his excellent personality and convicting. Again, the Burma Area Army, on its part, took all steps possible to incorporate the plan of Bose in drawing up the Imphal operation, and under such a situation it negotiated for shifting the provisional government to Rangoon.

On 7th January, Bose attended a dinner party given by the top commander of the Japanese forces along with his cabinet ministers and top official of the provisional government. The Japanese ambassador Sawada was also present here. Here also he reaffirmed his resolution to lay down his life for the Independence of India.

After coming to Burma, Bose took all possible step to step up his propaganda campaign.

Indian National Army Crosses the Border

The provisional government of free India moved to Rangoon in early January 1944 when the Burma Area Army was busy preparing for Imphal operation. The enemy counter offensive in Akyab front was repulsed by the 55th Division around this time. But the enemy did not relax its pressure on the 55th Division. As a diversionary tactics, the 55th Division attacked the superior enemy in order to attract as many enemy troops from Imphal area as possible. In Hukon area of North Burma, Chinese forces under the command of Gen. Stilwell was mounting attacks on the 18th Division in order to open the Ledo Road. Again, a Chinese force armed by American arms was poised for an attack from Salween river side to meet the Stillwell forces.

The enemy air force became more and more active with the passing of days, and the Japanese air units were no match to cope this. Not only land and water transport in Burma was virtually disrupted, even the rail road construction between Burma and Thailand and sea convoys came increasingly under enemy air attacks. The gap in the relative strengths of the two forces increased with the passing of days.

Even then the preparations for Imphal operation went on in great secrecy and slowly the troops assembled in the front line. The operations was entrusted to the 15th Army reinforced by a number of divisions.

Simultaneously with this the Indian side pressed the demand for advance of the INA to the front, and Bose was very unhappy over the delay of the Burma Area Army in finalizing the matter. His intention was to deploy two of his divisions in an independent front and lead it personnel by no means this could be fitted into the strategic planning of the Japanese army, and despite all sympathies the operation plan, could not changed. Both the army leaders and Hikari Kikan had to take a lot of troubles in consoling Bose.

For about a year prior to this the Hikari Kikan had also undergone reorganization to become the Headquarters of the Guerilla Units of the Southern Forces. Lt. Gen. Isoda was appointed as its head, and it was allotted the task of carrying out guerilla operations jointly with the INA. The set up was also changed into divisional headquarters set up, and the headquarters shifted to Rangoon around the time the Indian provisional government shifted to Rangoon. It maintained close contact with the provisional government and preparing for guerilla operations.

A joint committee of Japanese, Indian and Burmese officials was also set up for streamlining the joint Indo-Japanese operation. This committee acted as the liaison committee of the three armed forces. Quite often the commander of the Japanese forces, Bose and Aung Sen, the Burmese Defence Minister, attended the meeting of this committee as observers.

The main questions this committee deliberated were (a) transportation of the INA soldiers from Singapore to the front, (b) their accommodation during stay in Burma, and (c) the relation between the Japanese and the Indian forces after the capture or Imphal and Manipur area. Bose was not very happy with the delay in sending the Indian troops to the front but the Japanese side could not help this out of operational considerations on the question of accommodating the Indian soldiers, the Burmese side showed very little enthusiasm. Although prime minister Ba Maw was a personal friend of Bose, y et the Burmese in general had great antipathy towards the Indians and this was reflected in all the government policies.

The question of policy coordination regarding the occupied territories also raised a lot of controversy. As this meant the first administrative territory on the Indian soil proper, Bose wanted to have a concrete policy agreement with the Burma Area Army in order to avoid future troubles. Conforming to the basic policy, the Japanese side agreed to place the occupied territory under Indian administrative control, and the Indian side was given the right of even collecting the arms. The Japanese side agreed to be responsible for the operations alone. Although the above policy agreement was a signed, yet trouble arose again when the question of selecting the chairman of the Indo-Japanese joint committee came up. The Indian side asserted the claim of Bose, whereas the Japanese side wanted to have a Japanese as the head. Finally this question was left unresolved. This incident reflected the hardened attitude of the Japanese side.

In the mean time the Indian provisional government was also making steady preparations for administering Manipur area. People were recruited to repair electric lights, taps, construct houses, and for helping farmers etc. and hence the whole set up became what can be termed as military administrations organization.

Despite the above mentioned hurdles, preparations for war went on steadily. In early March three divisions of the 15th army were deployed on the left bank of Chindwyn river for capture of Manipur. The 31st Division took up position on the extreme right with Kohima as the objective; the 15th Divisions took up position in the middle and the 33rd Division took up position on extreme left, both having Imphal as the target. The last mentioned division was to launch offensive one was ahead of the main strength.

The Indian National Army was also getting ready for playing its historical role. A section of the army was deployed at the extreme left flank of the 33rd Division for capturing Haka-Falam area. The main strength of the INA, Col.. Kiani's Division was at that time on the way to front for attacking Manipur in conjunction with the 15th Division.

When the above division passed through Rangoon, Bose himself saw it off. When the troops were parading in front of Bose, suddenly siren rang and about ten planes appeared overhead. The Burmese officials present in the function ran helter skelter for their life. The Japanese staff officers looked resigned. But Bose was standing on the dias unperturbed, and ordered his officers to disperse the soldiers. He came down only after all had dispersed.

The operation took the enemy by surprise. Chindwin river was crossed successfully, and the front line troops advanced towards the Indo-Burma border. The operation was launched on the fifteenth of March 1944 at 9.3. P.M.

Prior to this one regiment of INA under Lt. Col. Saigal had launched attack on Haka-Fallam area in the beginning of February; and as the regiment under the direct command of Bose had successfully occupied a small territory within the Indian boundary. Although a little behind the scheme. The main strength of the Japanese army advanced steadily against stiff enemy resistance, and advanced towards Imphal for encircling it after crossing the Indo-Burma border on the 22nd of March.

As soon as the INA crossed the Indo-Burma border, Bose released his strongest weapon, propaganda. On 20th March he announced this achievement over the Rangoon Radio. This speech reflected the great confidence he had in himself and in the INA.

Responding to this speech, premier Tojo made the following statement on the 22nd. The keynote of this speech was that the Indian territories over which the INA would be placed under the administration of the provisional government of free India.

"...........The objective of the Empire is to crush the military might of the enemy and hand over India to the Indians. The territories occupied by the Indian National Army should be placed under the administration of Provisional Government of Free India without any delay. The penetration of the INA will rouse the patriotic Indian people and the liberated territory will swell in no time ultimately realizing Indian independence.

All the Asian people want to see India free, and this is the most righteous cause in the world......I earnestly hope and pray that the Indian army and people will cooperate with each other, overcome all the difficulties and attain success in no time. I want to declare here once again that the Empire will give all possible help to this noble fight."

Bose immediately expressed his gratitude in the following terms : "Beside carrying out war we shall set up new administration of free India. This new administration will show clearly how different self-government is from foreign rule. The panicking enemy will increase its anti-Japanese propaganda. I take this opportunity to express the sincere gratitude of the provisional government, INA and the Indian people in general."

Two following points became very clear when one sees the above statements of the two leaders in historical perspective. One is that this operation was of great significance so far as political strategy was concerned. Although this operation was conceived initially out of purely military strategic consideration, yet later on special character was appended to it. The other concerns military administrate of the occupied territories. Till now the normal practice had been to set up military administration for the occupied territories, which were good target for enemy propaganda. In this operation, this intermediate step was by passed, handing over the occupied territories directly to the provisional government. The policy of the Japanese government and of the Japanese army on the spot was drawn up under the above consideration and the characteristic features of cooperation with the Indian side can be seen here clearly.

The Japanese army mounted greater pressure in April, and by 6th April Kohima was captured by the 31st Division. The next objective was Imphal. The main strength of the 15th Army advanced towards it from north, one detachment of this division along with Kiyani Division of the INA proceeded from the Palel direction in the East, and the 33rd Division moved in from the South. It appeared that strategic encirclement was complete, and occupation of Manipur was now a matter of time.

At this stage Bose intensified his propaganda, and on 4th of April he made an appeal to the Indian masses outlining the stand of the provisional government, which he said would immediately follow the advancing forces, He also explained the administrative policy his government would follow.

".........Your government, the provisional government of free India has only one mission before it. It is to drive away the British forces from India with arms, and set up the government of Indian people which the Indian people have been aspiring so long.....the provisional government of free India will carry out war on hand, and take all the steps to rehabilitate the liberated territories on the other. The provisional government is the only legal government of Indians people. The provisional government appeals to the people in the liberated territories to give all possible assistance to the administrative officials appointed by the INA and the provisional government....."

He also guaranteed the safety of life and properties of the Indian living within the liberated territories, but warned that those collaborating with the enemy or trying to disrupt the activities of the provisional government would be dealt with severely. He made it clear repeatedly that he was relying on the promises made by Japan, and was accepting arms which Japan was giving out of good will. Japan wants that the people living in the liberated Zone should cooperate with the Japanese forces. Although it was the policy to have our own currency, yet this could not be done due to lack of time. Hence as a provisional step, Japanese currency would be used for the time being and this would be replaced as soon as arrangements could be made.

Round about the time this declaration was made. Lt. Col. Chatterjee, The finance minister, was appointed as the first Governer of the Liberated are :

Immediately after the above declaration of Bose, Premier Ba Maw of Burma made a very important broadcast, in which he explained the historical significance of penetration into India landing the role of the INA. He stressed the spiritual and material significance of this and termed it as the event of the century. In this struggle he expressed unqualified support of the Burmese people and army.

Around this time an aeroplane was presented to Bose by Japan.

On 5th April, Bose shifted part of his government to Maymyo, the headquarters of the 15th Army. This was an expression of his long cherished desire to lead the frontline troops. However, after some time he was forced to withdraw to Rangoon leaving a section of his government as the operation bogged down and also as he found the place unsuitable for his purpose.

During this time a controversy was raging in Tokyo over recognizing the provisional government as the official government of India. The Burn Area Army sought Bose's views over the matter. His attitude was very cautious. His reply was that he had no objection in dropping "Provision of 'provisional government' of free India' and make it 'government of free India', but care should be taken to avoid all trifling controversial so that wholehearted attention could be paid to war. It appears that the Japanese leaders had in their mind to exploit the success of Imphal operation and establishment of Bose' government on the Indian soil for propaganda purpose. However, Bose said that nothing but war must be the primary objective till the Indian tricolour fluttered from the Red Fort he stuck to the objective which he had propagated till that time. The Burma Area Army, in turn, sent the views of Bose to Tokyo.

On 8th April the Imperial Headquarters made the following announcement on the war situation in Burma.

(a) the Japanese forces in cojunction with the Indian and with the Indian National Army has captured a strategic point Kohima on the Imphal Dimapore highway on 6th April early morning.

(b) the operations against the enemy airbourn units in Katha area is going on smoothly.

This announcement of the Imperial Headquarters had a great importance on the people within the country. The Japanese people in general became aware that the historical event of penetration into India has taken plan and that in this operation the Japanese forces had an ally, The Indian National Army. This came just at the time when fortunes of war had turned against Japan in other fronts. This operation had its desired impact on the people as the government could give at least one positive action to the people.

However, a grave danger was lurking behind the shadow of Imphal operation on which both the Japanese government and people as well as the provisional government were banking up on. It was the appearance of air bourn units on the scene.

About a month prior to this, on 5th March, suddenly a strong enemy unit landed on a spot midway between Mandalay and Mitkyina along the railway line behind the 15th Army which was getting ready for operation. This is known as Katha landing. The 15th Army did not have any reserve to deal with this enemy. As they destroyed the railway line, supply to the 18th Division located to the north was cut off. Moreover the enemy succeeded in establishing strong base here and repulsed repeated attack of the defenders.

The Burma Area Army was taken off guard by this air bourn unit. It decided that the 15th Army should proceed with operation preparation undisturbed, and hence it took more than a month to destroy this enemy by deploying the 53rd Division.

The Burmese and the Indians were very sensitive to the assult by this air bourn unit. However, Bose was totally unperturbed, and the incident only hardened his attitude all the more.

The enemy could take such a daring step like dropping air bourn unit behind the Japanese line just because the Japanese air force had been neutralized by the enemy. The enemy air superiority soon exposed the air, water and land supply routes in the operational zone as well as in the rear to enemy raids. The enemy succeeded in maintaining constant supply of men and material to its forces encircled in Imphal by air. Japanese forces were helpless to check this development. Although Imphal was very weakly defended initially, yet slowly enemy built up considerable strength there, and the strategy of surprise became totally ineffective. Thus the essential nature of the operation. Element of surprise, totally changed and the Japanese found themselves engaging strongly entrenched enemy. But the Japanese forces had neither the strength nor the capacity to deal with such a situation. Moreover the preparations were for a different objective altogether.

As such the operation came to a standstill. Simultaneously with this the rainy season started which disrupted the supply route completely. The soldiers were down with fever, and hunger had its toll. The INA force were also passing through similar difficulties.

Just at that time there were incidents of surrender from the Kiyani Division which was manning the front in Palel area. Bose who had always been thinking of going to the front to lead the forces in person grabbed this chance and requested the Japanese side to make arrangement for his travel to the front. With great difficulty the Japanese side could dissuade him and finally Isoda, the head of the Hikari Kikan and a number of ministers of the provisional government went to the front.

The Japanese command tried all method for improving the situation. The divisional commanders were sent to the field, points of attack were changed a number of times, and all possible steps were taken. The fighting forces as well as the logistics forces did as much as they could. But all failed before enemy resistance.

Towards the end of May the commander of the Burma Area went to the front for studying the situation. He came back to Rangoon, his headquarters, with heavy heart. Mutaguchi, the commander of the 15th Army had advised him retreat to save the soldiers. He could not forget Kiyani, the commander of the INA division and the INA soldiers rushing to the front. The position was untenable. But all the telegrams which came from the Supreme command of the Southern Forces and Tokyo expected only good news of the operation. It was obvious that the objective of the operation was more political. He had no other alternative but to fight till the end. The fate of Japan and India was hanging on this operation. All the resources had to be mobilized for helping Mutaguchi.

The commander of the Burma Area Army visited Bose in his headquarters. After the commander had briefed Bose on the situation on the front, Bose repeated his request to visit the front, and demanded that the remaining forces of the INA and the Rani of Jhansi Regiment be rushed to the front. Finally Bose said that during his recent visit to Singapore he found the Indians not all disappointed over the war situation, and longer war meant greater determination. They were ready to face any adverse situation and were determined to fight till the end to achieve their goal under the leadership of Japan. These words of Bose only increasing his agony.

At that time Bose was contemplating to reorganize his government for expanding its activities as he expected smooth progress of operation. This was in order to give a material shape to his speech he delivered when he became the head of the provisional government. He divided the field of activity into three zones. East Asia, this was to remain the base for political and military activities as usual; liberated zone; the problems here involved political and reconstructional aspect coupled with preparations for future; Indian Territories Under Enemy Occupation: this was the territory to be liberated and where the activities of the INA was to be concentrated. The idea was to establish three section in the provisional government with ministers and advisor with clearly specified responsibilities.

The 1st Section was to supervise the activities in East Asia and was named as East Asia Committee of the cabinet. Maximum efforts were to be made in this area to mobilized men, material and funds. For the purpose it was decided either to set up a new administrative unit or to expand the already exiting administrative unit to suit the purpose.

The scope of the finance division was to be expanded. A new mobilization division was set up for recruiting people for the INA and the women's unit. It was also allotted the duty of training people for administering and rehabilitating the liberated areas as well as IIL workers. The supply division established a little earlier was to be expanded. It was decided to entrust all the matters of grave importance to the above three division finance, mobilization and supply, in future. The affairs of the East Asia Committee were entrusted to the minister normally looking after the East Asian affairs and his advisors.

The IInd Section was to be responsible for the liberated areas and was named liberated Area Committee of the cabinet. Plans for administering and rehabilitating the liberated areas wore already under preparation and their implementation was now only a question of time. Officials to supervise reconstruction work in the liberated areas were already posted in the border areas. The Liberated Area Committee was to be constituted by hand picked ministers and advisors.

The IIIrd Section was to look after the affairs of the areas under enemy occupation and was named War Committee of the cabinet. This committee was entrusted the job of dealing with various problems concern war and propaganda in the enemy held territory. It was also to study revolutionary movement and administrations in the enemy held areas. It was to be constituted with a minister and his advisors.

The affairs of the three committee were to be conducted from the centre with close liaison and cooperation among them. The keynote was to maintain the cohesion of the provisional government.

The above reorganization will show clearly how serious and thorough the thinking of Bose was.

Finally the Dooms Day came. The enemy counter offensive from Dimapore side proved to be too strong for the Japanese forces defending

Kohima, and the Kohima-Imphal road was breached by the enemy in a number of places. The 15th Army was more or less squeezed in to defensive posture. The commander of the Burma Area Army was gravely ill at that time. He called his staff officer at his sick bed and after a thorough discussion decided to send a staff officers to Manila, at that time the headquarters of the Southern Command, to explain the situation.

On 3rd July night, the Burma Area Army received telegraphic order that the enemy should be contained in the Manipur front at any cost. The next day Bose paid a visit to the sick commander, but he refused to see Bose under the pretext of illness.

On 5th July the Burma Area Army ordered the suspension of Imphal operation. Thus the offensive which was lunched by the Japanese and the Indian forces four months earlier came to a halt, and the forces fell back on defensive line to contain the enemy. The grand scheme of Bose pathetically, ended up in a vain dream.

Bose showed a good understanding of the situation to the chief of staff who went to communicate the decision of suspension of Imphal operation. He expressed his desire to keep the INA forces as close to the Indian border as possible, at least at points north and west of Mandalay. Although the feeling of Bose was very clear, yet cold logic of war made it plain that there was no chance of his dream being fulfilled.

Even under such a situation he sent a message to Gandhi on the 6th of July. In this message he explained his stand and steps he had taken, confidence he placed on Japan, the sincerity of the Japanese government, and establishment of the provisional government of India in order to fulfil his mission as a humble servant of India. Finally he declared his intention to fight till end with arms for throwing the Britishers out of India.

The tragedy did not strike at Imphal alone. The enemy launched strong attack on the 33rd Army from Hukon side on the west and from Yunan side on the east with superior and armoured unit for opening up the Indian China road.

The war situation had become very grave in other theatres as well around this time. Saipan fell to the enemy on the 18th of July, simultaneously with the premier Tojo resigned.

In Europe, the Anglo-American forces succeeded in landing in France in early June and thus opening second front against Germany long demanded by Russia. In Russian front also the Russians wrested the initiative from the Germans, reducing them to defensive posture.

Even under such an international development, Bose's fighting spirit remained quite high. He made the following comment to the staff officer of the Burma Area Army who went to communicate the resignation of Tojo to him— ".....I can well imagine that the new cabinet is committed to pursuer war more vigorously. The enemy will make a capital out of this resignation ...... It is indeed regrettable that Gen. Toja had to give up his post ......" His faith in Japan was unshaken.

Again, on 22nd, when the Koiso cabinet was formed, he sent a message of felicitation where he expressed the hope that there would be no shift in the policy of Indo-Japanese cooperation. This attitude of Bose was quite different from that of Ba Maw, the premier of Burma. In private, however, Bose expressed grave doubt about the coherence of the Koise cabinet. He was an admirer of strong policies of Tojo.

Under such gloomy situation the provisional government gave a party on 2nd August felicitating the 1st anniversary of Burma's independence. The Japanese side was so engrossed with war that such an important incident totally escaped their notice. That Bose did not forget the occasion shows clearly how conscious he was of international situation and politics.

On 30th August Gen. Kawabe, the commander of the Burma Area Army was recalled to Japan. Although the general was seriously ill, yet he supervised all the operations in order to stabilize the situation in the front. Before leaving, the General paid a visit to Bose to bid farewell. Bose entrusted the following message to him for communication to the authorities in Tokyo.

That he personally took a grave view of the overall situation, but even then his decision to fight the Britishers to the end had remained unchanged. Again, intermediate organs like Hikari Kikan should be abolished, and steps should be taken for establishing direct liaison between the Japanese army and the INA.

In this discussion he brought forward even such business matters like supply of military hardware and parts from the Japanese side etc. Bose showed steadfast attitude till the end during this meeting. Of late he had been showing signs of tiredness, but this day he was full of energy.

In his return visit to Gen. Kawabe, Bose expressed his thanks for the money given by the Japanese army for treatment of the wounded INA soldiers. Bose also said that he was going to convene a meeting of the Indian leaders of various regions in order to inspire them to fight the Britishers. This also was a proof that Bose was serious about what he was talking.

Although all the formalities called for at the time of such a farewell were completed, yet Bose went one stop further and held a tea party in the general's honour where he called the Burmese premier Ba Maw as well, in order to impress the general. Of course his sincerity impressed not only the general, but all the Japanese also. A few days before the general left, Bose sought an interview along with a number of INA officers and men who had received decorations. Although this meeting was agreed upon by the general, yet this shows clearly how seriously Bose tried to foster better understanding with the Japanese armed forces.

This change in the top level leadership of the Japanese forces in Burma formed the background of the final scene of Bose's activities in Burma. However, before describing it an attempt will be made to have an overall review of Japan's policy towards India vis-a-vis the tragic Imphal operation.

The point that need be mentioned first is that the Imphal operation was conceived out of strategic consideration alone. The only objective was to neutralize enemy's desire to launch counter offensive for recapturing Burma. This plan was not conceived as a part of India policy of Japan. A careful study of the whole course of operation will make this aspect amply evident. Now that Japan has been defeated stratagem; but this is nothing but a rash conclusion without proper understanding of the situation. Criticism levelled against the Tojo government that it took the adventurous step of Imphal operation under pressure from Bose are also not correct. However, it is true that great care was taken at the time of drawing up this operation to synchronize it with the operation of attacking India earnestly advocated by Bose's provisional government, thus giving the whole operation the colouring of a joint operation. Thus the operation was basically planned out of purely military strategy, although political significance was added to it at a later stage. The addition of political significance to the purely military operation brought a number of problems at its wake. When the operation was planned, war situation was in the favour of Japan, and it was evident that the capture of Imphal was only a matter of time. So not only the provisional government of India, even the Japanese authority and the Burmese leaders were of the view that the golden opportunity should not be lost. This being the situation, all efforts were concentrated to exploit the propaganda value of the political significance of this operation. The operational leadership also succumbed to the political aspect of the operation, forgetting the essential objective under which the operation, forgetting the essential objective under which the operation was conceived. Unfortunately this coincided with the time when the tide of war had turned against Japan, and hence the Japanese leaders from top to bottom secretly hoped to achieve success at least in this operation. The final manifestation of this expectation on the part of the Japanese leaders can be seen in the problem that arose when the question of ending the operation came up. Even though the position was hopless, the front line units were told to hold on and fight to the last; a natural outcome indeed. It is the responsibility of the higher level leadership to make the ultimate judgement of the situation after thoroughly evaluating the developments in the war situation. Even though the top leaders knew fully well that the front line forces had tried their best, and persistence meant total annihilation, yet they delayed the decision to end the operation as long as possible, a conclusive proof of the political significance attached to the operation by the Japanese leaders. In short, the reluctance to leave the grand plan of Bose to its own fate influenced the purely strategic judgement of the top leaders to a considerable extent. Although the front line leadership was restive and in many cases the orders from the top were not carried out, yet message of encouragement through wireless and occasionally through personal envoys poured in to the front line troops from the top level military leadership and the central leaders, and that also bypassing the normal channel. Naturally a stage came when the balance between the strategic judgement of the situation and political imposition broke down, and first signs of this appeared in the form of close of Imphal-Kohima road. Although Bose cannot be held directly responsible for initiating the Imphal operation, yet the decision to order the Japanese force to fight to death by the top leadership was considerably influenced by Bose's attitude towards this operation. That Japan had tried to fulfil its international obligation even by sacrificing thousands of soldiers will surely be a great contributory factor in cementing Indo-Japanese friendship and co-operation in future.

Bose's Third Visit to Tokyo

In September 1944, Gen. Kimura was appointed the commander of the Burma Area Army. The enemy kept up incessant pressure with vastly superior air force and mechanized units, leaving very little scope and time for the Japanese forces to take up defensive position for containing the enemy and bogging them down to protracted warfare. The INA forces also shared the fate of the Japanese, and started retreating towards Irrawadi.

This turn of fortune, however, failed to tone down the fighting spirit of Bose. It had very little repercussion on Bose who had fought bitterly all through his life against the British Government. When the Koiso cabinet was formed and the first Diet session was convened under the new prime minister, Bose sent the following telegram to him expressing his firm resolution of not to retreat.

"I want to express here once again my firm resolution to fight shoulder to shoulder with the Japanese forces till our common enemy is crushed and India is made completely free."

In reply to this message, premier Hoise also expressed his resolution to fight till Britain and USA were crushed, and conveyed his appreciation on the resolution of the provisional government and the INA. He promised all possible help to Bose.

Bose did not stop by sending the telegram alone. He donated five lakhs Yens each to the army and navy of Japan for building military planes through the local Japanese forces, describing this action as the token of friendship of the two countries in fighting the common enemy. This also is a proof of his rigid stand. Just before launching Imphal operation he had donated his personal plane to the Japanese forces. Indeed he was very much worried about the weak points of Japan.

Around this time, guessing the distress of Bose, Rear Admiral Chudo, the naval attache in Burma, proposed another line of action to Bose. His proposal was to give up the fight for Indian independence from the east in view of existing situation, and to seek cooperation of Russia for launching the struggle from the north. The admiral volunteered to accompany Bose to Samarkand as the representative of Japan. Bose received this proposal with great enthusiasm, and hence the admiral immediately sought instructions from the central authorities on the subjects. The response was in negative, which disheartened both of them considerably. However, this was not the first occasion when Bose showed his interest in Russia. Sometimes before this, when Col. Yamamoto was returning to Tokyo in September after completing his assignment as the head of the Hikari Kikan, he asked Bose whether the latter had any plan to launch his struggle from north west as the war situation in the Imphal front was slowly turning to worse. After keeping silent for about five or six minutes, he gave his approval, and said that he would like to have a try provided the Japanese government agree. This was also disapproved by Tokyo. The sole objective of Bose was independence of India, and any proposal having a positive bearing on it was welcome to him. It can be imagined what a great impact such a proposal would have on his thinking especially when such a proposal came from the Japanese side, although it was just a personal view.

It will not be wrong to say that from around this time Bose secretly thought of Russia as his future field of work, to which he attached top priority in the closing days of the war.

It will be appropriate here to have a review of the situation in India around this time. It was a matter of grave anxiety to Bose. The leaders of the Indian National Congress had started showing signs of compromise with the British government. Reconciliation with Muslim League was an essential precondition for compromise with the Britishers. And for reconciliation with Muslim League it was necessary to accede the demand of Pakistan. It was his pet theory that such a step would bring about division between the Hindus and the Moslems, a trap designed for perpetuating British rule in India. Thus it was natural for him to get upset over this development. On 13th September he appealed to his compatriots in India over Rangoon Radio not to be deceived by the British plan which would produce the tragedy of division of the country, and urged them to join hands with their compatriots abroad and fight for the ultimate victory.

"....... Patriotic Indians do not discriminate whether one Sikh or Moslem, Hindu or Christian or Parsee. In reality India cannot be divided. A real Indian can never agree to the demand of Pakistan. We have decided to develop powerful armed struggle and shed our blood for purchasing our freedom."

However, the actual developments in India went contrary to his expectation. Indeed the present independent India has little to console his soul. The only way to console his spirit now is to form a confederation between India and Pakistan, and revive the glorious days of ancient India.

At last 21st October, the first anniversary of the provisional government of Free India came. Bose personally supervised the preparations for celebration. Within a brief period of one year the government had to undergo a lot of changes. It became apparent that his grand dream was going to fail at least for the time being. The only torch in this gloom was his patriotism, belief in ultimate victory and faith in the friendly countries. Both Premier Koiso and the commander of the local force felicitated him on this occasion, pledging all possible assistance. On this day, the Indians of the Tokyo-Yokohama area and about thirty five Indian students went to Yasukuni Jinja shrine and prayed to the soul of the Indian and Japanese soldiers fallen in the Indo-Burma front. Here they pledged anew their firm resolution to fight till victory.

Towards the end of October, information reached through confidential sources that the Japanese government had decided to award the decoration of Asahi Class I to Bose. Incidentally, this was the time he was planning to visit Japan. But his reply took the Japanese authorities by surprise. He replied that he was very happy over the award, but he intended to receive it at the dawn of Indian independence along with his soldiers. He showed the same attitude he had shown earlier when he received presents at the house of the Shibusawa family.

Bose paid a visit to Tokyo by air on 1st November. The purpose of this visit was to acquaint himself with the new cabinet and military leaders, and to seek closer cooperation for the provisional government. On the Indian side, Col. Chatterjee, his minister without portfolio, Col. Kiani, the commander of the 1st Division of the INA, and Lt. Col. Habibur Rehman, his deputy chief of staff, accompanied him; and on the Japanese side, Lt. Gen. Isoda, the head of the Kikan accompanied him along with his associates. The party was received at the air port by Ram Murti and other members of the Indian Independence League of Tokyo, as well as a number of Indian students.

The appearance of Tokyo was totally changed. Enemy air raids had taken their toll. The enemy had landed at Layte in Philippines. The deteriorating war situation was amply evident. Immediately on reaching Tokyo he made the following speech in a meeting arranged in his honour at Hibiya Public Hall illustrating his conviction.

"........The enemy is striving hand to finish the war before its own people lose heart to fight. In leading my soldiers against the enemy, my slogan had been 'together we sink. Together we float'. We have taken a pledge to fight shoulder to shoulder with the Japanese army. In reality we have not to sunk. The fight cause will prevail at the end. According to the divine will we shall float together and also we shall together win victory".

The Hibiya Public Hall was packed with people who came to hear his speech, and for two hours they listened to him with rapt attention. In the end they raised cheers 'Banzai' to Bose.[3]

After routine visits to the government and military leaders, Bose met premier Koiso on the 4th and discussed various issues for two hours. The premier gave a dinner party in Bose's honour at his officials residence where ex-premier Gen. Tojo was present in civilian dress. Bose did not let this chance slip, and in his table speech recalled the role of Gen. Tojo and

3. For his speech see the douments in Volume IV

the important decisions taken at the Great East Asia Conference, which impressed all those present.

On the 6th, His Majesty the Emperor received Bose in audience. Unfortunately nobody asked Bose about his impression on this meeting. However, considering that on the following emperor's birthday he sent one of his sides to the headquarters of the Burma Area Army with message of felicitating although he was very busy with Imphal operation, it can be assumed that the emperor could impress him about Japan's sincerity.

Although Bose stayed in Tokyo for four weeks during this visit, yet he spent all his available time in negotiating with the government and military leaders. During these talks he tried to impress the Japanese side to give more arms to the INA in order to raise the fighting capacity and on the necessity of readjusting the relation with the Japanese army, the necessity for which he keenly felt before and after the Imphal operation. During these discussion he never uttered a word of complaint or discontent; everything he said was frank and constructive. The Japanese authorities concerned were taken away by his sincerity and forceful arguments.

On the government side, this was the first meeting between premier Koiso and Bose. Contrary to the case of premier Tojo, the new premier failed to understand Bose properly. Again, the chief of the general staff Gen. Umezu was new to his job, and business talks over military matters were confined to the bureau and section chief level.

Bose believed that the difficulties encountered during Imphal operation could be solved only by strengthening the INA and increased quantum of military aid from Japan. Hence he strongly asserted that the immediate duty was to strengthen the INA. Although the urgent issues were military hardware and training, yet the Japanese side showed very little interest on these points. The INA solider were equipped with rifles alone, and that also those captured from the enemy. They neither had tanks nor had anti-aircraft guns. With great difficulty the Hikari Kikan could be persuaded to agree to forty thousand as the maximum strength of the INA. This was much smaller than the strength contemplated by Bose. Again, he was unhappy because the Japanese army employed the INA troops in road construction work etc. in the rear rather than sending them to the front.

Ever since Bose came to east, he was unhappy over the lack of arms. Of course he could not expect the INA forces to be equipped with same type of arms with which he could equip the Indian volunteer unit in Germany. Yet what distressed him much was that even the Burmese forces were much superiorly equipped compared to the INA soldiers. Again, after Imphal operation, the Japanese army went as far as trying to negotiate the surrender of rifles possessed by the INA forces. Of course, Japan was at that time reduced to such as position, and the authorities had a very hard time in hiding facts from Bose.

Bose regretted very much that he did not go to the front; and he often cited this as one of the causes for the failure of Imphal operation. The propaganda warfare in the front was much inferior to that of the enemy; and the reason for this can be attributed to lack of preparation. Indeed his presence in the front could have improved the situation. Improper handling of the surrendered enemy soldiers often led to their desertion to the British side. He was also not very happy with medical facilities and food rationing.

Regarding commanding the INA forces, he wanted the Hikari Kikan to be reduced to the status of mere liaison body. Again, he kept alive the controversy of right of military trial till the end.

He raised these issues during his stay in Tokyo. Thorough discussion were needed till a formula satisfactory to Bose could be evolved. Indeed the relation between the two armies was not very rational, and many of the points raised by him could not be accepted readily in view of the tight war situation. Yet his attitude was very serious, and the authorities concerned also showed equal understanding to the tricky problems raised by him. As a result both sides could reach good understanding by the time Bose left Tokyo on the 27th.

Apart from the status of Hikari Kikan, the issue of diplomatic mission was raised during the visit. As fighting was according top priority by the provisional government, the question of diplomatic representation did not come up in the early stages. The Japanese Foreign ministry had posted one of its officials, Asada, as the councellor with the Hikari Kikan. However this official later on fell ill, and with the provisional government putting its house in order, the question of diplomatic representation came up. During Bose's visit to Tokyo, he took up this point with the Japanese foreign ministry, and an agreement was reached under which Hachiya was appointed Japan's ambassador to the provisional government, the formal announcement of which came just before Bose left Tokyo.

During this visit Bose also proposed an agreement on Indo-Japanese loan. Although he had been trying to persuade the Japanese side to treat the funds provided by Japan for running the provisional government IIL and the INA as loan and not as gift, yet during this visit he made all out efforts for reaching a formal agreement on the subject. The motive was to prevent Japan from setting any condition taking advantage of these funds at the time of Indian independence. Japan readily agreeed to his proposal, and an unofficial decision and agreement was reached on the subject.

Bose pursued the topics of loan agreement and establishing relation with Japan in ambassadorial level earnestly in order to aviod the danger of being reduced to the status of puppet government of Manchukuo. Here one can see cleraly his non-compromising attitude which he had develped through his bitter struggle against the cunning British policy of appeasement and deception.

Although the objective situation was not very encouraging at the time, yet his attitude was full of optimism, and in his negotiations with Japan, he took a firm line leaving no scope of compromise. For example, on the last day of his meeting with the military authorities, the meeting was interrupted a number of times due to B-29 bombing raids. During this time he was very calm and never showed any nervousness. However, signs of tiredness could be seen on his face, and Tojo was taken aback seeing him after one year. Again, when he gave a party at the end of his visit, his guest were a little surprised to see him talk very little.

Although Bose had a very tight schedule in Tokyo, yet he did not forget the youth. He met the Indian students in Tokyo, and was very pleased to hear about their excellent academic records.

Again, Bose never for a moment foreget his social obligations. His visit to Tojo at the latters private residence can be cited as one of the examples. The Tojo family still recollect this meeting with tears in eyes. By chance, Senda, his political advisor and a member of Hikari Kikan, died during his stay in Tokyo. He visited the family of the deceased and paid homage to the departed soul.

Bose also visited Rash Behari Bose who was bed ridden at that time. He consoled the old and sick fighter by assuring that the day of independence of India was not very far. Rash Behari passed away the following January, and Bose sent his message of condolence from Rangoon.

Another tragedy occurred during this visit of Bose. Wang Ching Wei, the head of Nanking government, died at Nagoya after protracted illness. The memory of their meeting at the Great East Asia conference one year ago in which they became intimate friends at the first sight and visited to Nanking on Wang's invitation as state guest was still very fresh. What fascinated Bose in Wang Ching Wei was the latters life as a revolutionary politician.

Resolving to save his country through peace Yang left Chungking risking his life, and had established a government in Nanking which was in no way a puppet government. In the mean time he attacked the worng policy of Chungking government in relying too much on the allied power for fighting the Japanese. Many of his actions were in common with those of Bose. He felt unity of China to be a basic precondition for peace in Asia, and had sent advise to Chungking government on a number of occasions over radio. He grieved too much at the death of this great leader.

Thus ended the Tokyo visit to Bose. What was the net achievement of this visit? There is no doubt that he could ascertain personally Japan continued desire to assist him, and he on his part could apprise Japan of his earnest desire to accomplish his mission. However, his concrete acheviement was not so encouraging. He did not get any satisfactory response to his demand for an overall Japanese plan for the liberation of India. He made this demand repeatedly to the government and military leaders of Japan. It was indeed necessary that he should have broadened his outlook a little while drawing up his policy.

During they stay Bose also tried to have a meeting with the Soviet ambassador several times. After getting the approval of the military authorities he sought a letter of introduction from the Foreign Minister Shigemistu, which was however declined. Ultimately he sent a letter directly to the Soviet ambassador, which was however returned to him undelivered. This move of Bose leaves little doubt that plan for future course of action was already crystallizing in his mind.

Bose left Tokyo on 29th November, and flew direct to Burma. Little did he know that this was going to be his last visit to Japan. His mind was full with the problems of liberation of India, and he had resolved to fight to last.

Bose returned to Burma at a time when the weather was excellent, thus leaving the air space at the mercy of enemy aircraft, and land to the on slaught of enemy tanks. The enemy had captured Ledo road and was advancing towards Irrawady river after crossing the Chindwin river.

Six months of fierce fight and lack of arms and ammunitions had left the soldiers utterly tired, and whatever air units were left were diverted to the Pacific front leaving the soldiers without any air cover. Attempt to contain the enemy had failed utterly, and the Indian and Japanese forces were retreating towards the left bank of Irrawady for establishing defence line around Mandalay. Even this retreat was not smooth as quite often the units found the rear areas already captured by the enemy.

The situation had worsened much quicker than expected by Bose.

Around this time the British warships were seen frequently off Remree, making it clear that a landing was on the offing. Strategically speaking, this was a natural step, and it was strange that it had been put off till that time. The 28th Army under the command of Lt. Gen. Sakurai was already deployed there to nullify such a move, and one division was kept in reserve north east of Rangoon to assist this army.

Bose remained in Rangoon disregarding heavy enemy air raids both day and night, conducting the affairs of his government and leading the INA. Fortunately, the front line INA forces constituting the left wing of the retreating 15th Army maintained a cool and orderly retreat. If possible he wnated to maintain the Indian units on the right bank of river Irrawadi in order to cover the retreat of the Japanese forces. For this he wanted to proceed to the front and assume and command personally. But the situation then did not permit him such a step. His immediate job was to revive the spirit of the disheartened Indians. Although his attitude was uncompromising, yet it was difficult to imbush such a spirit in the overseas Indians. They were especially susceptable to the feeling of the Burmese people among whom they were living, who were in turn very sensitive to the development of war.

At last December also passed in vain. During the middle of this month the defenders of Bhamo area consisting of one battalion finally capitulated to the fierce attack of two divisions of the newly organized Chinese 1st Army equipped with American arms. The 33rd Army defending Lashio area under the command of Lt. Gen. Honda helped the 15th Army as much as possible in setting up the defence line along the banks of river Irrawadi. With almost all the soliders sick or too exhausted, this defence line remained a matter of imagination. The enemy had already reached the opposite bank of Irrawadi, and was probing the establish bridgehead for crossing.

When the situation was deterioriating like this, an incident occurred which made Bose feel all the more lonely. It was the transfer of Maj. Gen. Yamamoto from Hikari Kikan. They were old friends since Berlin days, and in East Asia, both worked hand in hand with perfect understanding. Both were very much moved at this parting.

On 31st December, the British forces made a sudden landing near Akyab. Akyab-Chittagong: this was the route Bose had in mind for advance into Delhi. Although he had to modify his plan in view of the existing situation, yet Akyab, had a special place in his mind.

1945 dawned. It was a fateful year not only for Japan, but also for Bose. He had no time think about this. He was too preoccupied with devising plans that would take him nearer to his goal. As usual, the new year brought new hopes to him. His ultimate aim was to lay down his life for the country. He had already transcended above the question of life and death.

23rd January was the birth day of Bose. Although Rangoon was exposed to incessant enemy bombing raids, yet the local Indians celebrate it in a grand scale; and the gold and jewellary he received on the occasional weighted one and half times his body weight.

On 12th January the 25th British Indian Division started landing at Myebon peninsula after heavy naval bombardment. Taking advantage of the vacuum created as the Japanese forces hurried to repulse this landing the 26th Division of the British Indian army started landing on Ramree island on the 26th January.

The 15th Army also fought a number of engagements in order to prevent the enemy from crossing Irrawady. The INA constituting the extreme left wing of the 15th Army also fought bitterly, but slowly started getting disheartened. Unable to bear this development, Bose decided to go to the front to lead the soldiers personally. Isoda, the head of Hikari Kikan also accompanied Bose in this trip. Bose's role as the supreme commander at this time revealed his firm resolution clearly. A good profile to Bose can be seen in the following words of Maj. Takahashi of Hikari Kikan who accompanied Bose to the front.

".....We left Rangoon towards the end of January. Bose himself supervised the allocation of vehicles and duties. The movement was restricted to night in order to avoid enemy aerial raids. On the following night we reached Pyinmana. The next day he met the leaders of the local Indian community and listened to their problems, giving the necessary instructions. Nex he met the woman's unit of the INA posted there and had lunch with them. In the afternoon he inspected the 1st INA division posted there under the command of Col. Kiyani. The colonel showed considerable nervousness over this inspection. During this inspection all the commands were issued by Bose himself. He passed the whole day without any rest.

After leaving Pyinmana we advanced forward. We halted for rest usually in the Indian settlements on the way. We avoided roads and houses during the day time. He rested under trees reading a book. He told me that the book was on independence of Ireland.

We reached Meiktila on 1st February. After gathering information we went to an Indian settlement about 6 km from the town. There we came to know that two companies of the INA had surrendered to the enemy, and a battalion was regrouping after retreating from the front. Hearing this Bose said that he would go to the front to encourage the battalion commander personally. We tried to dissuade Bose as the whole zone had become the scene of brisk enemy tank activity. But Bose stuck to his point asserting that the enemy armoured units were active only along the roads. After coming all the way to encourage his soldiers he found it too much to give up the idea of going to the front line because of the danger involved. Again, the battlion was regrouping right at the moment. We advised Bose to watch the situation for a while in order not to embarass the battalion commander. Bose retorted by saying that it was all the more necessary for him to be in the front now that the situation was deteriorating fast. Finally it was decided that Col. Kiyani and Maj. Takashashi would go to the unit to have a first hand view of the unit. In so far I can remember, Bose went as far as ordering Col. Kiyani to resume his duty immediately in order to have his way..........

The enemy tanks advanced along the roads as predicted by Bose. Out of tactical considerations Maj. Takahashi had said that the tanks would avoid the roads as they would encounter maximum resistance here. Probably the enemy got a wind that the Japanese forces lacked anti-tank guns, and hence the enemy armoured units penetrated deep inside the Japanese position during the day time retreating to safety at night.......

As the activitiy of the enemy armourned units became very brisk in Meiktila area, Bose was advised to retreat, but he refused. On the third day morning luckily a time bomb exploded, and by mistake it was reported as firing from tank guns. It was this point that Bose could be persuaded to leave Meiktila after much difficulty. He retreated to an Indian village about 4 km south west of Meiktila. The retreat look place during day time receiving enemy air attack a number of times. Bose went by horse coach, and other on foot. Enemy planes attacked Bose's coach when it was about to enter the village, and the raid continued for about half an hours.

During this retreat Bose suddenly demanded that the local Japanese command should be asked to reinforce the units in the area with one artillary battalion and two infantry battalion to check the enemy. He also said that he would personally command this force. It was a matter of common sense that the Japanese command was receiving such requests from all over the front, and it was not in a position to fufill the demands. So

Bose was informed that his request could not be communicated as the location of the local Japanes command was not known.

We reached Pyinmana around 8th February. The bridges and roads were closely watched by enemy planes, and any moving vehicle was attacked. Luckily, the party of Bose reached the headquarter of the 1st Division of the INA unscathed.

On the following day, Bose called the staff officers of the INA 1st Division and Maj. Takahashi and communicated his intention to take a decisive defensive stand. In view of that he ordered intensive patrol and reconnaisance. When the results of reconnaiscance was reported back to Bose he made the following comment.

Eversince I left this place the other day I have been reading the history of Irish freedom. Even though the patriots were killed to the last man, yet the spirit remained unvanquished. And they attained freedom after about seventy or eighty years, Considering the present situation, the future of Burma is also uncertain. I want to lay down my life here commanding the 1st Division. I think my sacrifice will keep alive the spirit of patriotism in the minds of the Indian people. So I want to make my final here.

All were at a loss over this decision of Bose. Col. Kiyani, who had just returned at that time also interceded advocating that the time was not yet ripe for making such a final stand. Moreover, there were a large number of units deployed in Rangoon area and the headquarters of the Burma Area Army was also located at Rangoon. So Bose should postpone his decision for the time being. But all arguments failed to move Bose. After four days of debates, Kiyani assured Bose that he would be absolutely responsible for defending the region, and that he would defend to the last man. He urged that Bose should immedaitely return to Rangoon for supervising the overall control. Only after this did Bose agree to return.

During these weeks of inspection tour, Bose had to change three of his sides. This was because all had collapse out of sheer fatigue. Bose slept for only three or four hours a day, devoting rest of the time in meeting the local Indian leaders and inspecting the units and installated. Thereupon his sides collapsed one after anohther out of exhuastion.

In Pyinmana Bose ordered the Women's unit to return to Rangoon along with him. As a result the vehicles were very crowded. On the way when a vehicle developed trouble, Bose stopped and redistributed the passangers to other vehicles. This shows how careful he was about the girls. This was indeed much different from the tradition of the Japanese officers and men.

"The way back to Rangoon was not so easy. The whole route was infested with spies, and every time two or three vehicles passed, they fired signal rockets inviting air attacks....."

The above reminiscences of Maj Takahashi give an idea of Bose's conception of war tactics. Again, he expressed his views on naval operation in the letters he exchanged with the commander of the 1st fleet operating in the south.

Towards the middle of July after Germany had capitulated, Bose sent a strongly worded letter to vice-admiral Fukutome, the commander of the 1st fleet making a fresh demand for transportation some of Bose's officials to Malaya from Andamans. In this letter he added:

"...... Had the Japanese fleet been active a little earlier as I had said, the condition in the Indian Ocean would not have dererioriated as today. It is indeed regrettable."

This only gave an impression of his haughty temperament. Here the navy had taken all the steps possible, and the admiral informed Bose of it. The question here was the later part of the operation. It is not known when and how the views of Bose were communicated to the fleet. The admiral informed him that the position in Indian Ocean was utterly hopeless.

The above are just a few of the examples. It is of course unreasonable to expect him to be an expert on military tactics an strategey. But he was too confident of himself. As the head of the provision government he was naturally the supreme commander of the INA. As the persons surrounding him were not very brilliant, he could easily impose his views on others, and his overbearingness became more and more marked with the passing of the days.

The position of the INA forces manning the extreme left flank of the front near river Irrawadi became clear after the inspection tour of Lt. Gen. Isoda, the head of the Kikan. This general left Rangoon along with Lt. Col. Gulzara Singh a little after the departure of Bose. The party reached Yenangyaung after three days. After one more night they reached the INA positions around Mt. Popa. They met retreating Japanese trucks on the way. There the division commander Shah Nawaz Khan and regiment commander Saigal briefed the party about the circumstances under work which the two companies surrendered, and the present position of the battalion. In the division headquarters also five or six staff officers and other officers had deserted. But the two commanders were confident that the position could be held. Proper reorganizations were already over. However, as the air was completely under enemy control, any slightest movement brought enemy retaliation. Air raid warning rang every ten to thirty minutes. The two commanders, again, and a wide front at their disposal, which had to be defend with too few soldiers. Shah Nawaz felt himself to be guilty and responsible for the surrender, and had resolved to defend his positions at all cost. Saigal also felt that the morale of the soldiers was quite party came under severe enemy aeroplane be held. During return trip this party came under severe enemy aeroplane fire in between Mt. Popan and Yenangyaung. The Japanese propaganda about the existence of a reinforced division in the area. The Japanese propaganda about the existence of a reinforced division in the area had apparently deceived the enemy.

Bose was very much relieved to hear the report on the front. Perturbed over mass surrender, Bose sent a message to the front line INA units ordering to shoot the deserters. Till then there had been no instance of surrender, and they had fought valiantly. The Japanese army was also surprised at the severity to the order.

Towards the middle of February, the enemy started crossing Irrawadi in strength. They establashed bridge heads at Myaung and Pakoku. To repulse this the Burma Area Army planned a strong counter attack. After crossing the river, the enemy army corps consisting of white soldiers overcame the extreme left flank and was threating the Shan Plateau. As the 15th Army did not have enough strength to repulse this attack, it thought to cut off the enemy line of retreat by advancing from the direction of Mandalaya. However, this line of action did not materialize ultimately, and Meiktila fell to the enemy armoured corps on 23rd February. Around this time to make the matters worse, one division was withdrawn from Burma and sent to Philippines as the situation there had become desperate.

The direct threat to Rangoon was posed by the enemy forces which had landed from the sea. The Burma Defence Army came forward to meet this enemy force, which was to become the maiden participation of the Burmese forces in the war. The Burma Defence Army had been trained all these years by the Japanese forces, and was very well equipped. It became a matter of speculation whether the performance of this army will match that of the INA.

On 15th March a grand ceremony was held in front of ShweDagon Pagoda to bid farewell to the soldiers going to the front. On the following day, the commander of the Burma Defence Army himself, Gen. Aung San, advanced towards Prome at the head of his forces. A few days after this the Burma Defence Army troops suddenly turned their guns and attacks

Japanese installations in the rear. The Burmese forces groomed with so much care have at last turned against the Japanese. Simultaneously with this, the cadets of the Rangoon military school deserted and attacked the Japanese installations, which ws however supressed without much difficulty by defence units composed by the local Japanese civilians. The revolting Burma Defence Army forces were suppressed without much difficulty, although a section continued guerilla activities after this debacle.

This rebellion of the Burmese army was carefully planned move. Aung San had collaborated with the Japanese army till the other day as the defence minister in to the Ba Maw cabinet. Moreover, as the head of the Burma Independence Army trained by the Japanese army he had cooperated with Japan eversince the Japanese forces entered Burma. His action can be excused when one considers the changed situation, but the line of action he chose was that of treachery.

Indeed it is difficult to suppress disappointment when this rebellion is viewed in the light of bitter struggle waged by the INA eversince Imphal operation under the leadership of Bose, although there had been occasions of misunderstanding. One of the factors responsible for this was the national character. The overall war situation and popular feeling also played an important role. Above all, the greatest responsibility was that of the leader.

Although such incidents were taking place in the rear, yet fierce engagements were continuing in the front around Mandalaya. The enemy armoured brigade which had established a strong base at Meiktila was repeatedly attacked by the 33rd Army which withdraw from Lashio area in order to shorten the length of front, but without any effect. Finally, the defence of Mandalay had to be abandoned towards the end of March.

The enemy closely persued the retreating Japanese forces spearheaded by armoured brigade. The Japanese forces were not in a position to check this advance as they had exhausted all their ammunition and provisions. Pyinamana area, where Bose had thought to contain the enemy at all cost, also fell to the enemy after about a month, around 21st April. Once this water shed is crossed, the road to Rangoon passes through plains along the Sittang river situated to the east of Rangoon. At last Rangoon, which Bose had dreamt of using as the springboat for attack on India and where he had located the headquarters of the provisional government, was also exposed to the enemy advancing from the east and from the west. The enemy was threatening the line of retreat.

On 20th April Bose was confidentially informed of Gen. Kimura's (the commander of the Burma Area Army) decision to abandon Rangoon.

It seems that a section in the Burma Area Army was against this retreat. Considering the overall situation Bose had no other alternative but to cooperate with the general. However, Bose had many units communication with which was disrupted. Again, the Women's unit just started retreating by train. It was impossible for Bose to retreat to safety along with his top aides immediately leaving all these people to fate. Thereupon Bose rejected the pleadfor immediate retreat. This had to serious misunderstanding with the commander of the Burma Area Army. Bose left Rangoon only after arranging the withdrawnofthe women's unit by trucks. Bose started retreat towards Moulmein on the 23rd night. Prior to this an emergency secret meeting of the cabinet was held in which oit was decided to leave Maj. Gen. Loganadhan in Rangoon to command the remnant INA units.

Although there was nothing to restraint Bose, why did he keep his government exposed to danger to till the last moment. As back as December some of his aides had advised him to shft the government to Bangkok or Saigon in view of the worsening war situation. Althugh he agreed to this as a logical step, by in practice he did not show any inclination be take such a step. Of course he had his own reason for this. When he took over the command of the INA as its supreme commander, he said to his officers and men.

"............ I pledge that I shall be with yu in you gloom and glory, in your distress an joy distress and joy, in your defeat and victory." Indeed he meant what he said.

Another tragedy was in store for Bose during this April. It was the death of his mother. Eversince he joined the Indeina independence movement, he was very careful about his activities , an did not marry. considering the hardships that his family would be forced to undergo, he vosed to remain bachelor till India attained independence. So of all persons his mother was closest to him. He was very sad that he could not remain by her bedside at her lost moment.

Bose started retreat towards Moulmein with about ten and odd motor vehicles. It was the time when the enemy planes were active all through day and night. This retreat route was full of withdrawing Japanese forces, and a mnumnber of big rivers had to be crossed. Movreover, th eunits of th rebelling Burmese forces were carruing out brisk guerilla activities in the area. Thus Bose's retreat through such confusion was indeed fraught with grave danger. Just after leaving Rangoon Bose's party came under enemy fire,. and he thought that the retreat was matter of shame. He harassed his companions by saying repeatedly that he would go back to

Rangoon fight till last together with Loganandhan. Whenever a river had to be crossed, the girls crossed first, and he crossed after all had crossed. When the number of cars decreased, some advised him to go ahead by car, but he refused resolutely. Ultimately, he marched for a few days carrying a gun ahead of his party. When Moulmein was approached, the cars shuttled the girls to Moulmein. He was the last men to get in the last car. This difficult march took one week, and he reached Moulmein towards the end of April. During this march the only thing that occupied his mind was neither death not life; just to be together with the companions whom he loved so much.

After reaching Moulmein Bose tried to pay a courtesy visit to Gen. Kimura, the commander of the Burma Area Army, who had already reached there. The general refused under the pretext of secrecy. However he accepted wine that Bose sent and expressed thanks for it. From here Bose arranged the trasportation of the Women's unit and the remaining INA forces to Bangkok by motor vehicle and train, and himself left aftrer all had departed, on the 9th of May.

In this trip from Moulmein to Bangkok, Bose was accompained by a number of provisional government officials, ambassadors Hachiya, Isoda, the Kikan head, and a few other Kikan members. The motor convey was escorted by one equal of INA soldiers, five Japanese soldiers and one military police. The journey was restricted to night as the enemy was very active in air during the day time. The road was bad, and moreover the rain had started. So the group had to repair road while proceeding. At last attempt was made to travel by Thai-Burma rail road, but as the sick and injured soldiers got priority, the idea had to be abandoned. The party after great difficulty reached Kanchanburi, making th journey partly by horse coach, partly by car and partly by Thai-Burma rail. From Kanchanaburi the party reached Bangkok by car. It took about one week to reach Bangkok. Bose spoke very little during this journey, and with great relish took the simple food prepared by the soldiers. Sometimes he helped the soldiers repair the motor vehicles by holding lighted torch. Often he shared his food with sick and wounded Japanese soldiers. Despite hardships and disappointments, he never forgot his warm humane feeling even for once. Usually the Indian officers had a tendency to assume airs, but Bose had brotherly attitude to the soldiers, and the soldier respected him like a kind and benevolent father.

Just after Bose reached Bangkok, he received a courtesy call from one time aides of Gen. Terauchi, the commander-in-chief of the Southern Forces, who delivered a message from the general. The good will of the general impressed Bose very much. One of these aides was Rear-Admiral Chudo, who had proposed going to Samarkand to Bose the year before in Rangoon.

Bose did not get even a day's rest in Bangkok as he was deeply engrossed with his future plans. Although he was throughly convinced of Japan's good will, yet he had to give up the idea of attacking India from the east for the time being. However, this did not mean that he had lost his spirit. He still had units retruning from Burma front, and a considerable force in Malaya at his disposal. He was thinking to take this force along with him and start the fight once again from some other direction. He was trying out all possibilities.

The supreme command of the southern forces advised Bose to shift the provisional government to Saigon. Bose did not agree to this, but rather expressed his desire to shift the INA to Saigon and then to China, and the provisional government to a convenient place where negotiations with the Soviet Embassy or consulate could be carried out without any interruption. On coming to know the intension of Bose, the Imperial Headquarters sent an emissary to inform him the basic policy of the Japanese army, which had decided to order the armies located in South Asia, China and Japan proper to fight the enemy till the end. As the provisional government was techincally under the jurisdiction of the Southern Command, it should a bide by the decisions of the command. This emissary, staff officer Takakura of the Imperial Headquarters, met Bose on 18th June, and the discussion continued till about 3 a.m., but without any softening of Bose's attitude. At any rate, Bose finally agreed to abide by the desire of the Imperial Headquarters. After this Bose decided to strengthen the branches of the Indian Independence League at Shanghai and other cities of China, and establish contact with the Soviet diplomatic missions through these branches.

Thus August came. Around 10th head of the Hikari Kikan deduced on the basis of all the available information that a very important development was on the offing. He informed his evaluation to Bose who was at that time on an inspection tour of Singapore, urging Bose to return immediately. However, Bose did not show any inclination of immediate retur. Thereupon, the Indian Chief of staff Bhonsle was informed of the views of the Japanese government and armed force, hinting him to be prepared for any exigencies. Two or three days passed in no time, and then the final decision was made known. After repeated telegrams, Bose returned to Saigon. His final request was as follows:

"I want to go to Soviet Union along with other Indian leaders. If this is difficult, I want to go alone. In that case I shall request the Japanese government to provide facilities for my aides to go to Russia."

The Southern Command sought the opinion of the Imperial Headquarter on this request of Bose. The reply from the centre was that it was outrageous on the part of Bose to abandon Japan at this stage and go to Russia after having received such enormous aid. Terauchi, the C-in-C of Southern Command felt delicate to communicate this to Bose. He decided to let Bose have his way at his own risk. As a result he decided to send a special plane to Manchuria, which was also to carry Lt. Gen. Shideifrom Saigon, as the latter was appointed to a post there. The plane was to fly to Manchuria, where Bose was to surrender to the Soviet forces moving south. The departure was fixed opn the 17th August.

The Hikari Kikan however disapproved the idea of Bose's journey alone. They advocated that at least some of the top leaders of the provisional government should accompany Bose. But as the situation did not permit this, it was decided to allow only one of his sided to accompany him. Bose on his apart also disapproved the idea of going alone leaving all his associates, and all intercession of the head of the _Kikan was in vain. In the mean time the time of departure approached. Finally he said to delay the departure till he held the final meeting with the leaders of the provisional government. Here he decided to leave alone, requesting the Japanese side to help others to hide in Japan or in some other appropriate place.

At last Bose reached the aeroplane in great hurry. As putting this luggage on board took time, the departure was delayed by one hour. As the plane was about the take off, suddenly an Indian came running and pleaded with Bose to take the last token present from the three million Indians living in South Asia. The plane departure was delayed further by about fifteen minutes. The man brought two very heavy suitcases.

At last the plane took off. Bose was seen off by the top officer of the Southern Command, the members of Hikari Kikan and the leaders of the provisional government and other local Indians. The plane was Type 2 Heavy Bomber of the Army, put into operational use about a month earlier. All the crew members had excellent records.

The plane reached Taipei on the 18th, and after taking fuel was about to take off for Manchuria at about 2 P.M. Just at the moment it was about to take off, the left propellor came off. As the plane started taxining again, it crushed against an embankment, the plane body broke into two, and the gasoline tank caught fire. The pilot Maj. Taki, Lt. Gen. Shidei, and another person died instantaneously, and Bose received grave injuries.

Those sitting at the rear of the plane receive only minor burn injury. Lt. Col. Habib-ur-Rahman, who accompanied Bose on this fateful journey, was one of the lucky to escape with minor injury.

Whole body of Bose was on flame, yet he succeeded to extricate himself from the plane, and was soon sent to Taipei military hospital. The diagnosis of Cpt. Yoshimi, the doctor who looked after Bose, was third degree burn. Although all possible steps were taken, like blood transfer saline injection etc., yet the condition worsened around midnight. All this time Habib-ur-Rehman was by the side of Bose. The whole body of Bose was in bandage, and although he was suffering unbearable pain, yet he did not utter any cry of pain. Just he said "water, water" once in broken Japanese and another time told to raise the pillow.

At a later date Habib-ur-Rehman confided to Lt. Gen. Isoda that Bose did not say anything which could be treated as his last will. He just murmured that he regretted to die without seeing India free. However he was sure that India would be free before long. He had dedicated his life for India's freedom, and he had nothing to regret. He was very happy to die for India's freedom.

Again, according to one, who had attended Bose all the time in the hospital, Bose wanted to have curry rice when asked about food. So all the cooks in the hospital refectory were mobilized, and the curry rice prepared was relished very much by Bose. Bose died shortly after taking this meal.

Bose breathed his last at 11.40 P. M. on the 18th August on the Japanese soil, nursed by the Japanese doctors. Just before death he said something like 'My best wishes to C-in-C Terauchi'. This was his parting speech.

Hearing this plane disaster in Taipei, the Southern Command sent Ota, the staff officer who had looked after this journey, to do the needful.

His bones were put in a tea pot, and was sent to the War Office on the 7th September. His funeral rites were held in great secrecy at Renkoji temple of Nakeno, in the presence of the leaders of the local branch of IIL and the local Indian students.. Next the quesion of safe custody of the bones came up. As Japan was under enemy occupation. British seriously trying to locate Bose hiding somewhere in Japan. So none was willing to take custody of the bones in view of the risk involved. Luckily, the head priest of Renkoji temple of Nakano ward of Tokyo came forward and took the bones for safe custody in the temple. Since then the bones have been kept there, the monks of the temple praying for the departed soul every day. As soon as the location of the bones became known, it became a place of pilgrimage of the Indians and a section of Japanese with interest on India.

Index